T0214612

Communications
in Computer and Information Science   1008

Commenced Publication in 2007
Founding and Former Series Editors:
Phoebe Chen, Alfredo Cuzzocrea, Xiaoyong Du, Orhun Kara, Ting Liu,
Dominik Ślęzak, and Xiaokang Yang

More information about this series at http://www.springer.com/series/7899

Cyrille Artho · Peter Csaba Ölveczky (Eds.)

Formal Techniques for Safety-Critical Systems

6th International Workshop, FTSCS 2018
Gold Coast, Australia, November 16, 2018
Revised Selected Papers

 Springer

Editors
Cyrille Artho
KTH Royal Institute of Technology
Stockholm, Sweden

Peter Csaba Ölveczky ⓘ
University of Oslo
Oslo, Norway

ISSN 1865-0929   ISSN 1865-0937 (electronic)
Communications in Computer and Information Science
ISBN 978-3-030-12987-3   ISBN 978-3-030-12988-0 (eBook)
https://doi.org/10.1007/978-3-030-12988-0

Library of Congress Control Number: 2019930853

This Springer imprint is published by the registered company Springer Nature Switzerland AG
The registered company address is: Gewerbestrasse 11, 6330 Cham, Switzerland

Preface

This volume contains the proceedings of the 6th International Workshop on Formal Techniques for Safety-Critical Systems (FTSCS 2018), held in Gold Coast on November 16, 2018, as a satellite event of the ICFEM conference.

The aim of this workshop is to bring together researchers and engineers who are interested in the application of formal and semi-formal methods to improve the quality of safety-critical computer systems. FTSCS strives to promote research and development of formal methods and tools for industrial applications, and is particularly interested in industrial applications of formal methods. Specific topics include, but are not limited to:

- case studies and experience reports on the use of formal methods for analyzing safety-critical systems, including avionics, automotive, railway, medical, and other kinds of safety-critical and QoS-critical systems;
- methods, techniques, and tools to support automated analysis, certification, debugging, etc., of complex safety/QoS-critical systems;
- analysis methods that address the limitations of formal methods in industry (usability, scalability, etc.);
- formal analysis support for modeling languages used in industry, such as AADL, Ptolemy, SysML, SCADE, Modelica, etc.; and
- code generation from validated models.

The workshop received 22 regular paper submissions. Each submission was reviewed by at least three referees. Based on the reviews and extensive discussions, the program committee selected ten papers for presentation at the workshop and inclusion in this volume. Another highlight of the workshop was an invited talk by César Muñoz on the use of formal methods at NASA during the development of highly assured software for unmanned aircraft systems.

Many colleagues and friends contributed to FTSCS 2018. We thank César Muñoz for accepting our invitation to give an invited talk and the authors who submitted their work to FTSCS 2018 and who, through their contributions, made this workshop an interesting event. We are particularly grateful to the members of the program committee, who provided timely, insightful, and detailed reviews. We also thank the editors of *Communications in Computer and Information Science* for agreeing to publish the proceedings of FTSCS 2018 as a volume in their series, and Jin Song Dong for his help with the local arrangements.

January 2019

Cyrille Artho
Peter Csaba Ölveczky

Organization

Program Chairs

Cyrille Artho   KTH Royal Institute of Technology, Sweden
Peter Csaba Ölveczky   University of Oslo, Norway

Program Committee

Étienne André   Université Paris 13, France
Toshiaki Aoki   JAIST, Japan
Cyrille Artho   KTH Royal Institute of Technology, Sweden
Kyungmin Bae   Pohang University of Science and Technology, Korea
Daniel Fava   University of Oslo, Norway
Sabine Glesner   TU Berlin, Germany
Osman Hasan   National University of Sciences and Technology,
                                 Pakistan
Klaus Havelund   Jet Propulsion Laboratory, USA
Jérôme Hugues   ISAE, France
Marieke Huisman   University of Twente, The Netherlands
Ralf Huuck   UNSW/SYNOPSYS, Australia
Fuyuki Ishikawa   National Institute of Informatics, Japan
Takashi Kitamura   National Institute of Advanced Industrial Science
                                 and Technology (AIST), Japan
Thierry Lecomte   ClearSy, France
Yang Liu   Nanyang Technological University, Singapore
Robi Malik   University of Waikato, New Zealand
Frédéric Mallet   Université Nice Sophia-Antipolis, France
Roberto Nardone   Mediterranean University of Reggio Calabria, Italy
Thomas Noll   RWTH Aachen University, Germany
Peter Csaba Ölveczky   University of Oslo, Norway
David Pearce   Victoria University of Wellington, New Zealand
Markus Roggenbach   Swansea University, UK
Ralf Sasse   ETH Zürich, Switzerland
Martina Seidl   Johannes Kepler University Linz, Austria
Graeme Smith   The University of Queensland, Australia
Sofiene Tahar   Concordia University, Canada
Carolyn Talcott   SRI International, USA
Tatsuhiro Tsuchiya   Osaka University, Japan

Mark Utting	University of the Sunshine Coast, Australia
András Vörös	Budapest University of Technology and Economics, Hungary
Michael Whalen	University of Minnesota, USA
Huibiao Zhu	East China Normal University, China

Additional Reviewers

Elderhalli, Yassmeen
Siddique, Umair

Formal Methods in the Development of Highly Assured Software for Unmanned Aircraft Systems (Invited Paper)

César Muñoz

NASA Langley Research Center, Hampton, USA

Abstract. Operational requirements of safety-critical systems are often written in restricted specification logics. These restricted logics are amenable to automated analysis techniques such as model-checking, but are not rich enough to express complex requirements of unmanned systems that involve, for example, the physical environment. This talk advocates the use of expressive logics, such as higher-order logic, to specify the complex operational requirements and safety properties of unmanned systems. These rich logics are less amenable to automation and, hence, require the use of interactive theorem proving techniques. However, they enable the formal verification of complex numerically intensive algorithms and the rigorous validation of their implementations. The proposed approach is illustrated with two cases studies from NASA's research on Unmanned Aircraft Systems (UAS): Detect and Avoid Alerting Logic for Unmanned Systems (DAIDALUS) and Independent Configurable Architecture for Reliable Operations of Unmanned Systems (ICAROUS). DAIDALUS is the reference implementation of detect and avoid for UAS in FAA DO-365. ICAROUS is a software architecture built on top of DAIDALUS that enables the development of autonomous UAS applications.

Contents

Model Transformation

Analysis and Verification of Safety-Critical Systems

Formal Stability Analysis of Control Systems

Asad Ahmed[1(✉)], Osman Hasan[1], and Falah Awwad[2]

[1] School of Electrical Engineering and Computer Science (SEECS),
National University of Sciences and Technology (NUST),
Islamabad, Pakistan
{asad.ahmed,osman.hasan}@seecs.nust.edu.pk
[2] Electrical Engineering Department, College of Engineering,
United Arab Emirates University, Al-Ain, UAE
f_awwad@uaeu.ac.ae

Abstract. Stability of a control system ensures that its output is under control and thus is the most important characteristic of control systems. Stability is characterized by the roots of the characteristic equation of the given control system in the complex-domain. Traditionally, paper-and-pencil proof methods and computer-based tools are used to analyze the stability of control systems. However, paper-and-pencil proof methods are error prone due to the human involvement. Whereas, computer based tools cannot model the continuous behavior in its true form due to the involvement of computer arithmetic and the associated truncation errors. Therefore, these techniques do not provide an accurate and complete analysis, which is unfortunate given the safety-critical nature of control system applications. In this paper, we propose to overcome these limitations by using higher-order-logic theorem proving for the stability analysis of control systems. For this purpose, we present a higher-order-logic based formalization of stability and the roots of the quadratic, cubic and quartic complex polynomials. The proposed formalization is based on the complex number theory of the HOL-Light theorem prover. A distinguishing feature of this work is the automatic nature of the formal stability analysis, which makes it quite useful for the control engineers working in the industry who have very little expertise about formal methods. For illustration purposes, we present the stability analysis of power converter controllers used in smart grids.

Keywords: Stability · Control systems · Polynomials · HOL-light

1 Introduction

Stability [15] is the most important design requirement of a linear time-invariant control system. An unstable control system deployed in a safety-critical domain, e.g., in nuclear power plants or aircrafts, can lead to disastrous consequences,

C. Artho and P. C. Ölveczky (Eds.): FTSCS 2018, CCIS 1008, pp. 3–17, 2019.
https://doi.org/10.1007/978-3-030-12988-0_1

including the loss of human lives, and therefore stability is considered as a safety-critical system specification.

Generally, the design and analysis of linear time-invariant control systems [15] is done in the frequency domain. The main idea is to convert a differential equation representation of the system into its frequency domain representation using a transform method, like Laplace or Fourier [4]. This transformation simplifies the modeling of interconnected subsystems and also generates a mathematical model of the system that algebraically relates the input to the output based on a transfer function,

$$TF(s) = \frac{O(s)}{I(s)} = \frac{a_m s^m + a_{m-1} s^{m-1} + \dots + a_0}{b_n s^n + b_{n-1} s^{n-1} + \dots + b_0} \qquad (1)$$

where, a_i and b_i are the coefficients representing system parameters, s is a complex-variable and m and n are natural numbers. Whereas, $max\{m, n\}$ represents the order of the transfer function. The order of the transfer function depends on the order of the corresponding linear differential equation in the time domain representing a physical system. As most of the variables of the physical system can be represented using differentials upto the fourth order, such as capacitor current, inductor voltage, acceleration, velocity and momentum, therefore, control systems upto fourth order cover a wide spectrum of applications, including safety and mission-critical applications. Moreover, there are model reduction techniques [20] to reduce the higher-order transfer functions into their equivalent lower-order representations to facilitate the control system design. The denominator and the numerator of a transfer function, in Eq. (1), are complex polynomials which are used to characterize the *zeros* and the *poles* of the system. These zeros and poles are roots of complex polynomials in the denominator and the numerator of the transfer function, respectively. In particular, the stability of the system solely depends on the location of the poles of the system, obtained from:

$$b_n s^n + b_{n-1} s^{n-1} + \dots + b_0 = 0 \qquad (2)$$

Equation (2) is also referred to as a *characteristic* equation of the system. The system is categorized as *stable, unstable* and *marginally stable* based on the location of the roots of Eq. (2) in the complex-plane. For a stable system, the roots of the characteristic equation lie in the left-half of the complex-plane, for an unstable system, the roots of the characteristic equation lie in the right-half of the complex-plane, and for a marginally stable system, the roots of the characteristic equation lie on the imaginary axis of the complex-plane.

Traditionally, paper-and-pencil proof methods and computer based tools are used to perform the stability analysis of control systems. The stability analysis using paper-and-pencil proof methods is based on the quadratic formula for the second order polynomial (quadratic), Cardano's method, Vieta's method and Lagrange's method for the third order polynomial (cubic), and Ferrari's solution, Descartes' solution and Euler's solution for the fourth order polynomial (quartic). Whereas, to the best of our knowledge, there does not exist any closed form solution to find the root for higher than fourth order polynomials. Routh-Hurwitz criterion [15] is another paper-and-pencil proof method, which is used for the stability analysis of control systems. It consists of building a table using the coefficients of the given polynomial following certain rules. This table can be used to find if the given system is stable or unstable on the basis of patterns exhibited by the rows and columns of the table [15]. The manual analytical analysis involved in these methods make them prone to human error. Moreover, these risks significantly increase with an increase in the system complexity.

Many computer-aided design tools based on the principles of numerical methods and simulation have also been introduced for the modeling and analysis of linear time-invariant control systems. For example, MathWorks Simulink [13] and MathWorks Control System Toolbox [12] facilitate finding the poles and zeros of the system and are thus frequently used in the design and analysis of control systems. They provide a scalable option to handle large and complex systems as well. However, these computer based techniques cannot capture the continuous aspects of the system in their true form and are based on the discrete frequency models. The completeness of the model is thus lost while dealing with the continuous time behavior. Moreover, the numerical values of roots computed using computer based arithmetic, like floating or fixed point numbers, are subject to truncation errors, and hence may not be accurate. Another alternative for analyzing the stability of control systems is computer algebra systems, such as Mathematica [26], Maple [10] and Maxima [21]. These methods are very efficient for computing the roots of a system, symbolically, but they are not reliable as well [8] due to the presence of unverified huge symbolic manipulation algorithms in their core, which are quite likely to contain bugs. Thus, given the above-mentioned inaccuracies, these traditional techniques should not be relied upon for the stability analysis of control systems used in safety-critical applications, such as nuclear plants, electric vehicles or auto-pilot systems, where an inaccurate or erroneous analysis could result in unfortunate catastrophic events that may even lead to the loss of human lives.

The main motivation of this paper is to develop a formalization for the stability analysis of linear time-invariant control systems, represented by characteristic equations of order upto four, with minimal dependence on conventional analysis techniques. We consider complex polynomials with real coefficients, for the purpose of formal analysis in higher-order logic, which allow us to express the cubic and quartic complex polynomials in terms of the quadratic polynomials. However, this choice does not limit the scope of the applicability of our formalization as these coefficients are usually real numbers as they represent the different parameters of the system, e.g., resistance in electrical and electronics systems. The formally verified roots, which are poles of the system, are then formally analyzed to check for the stability condition, i.e., if they lie in the left-half of the complex-plane, in the sound core of the higher-order-logic theorem prover HOL-Light [7]. The main motivation of this choice is the extensive reasoning support available in HOL-Light about multivariate complex, real and transcendental theories, which are required for the formalization of stability analysis of control systems.

The rest of the paper is organized as follows: In Sect. 2, we present a review of the related work. This is followed by the description of the proposed methodology about stability analysis in Sect. 3. The formalization of the quadratic, cubic and quartic characteristic polynomials is described in Sect. 4. We utilize this formalization to formally verify voltage and current controllers designed for the power converters for reliable and efficient smart grid operation in Sect. 5. Finally, Sect. 6 concludes the paper.

2   Related Work

The formalization of Laplace transform [24] has been proposed to formally reason and verify the transformation properties, e.g., existence, linearity, frequency shifting and differentiation and integration in time domain. This formalization framework allows to verify the correspondence of the time domain representation of the system, i.e., linear differential equation, to the frequency domain representation of the system, i.e., transfer functions. This existing work can be used along with the formalization proposed in this paper to analyze the stability analysis of control systems, expressed in terms of their dynamical behaviors using differential equations.

Block diagrams formalization has been proposed [1,9] to conduct steady-state error analysis, i.e., when $s \to 0$, for feedback and unity feedback control systems, in frequency domain. However, this formalization does not explicitly deal with the stability analysis of control systems. Formal stability analysis has also been proposed for some particular safety and mission-critical applications. The formal stability analysis of optical waveguides [19] has been performed by defining the stability condition in terms of the boundedness and orientation of a ray in a wave guide using multivariate theory in HOL-Light. A logical framework for the formal verification of various strategies for the platoon vehicle controllers [17] is proposed and is then used for developing a runtime monitor which can be used for automatic monitoring of the vehicles for stability violation. Similarly, another comprehensive logical framework for the analysis of control systems [16] considers the system differential equations and obtains their corresponding transfer functions using Laplace transformation and it also provides a support for the block diagram analysis of the system in frequency domain. On the basis of this framework, formal analysis of active realizations of various controllers, Proportional Integral-Derivative (PID), Proportional-Integral (PI), Proportional-Derivative (PD), Proportional (P), Integral (I) and Derivative (D) and various active and passive compensators, such as lag, lead and lag-lead is conducted. However, the aforementioned formalizations for the stability are application specific and do not provide a generic treatment of the stability of the control systems. The formally verified quadratic roots [18] have been used for the formal analysis of cyber-physical systems using the real number theory in the HOL4 theorem prover. However, this formalization of the quadratic formula in real number theory cannot be used to analyze the complex-domain of the control systems. Whereas, our formalization directly incorporates the transfer function of a control system, as a complex polynomial, for the stability analysis of a control system and thus provides the flexibility to be applied on any control system. A distinguishing aspect of our formal analysis is the explicit availability of an exhaustive list of side assumptions besides every theorem which is not possible in the informal analysis methods, which can be quite useful for the analysis of safety-critical application designers.

3 Proposed Methodology

We propose to use higher-order-logic theorem proving, as shown in Fig. 1, to formally verify the stability of linear time-invariant control systems. The analysis is primarily based on the characteristic equation of the system, of the fourth order at most, in the complex-domain. The first step in the proposed methodology is to formally verify the roots of the complex quadratic, cubic and quartic polynomials, which represent poles of a given control system. Therefore, these polynomials are described as higher-order-logic functions and the formal verification of their roots are performed using the multivariate complex, real and transcendental theories available in the library of HOL-Light theorem prover, interactively, as shown in Fig. 1. In the next step, the stability condition is formally modeled in higher-order logic to formally verify the stability of these roots, as higher-order-logic theorems, using the formally verified results from the first step, as shown in Fig. 1. Finally, the above-mentioned formalization can be utilized to formally analyze the stability of any control system almost automatically.

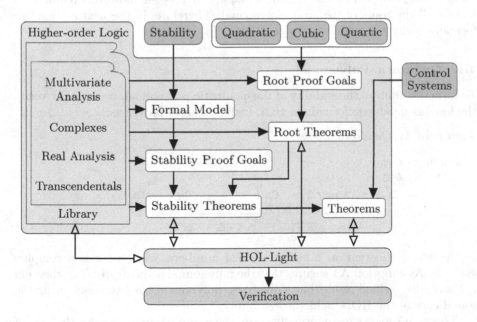

Fig. 1. Proposed methodology for stability analysis in HOL-Light

4 Stability Formalization

This section provides a formal definition of stability of a root of a polynomial, formally verified results for the close form solutions or roots of polynomilas upto fourth order and formally verified results on the stability of these polynomials in the HOL-Light theorem prover. The stability of a root is defined, as a higher-order logic function, as:

Definition 1: *Stability*

⊢ ∀ f. stable f = ∼({ x | f x = Cx (0) ∧ Re (x) < 0 } = EMPTY)

In Definition 1, $f : R^2 \rightarrow R^2$ represents a complex function, which is a polynomial in our case, $x : R^2$ is a complex variable, which in our case is the root of the given polynomial, and Cx and Re are HOL-light functions, which are used to convert a real number into a complex number and to retrieve the real part of a given complex number, respectively.

The predicate stable:$(R^2 \rightarrow R^2) \rightarrow bool$ accepts a polynomial and returns a *boolean* output, which is true for a stable root of the polynomial of the considered system and false otherwise. Definition 1 formally models two conditions for the stability of a root of the given complex polynomial, i.e., f x = Cx (0) and Re (x) < 0. These conditions ensure that a complex-variable, x, is a root of the given polynomial and its real part lies in the left-half of the complex-plane. Furthermore, these roots are formally defined as the member of a set which should not be empty if the polynomial has any stable root. To ensure that all roots of a given polynomial are the members of this set, however, requires us to find all the roots of the given polynomial. Therefore, in the next section, we formally verify the roots of a polynomial.

4.1 Quadratic Polynomial

To formally analyze the stability of the quadratic polynomial, we formally verify the famous quadratic formula in HOL-Light theorem prover as:

Theorem 1: *Quadratic Roots*

⊢ ∀ a b c x .
   A1: a ≠ 0
$$\Rightarrow \text{Cx a} * \text{ x pow 2} + \text{ Cx b} * \text{ x} + \text{ Cx c} = \text{Cx 0}$$
$$x = \frac{-\,\text{Cx b} + \sqrt{\text{Cx b pow 2} - \text{Cx 4} * \text{Cx a} * \text{Cx c}}}{\text{Cx 2} * \text{Cx a}} \lor$$
$$x = \frac{-\text{Cx b} - \sqrt{\text{Cx b pow 2} - \text{Cx 4} * \text{Cx a} * \text{Cx c}}}{\text{Cx 2} * \text{Cx a}}$$

In the above theorem, a, b and c are real numbers, whereas, x is a complex variable. Assumption **A1** ensures that the polynomial is quadratic. The theorem is a formally verified result that a quadratic polynomial has two roots, using the sound core of the HOL-Light theorem prover.

Theorem 1 allows us to formally verify the stability conditions for the case of two roots, using Definition 1, as:

Lemma 1: *Complex Root Case*

$\vdash \forall$ a b c x .
    A1: a $\neq$ 0 $\wedge$
    A2: b pow 2 $-$ 4 $*$ a $*$ c $<$ 0 $\wedge$
    A3: 0 $< \frac{b}{a}$
    $\Rightarrow$ stable (λx. Cx a $*$ x pow 2 $+$ Cx b $*$ x $+$ Cx c)

Lemma 2: *Real Root Case 1*

$\vdash \forall$ a b c x .
    A1: a $\neq$ 0 $\wedge$
    A2: b pow 2 $-$ 4 $*$ a $*$ c $=$ 0 $\wedge$
    A3: 0 $< \frac{b}{a}$
    $\Rightarrow$ stable (λx. Cx a $*$ x pow 2 $+$ Cx b $*$ x $+$ Cx c)

Lemma 3: *Real Root Case 2*

$\vdash \forall$ a b c x .
    A1: a $<$ 0 $\wedge$
    A2: 0 $<$ b pow 2 $-$ 4 $*$ a $*$ c
    A3: b $< \sqrt{\text{b pow 2} - 4 * a * c}$
    $\Rightarrow$ stable (λx. Cx a $*$ x pow 2 $+$ Cx b $*$ x $+$ Cx c)

Lemma 4: *Real Root Case 3*

$\vdash \forall$ a b c x .
    A1: a $<$ 0 $\wedge$
    A2: b pow 2 $-$ 4 $*$ a $*$ c $<$ 0 $\wedge$
    A3: $\sqrt{\text{b pow 2} - 4 * a * c}$ $< -$ b
    $\Rightarrow$ stable (λx. Cx a $*$ x pow 2 $+$ Cx b $*$ x $+$ Cx c)

Lemma 5: *Real Root Case 4*

$\vdash \forall$ a b c x .
    A1: 0 $<$ a $\wedge$
    A2: 0 $<$ b pow 2 $-$ 4 $*$ a $*$ c $\wedge$
    A3: $\sqrt{\text{b pow 2} - 4 * a * c}$ $<$ b
    $\Rightarrow$ stable (λx. Cx a $*$ x pow 2 $+$ Cx b $*$ x $+$ Cx c)

Lemma 6: *Real Root Case 5*

$\vdash \forall$ a b c x .
    A1: 0 $<$ a $\wedge$
    A2: 0 $<$ b pow 2 $-$ 4 $*$ a $*$ c $\wedge$
    A3: $-$ b $< \sqrt{\text{b pow 2} - 4 * a * c}$
    $\Rightarrow$ stable (λx. Cx a $*$ x pow 2 $+$ Cx b $*$ x $+$ Cx c)

Lemmas 1–6 are formally verified using the multivariate complex, real analysis and transcendental theories available in the library of the HOL-Light theorem prover. The above formally verified results cover all possible conditions on coefficients, of the second order polynomial, and on the discriminant of the quadratic formula for the stability of roots, as shown in Fig. 2.

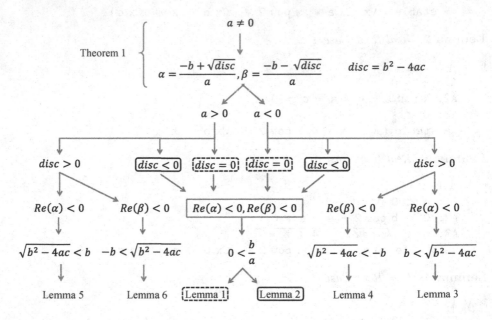

Fig. 2. Stability of quadratic polynomial

Now, Lemmas 1–6 are used to formally assert the stability of a quadratic polynomial as:

Theorem 2: *Quadratic Stability*

```
⊢ ∀ a b c x .
    A1: a ≠ 0 ∧
    A2:  0 < b/a ∧ ( b pow 2 - 4 * a * c < 0 ∨   b pow 2 - 4 * a * c = 0 )
∨
         0 < b pow 2 - 4 * a * c ∧
            ( a < 0 ∧ ( b < √b pow 2 - 4 * a * c ∨
                        √b pow 2 - 4 * a * c < - b ) ∨
            ( 0 < a ∧ ( √b pow 2 - 4 * a * c < b ∨
                        - b < √b pow 2 - 4 * a * c )
         ⇒ stable ( λx. Cx a *  x pow 2 +  Cx b *  x +  Cx c )
```

Theorem 2 provides a formally verified comprehensive result for the stability of the quadratic polynomial under all possible cases that may arise due to the nature of discriminant, nature of real coefficients of the polynomial using HOL-Light. The formalization of the quadratic polynomial plays a key role in the formal stability analysis of cubic and quartic polynomials as will be observed in the next two subsections.

4.2   Cubic Polynomial

In this section, we provide the formally verified results for the roots of a cubic polynomial, and their stability, using Definition 1 and Lemmas 1–6. To formally analyze the stability of the cubic polynomial, we formally verify the factor decomposition of a cubic into its linear and quadratic factors in HOL-Light as follows:

Theorem 3: *Cubic Factors*

$\vdash \forall$ a b1 c1 d1 r x .
   A1: Cx b $=$ Cx b1 $+$ Cx a $*$ Cx r $\wedge$
   A2: Cx c $=$ Cx c1 $+$ Cx b1 $*$ Cx r
   A3: Cx d $=$ Cx c1 $*$ Cx r $\wedge$
     $\Rightarrow$ Cx a $*$ x pow 3 $+$ Cx b $*$ xpow 2 $+$ Cx c $*$ x $+$ Cx d $=$
     (x $+$ Cx r) $*$ (Cx a $*$ x pow 2 $+$ Cx b1 $*$ x $+$ Cx c1)

In the above theorem, a, b1, c1, d1 and r are real-valued random variables, which represent coefficients of the cubic factors. Whereas, x is a complex variable. Assumptions **A1–A3** formally represent the factor decompositions of the cubic polynomial.

Next, we present formally verified roots of the cubic polynomial using Definition 1, Lemmas 1–6 and Theorem 3 in HOL-Light as:

Theorem 4: *Cubic Roots*

$\vdash \forall$ a b1 c1 d1 r x .
  A1: a $\neq$ 0 $\wedge$
  A2: Cx b $=$ Cx b1 $+$ Cx a $*$ Cx r $\wedge$
  A3: Cx c $=$ Cx c1 $+$ Cx b1 $*$ Cx r $\wedge$
  A4: Cx d $=$ Cx c1 $*$ Cx r
  $\Rightarrow$ (Cx a $*$ x pow 3 $+$ Cx b $*$ xpow 2 $+$ Cx c $*$ x $+$ Cx d $=$ Cx 0)
  $=$ (x $=$ Cx r $\vee$ x $= \dfrac{-\ \text{Cx b1} + \sqrt{\text{Cx b1 pow 2} - \text{Cx 4} * \text{Cx a} * \text{Cx c1}}}{\text{Cx 2} * \text{Cx a}}$ $\vee$
        x $= \dfrac{-\ \text{Cx b1} - \sqrt{\text{Cx b1 pow 2} - \text{Cx 4} * \text{Cx a} * \text{Cx c1}}}{\text{Cx 2} * \text{Cx a}}$)

In the above theorem, Assumption **A1** ensures that the leading coefficient of the polynomial is not zero, i.e., the given polynomial is cubic. Assumptions **A2–A4** provide the factor decomposition of the given polynomial. Based on these assumptions, Theorem 4 formally verifies that the cubic polynomial has three roots.

Finally, the above formalization is used to formally verify the stability of a cubic polynomial as:

Theorem 5: *Cubic Stability*

⊢ ∀ a b1 c1 d1 r x .
   A1: a ≠ 0 ∧ A2: Cx b = Cx b1 + Cx a ∗ Cx r ∧
   A3: Cx c = Cx c1 + Cx b1 ∗ Cx r ∧ A4: Cx d = Cx c1 ∗ Cx r
   A4: 0 < r ∨
      ((0 < $\frac{b1}{a}$ ∧ (b1 pow 2 - 4 ∗ a∗ c1 < 0 ∨
                              b1 pow 2 - 4 ∗ a∗ c1 = 0))) ∨
      (0 < b1 pow 2 - 4 ∗ a ∗ c1 ∧
             (a < 0 ∧ (b1 $\sqrt{\text{b1 pow 2} - 4 * a * c1}$ ∨
                        $\sqrt{\text{b1 pow 2} - 4 * a * c1}$ < - b1) ∨
             (0 < a ∧ ($\sqrt{\text{b1 pow 2} - 4 * a * c1}$ < b1 ∨
                        - b < $\sqrt{\text{b1 pow 2} - 4 * a * c1}$)))
   ⇒ stable (λ x. Cx a ∗ x pow 3 + Cx b ∗ x pow 2 + Cx c ∗ x + Cx d)

Theorem 5 provides a formally verified result for the stability of the cubic polynomial under all possible values of real coefficients of the cubic polynomial, and explicitly states the relationship among them for satisfying stability conditions.

4.3   Quartic Polynomial

In this section, we provide formally verified results for the roots, of a quartic polynomial, and their stability, using Definition 1 and Lemmas 1–6. To formally analyze the stability of the quartic polynomial, we formally verify the factor decomposition of a quartic into its two quadratic factors in HOL-Light as:

Theorem 6: *Quartic Factors*

⊢ ∀ a1 b1 c1 a2 b2 c2 x .
   A1: Cx a = Cx a1 ∗ Cx a2 ∧
   A2: Cx b = Cx a1 ∗ Cx b2 + Cx a2 ∗ Cx b1 ∧
   A3: Cx c = Cx a1 ∗ Cx c2 + Cx b1 ∗ Cx b2 + Cx a2 ∗ Cx c1 ∧
   A4: Cx d = Cx b1 ∗ Cx c2 + Cx b2 ∗ Cx c1 ∧
   A5: Cx e = Cx c1 ∗ Cx c2
   ⇒ (Cx a ∗ x pow 4 + Cx b ∗ x pow 3 + Cx c ∗ x pow 2 + Cx d ∗ x
      + Cx e = Cx 0) =
      ((Cx a1 ∗ x pow 2 + Cx b1 ∗ x + Cx c1) ∗
        (Cx a2 ∗ x pow 2 + Cx b2 ∗ x + Cx c2))

In the above theorem, a1, b1, c1, a2, b2 and c2 are real-valued variables, which represent coefficients of the quadratic factors of a given quartic polynomial. Whereas, x is a complex variable. Theorem 6 formally verifies the factor decomposition of the quartic polynomial given the Assumptions **A1–A5**.

Next, we present formally verified roots of the quartic polynomial using Definition 1, Lemmas 1–6 and Theorem 6 in HOL-Light as:

Theorem 7: *Quartic Roots*

⊢ ∀ a1 b1 c1 a2 b2 c2 x .
    A1: $a \neq 0$ ∧ A2: Cx a = Cx a1 $*$ Cx a2 ∧
    A3: Cx b = Cx a1 $*$ Cx b2 + Cx a2 $*$ Cx b1 ∧
    A4: Cx c = Cx a1 $*$ Cx c2 + Cx b1 $*$ Cx b2 + Cx a2 $*$ Cx c1 ∧
    A5: Cx d = Cx b1 $*$ Cx c2 + Cx b2 $*$ Cx c1 ∧
    A6: Cx e = Cx c1 $*$ Cx c2
    ⇒ (Cx a $*$ x pow 4 + Cx b $*$ x pow 3 + Cx c $*$ x pow 2 + Cx d $*$ x
    + Cx e = Cx 0) =

$$\left(x = \frac{-\text{Cx b1} + \sqrt{\text{Cx b1 pow 2} - \text{Cx 4} * \text{Cx a1} * \text{Cx c1}}}{\text{Cx 2} * \text{Cx a1}} \right. \lor$$

$$x = \frac{-\text{Cx b1} - \sqrt{\text{Cx b1 pow 2} - \text{Cx 4} * \text{Cx a1} * \text{Cx c1}}}{\text{Cx 2} * \text{Cx a1}} \lor$$

$$x = \frac{-\text{Cx b2} + \sqrt{\text{Cx b2 pow 2} - \text{Cx 4} * \text{Cx a2} * \text{Cx c2}}}{\text{Cx 2} * \text{Cx a2}} \lor$$

$$\left. x = \frac{-\text{Cx b2} - \sqrt{\text{Cx b2 pow 2} - \text{Cx 4} * \text{Cx a2} * \text{Cx c2}}}{\text{Cx 2} * \text{Cx a2}} \right)$$

In the above theorem, Assumption **A1** ensures that the leading coefficient of the polynomial is not zero and thus confirming that the given polynomial is quartic. Assumptions **A2–A6** provide the factor decomposition of the given quartic polynomial. Based on these assumptions, Theorem 7 formally verifies that the quartic polynomial has four roots.

Finally, the above formalization is used to formally verify the stability of a quartic polynomial as:

Theorem 8: *Quartic Stability*

⊢ ∀ a1 b1 c1 a2 b2 c2 x .
    A1: $a \neq 0$ ∧ A2: Cx a = Cx a1 $*$ Cx a2 ∧
    A3: Cx b = Cx a1 $*$ Cx b2 + Cx a2 $*$ Cx b1 ∧
    A4: Cx c = Cx a1 $*$ Cx c2 + Cx b1 $*$ Cx b2 + Cx a2 $*$ Cx c1 ∧
    A5: Cx d = Cx b1 $*$ Cx c2 + Cx b2 $*$ Cx c1 ∧
    A6: Cx e = Cx c1 $*$ Cx c2 ∧
    A7: ($0 < \frac{b1}{a1}$ ∧ (b1 pow 2 - 4 $*$ a1$*$ c1 < 0 ∨
                       b1 pow 2 - 4 $*$ a1$*$ c1 = 0)) ∨
    (b1 pow 2 - 4 $*$ a1$*$ c1 < 0 ∧
          (a1 < 0 ∧ (b1 < $\sqrt{\text{b1 pow 2} - 4 * \text{a1} * \text{c1}}$ ∨
                   $\sqrt{\text{b1 pow 2} - 4 * \text{a1} * \text{c1}}$ < $-$ b1) ∨
          (0 < a1 ∧ ($\sqrt{\text{b1 pow 2} - 4 * \text{a1} * \text{c1}}$ < b1 ∨
                  $-$ b1 < $\sqrt{\text{b1 pow 2} - 4 * \text{a1} * \text{c1}}$))) ∨
    ($0 < \frac{b2}{a2}$ ∧ (0 < b2 pow 2 - 4 $*$ a2$*$ c2 ∨
                     b2 pow 2 - 4 $*$ a2$*$ c2 = 0)) ∨
    (b2 pow 2 - 4 $*$ a2$*$ c2 < 0 ∧
          (a2 < 0 ∧ (b2 < $\sqrt{\text{b2 pow 2} - 4 * \text{a2} * \text{c2}}$ ∨
                   $\sqrt{\text{b2 pow 2} - 4 * \text{a2} * \text{c2}}$ < $-$ b1) ∨
          (0 < a2 ∧ ($\sqrt{\text{b2 pow 2} - 4 * \text{a2} * \text{c2}}$ < b2 ∨
                  $-$ b2 < $\sqrt{\text{b2 pow 2} - 4 * \text{a2} * \text{c2}}$)))
    ⇒ stable (λx. (Cx a $*$ x pow 4 + Cx b $*$ x pow 3 + Cx c $*$ x pow 2
    + Cx d $*$ x + Cx e)

Theorem 8 provides an exhaustive set of conditions for the stability of the quartic polynomial using the HOL-light theorem prover.

Theorem proving is a highly expressive and sound formal method technique and therefore resulted in an exhaustive set of assumptions for the formal verification of poles of the system and their stability, which is not possible using conventional analysis techniques. Moreover, these assumptions reveal the relationship among the coefficients of polynomials, representing system parameters, which provide useful insights from the perspective of a control system design. The formalization is generic, i.e., all the involved variables are universally quantified, and thus the verified theorems can be specialized to conduct the stability analysis of a control system in an almost automatic manner. The corresponding proof script, which is available for download at [2], has 5000 lines of HOL-Light code and required about 380 man hours of development time.

5   Application: Power Converter Controllers Used in Smart Grids

Smart grids are networks with intelligent nodes to produce, consume and share the energy efficiently by leveraging upon the advances in the fields of communication, electronics and computation [14]. There has been an enormous increase in the usage of smart grid technology over the world in the last decade or so [6]. Thus, an insecure and unreliable smart grid can even lead to disastrous consequences [3].

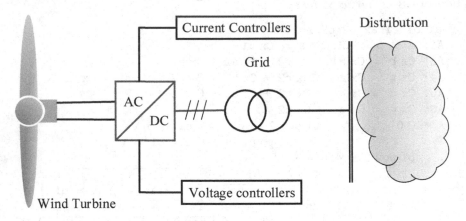

Fig. 3. Efficient energy harvesting using power converter controllers in smart grids

Energy harvesting and its processing, from unconventional sources, such as wind turbines and solar panels, is one of the key challenges in smart grids due to the intermittent nature of the produced energy [27]. To achieve a steady flow from these sources, power converters are designed to alleviate the problem. This objective is usually achieved by designing efficient current and voltage controllers for these power converters so that a smooth supply of power can be ensured, as shown in Fig. 3.

In this paper, we formally verify the stability of an H^∞ current, H^∞ voltage and H^∞ repetitive current controllers designed for the power converters to enhance the efficiency of smart grids [27]. H^∞ [23] and repetitive control [11] are control methods, which are used for designing suboptimal controllers and controllers, which enable the power converters to inject a clean power into the grid system and thus resulting in more reliable and secure grid operations.

The transfer function of an H^∞ current controller is given [27] as:

$$[TF]_i = \frac{1.7998 * 10^9(s + 300)}{s^2 + 4.33403 * 10^8 s + 1.10517 * 10^{12}} \tag{3}$$

The characteristic equation of above transfer function is of second order therefore we utilize Theorem 2 to formally verify the stability in higher-order logic as:

Theorem 9: H^∞ *Current Controller*

⊢ ∀ a b c s .
     stable (λx. Cx 1 * s pow 2 +   Cx 4.3340 * 10^8 * x +   Cx 1.10517 * 10^{12})

The transfer function of an H^∞ voltage controller is given [27] as:

$$[TF]_v = \frac{748.649(s^2 + 6954s + 3.026 * 10^8)}{s^3 + 10519s^2 + 3.246 * 10^8 s + 7.7596 * 10^7} \tag{4}$$

The characteristic equation of this transfer function is of third order therefore we utilize Theorem 5 to formally verify the stability in higher-order logic as:

Theorem 10: H^∞ *Voltage Controller*

⊢ ∀ a b1 c1 d1 r s .
   A1: a = 1 ∧ A2: b1 = 79669 ∧ A3: c1 = 3.043 * 10^8 ∧ A4: r = 2550
   ⇒ stable (λx. Cx 1 * s pow 3 +   Cx 10519 * s pow 2 +   Cx 3.246 * 10^8 * s
       +   Cx 7.7596 * 10^7)

The transfer function of an H^∞ repetitive current controller is given [27] as:

$$[TF]_{vr} = \frac{8.63 * 10^8(s + 10^4)(s + 1000)(s + 80)}{s^4 + 1.55 * 10^8 s^3 + 1.83 * 10^{13} s^2 + 1.43 * 10^{17} s + 1.08 * 10^{19}} \tag{5}$$

The characteristic equation of above transfer function is of fourth order therefore we utilize Theorem 8 to formally verify the overall stability in higher-order logic as:

Theorem 11: H^∞ *Repetitive Current Controller*

⊢ ∀ a1 b1 c1 a2 b2 c2 s .
     A1: a1 = 1 ∧ A2: b1 = 1.557 * 10^7 ∧ A3: c1 = 1.70538 * 10^3 ∧
     A4: a2 = 1 ∧ A5: b2 = 8.403 * 10^3 ∧ A6: c2 = 6.375 * 10^5
     ⇒ stable (λx. Cx 1 * s pow 4 +   Cx 1.55 * 10^8 * s pow 3 +
         Cx 1.83 * 10^{13} * s pow 2 +   1.43 * 10^{17} * s +   Cx 1.08 * 10^{19})

Theorems 9–11 formally verify the correctness of the power converter controllers for a smart grid and the reasoning process was very straightforward, i.e., only a few lines of code and almost automatic based on simple real arithmetic. The main distinguishing feature of these theorems, compared to the corresponding results obtained through the traditional methods, is the explicit availability of all the assumptions required for the results to hold. As can be noted from Theorems 9–11 many of these assumptions specify very important design constraints. If these constraints are not met then we may get an unstable controller, which can be very dangerous, given the safety-critical nature of smart grids.

6 Conclusion

This paper presents a formalization for the stability analysis of control systems, which are used in many safety-critical applications. We provided a formal definition of stability in higher-order logic and also formally verified the roots of *characteristic* equations, upto the fourth order, that are used for representing the control systems in the complex-domain. Our formalization is based on the multivariate complex, real and transcendental theories available in HOL-Light theorem prover and allows us to conduct the stability analysis of wide range of control systems almost automatically. For illustration, we also presented the analysis of voltage and current controllers of the power converters which are used to ensure the efficient and reliable smart grid operations. The formalization framework can be easily extended to incorporate the formal verification of marginally stable and unstable roots of the presented polynomials, which are also important for the design of many interesting control systems' applications. Based on the formalization presented in this paper, we are in the process of conducting the formal stability analysis of many other safety-critical applications of control systems, including smart grids [5], robotics [22] and smart cars [25].

Acknowledgments. This work is supported by ICT Fund UAE, fund number 21N206 at UAE University, Al Ain, United Arab Emirates.

References

1. Ahmad, M., Hasan, O.: Formal verification of steady-state errors in unity-feedback control systems. In: Lang, F., Flammini, F. (eds.) FMICS 2014. LNCS, vol. 8718, pp. 1–15. Springer, Cham (2014). https://doi.org/10.1007/978-3-319-10702-8_1
2. Ahmed, A.: System Analysis and Verification (SAVe) Lab. http://save.seecs.nust.edu.pk/projects/fsacs/. Accessed 12 Sept 2018
3. Amin, S.M., Wollenberg, B.F.: Toward a smart grid: power delivery for the 21st century. IEEE Power Energ. Mag. **3**(5), 34–41 (2005)
4. Dyke, P.: An Introduction to Laplace Transforms and Fourier Series. SUMS. Springer, London (2014). https://doi.org/10.1007/978-1-4471-6395-4
5. Ekanayake, J., Jenkins, N.: Comparison of the response of doubly fed and fixed-speed induction generator wind turbines to changes in network frequency. IEEE Trans. Energy Convers. **19**(4), 800–802 (2004)
6. Giordano, V., et al.: Smart grid projects in Europe. JRC Ref Rep Sy 8. Publications Office of the European Union, Luxembourg (2011). https://doi.org/10.2790/32946

7. Harrison, J.: HOL light: an overview. In: Berghofer, S., Nipkow, T., Urban, C., Wenzel, M. (eds.) TPHOLs 2009. LNCS, vol. 5674, pp. 60–66. Springer, Heidelberg (2009). https://doi.org/10.1007/978-3-642-03359-9_4

8. Harrison, J.: Theorem Proving with the Real Numbers. Springer, London (2012)

9. Hasan, O., Ahmad, M.: Formal analysis of steady state errors in feedback control systems using HOL-Light. In: Proceedings of the Conference on Design, Automation and Test in Europe, pp. 1423–1426. EDA Consortium, San Jose (2013)

10. Heck, A., Heck, A.: Introduction to MAPLE. Springer, New York (1993). https://doi.org/10.1007/978-1-4684-0519-4

11. Hornik, T., Zhong, Q.C.: A current-control strategy for voltage-source inverters in microgrids based on H^∞ and repetitive control. IEEE Trans. Power Electron. **26**(3), 943–952 (2011)

12. MathWorks: Control System Toolbox. https://ch.mathworks.com/products/control.html. Accessed 12 Sept 2018

13. MathWorks: Simulink. https://www.mathworks.com/products/simulink.html. Accessed 12 Sept 2018

14. Momoh, J.A.: Smart Grid: Fundamentals of Design and Analysis, vol. 63. Wiley, Hoboken (2012)

15. Nise, N.S.: Control Systems Engineering. Wiley, Hoboken (2007)

16. Rashid, A., Hasan, O.: Formal analysis of linear control systems using theorem proving. In: Duan, Z., Ong, L. (eds.) ICFEM 2017. LNCS, vol. 10610, pp. 345–361. Springer, Cham (2017). https://doi.org/10.1007/978-3-319-68690-5_21

17. Rashid, A., Siddique, U., Hasan, O.: Formal verification of platoon control strategies. In: Johnsen, E.B., Schaefer, I. (eds.) SEFM 2018. LNCS, vol. 10886, pp. 223–238. Springer, Cham (2018). https://doi.org/10.1007/978-3-319-92970-5_14

18. Sanwal, M.U., Hasan, O.: Formally analyzing continuous aspects of cyber-physical systems modeled by homogeneous linear differential equations. In: Berger, C., Mousavi, M.R. (eds.) CyPhy 2015. LNCS, vol. 9361, pp. 132–146. Springer, Cham (2015). https://doi.org/10.1007/978-3-319-25141-7_10

19. Siddique, U., Aravantinos, V., Tahar, S.: Formal stability analysis of optical resonators. In: Brat, G., Rungta, N., Venet, A. (eds.) NFM 2013. LNCS, vol. 7871, pp. 368–382. Springer, Heidelberg (2013). https://doi.org/10.1007/978-3-642-38088-4_25

20. Skogestad, S., Postlethwaite, I.: Multivariable Feedback Control: Analysis and Design, vol. 2. Wiley, New York (2007)

21. Sourceforge: Maxima. http://maxima.sourceforge.net/. Accessed 12 Sept 2018

22. Spong, M.W., Hutchinson, S., Vidyasagar, M., et al.: Robot Modeling and Control, vol. 3. Wiley, New York (2006)

23. Stoorvogel, A.A.: The H^∞ Control Problem: A State Space Approach. Citeseer (1992)

24. Taqdees, S.H., Hasan, O.: Formalization of Laplace transform using the multivariable calculus theory of HOL-light. In: McMillan, K., Middeldorp, A., Voronkov, A. (eds.) LPAR 2013. LNCS, vol. 8312, pp. 744–758. Springer, Heidelberg (2013). https://doi.org/10.1007/978-3-642-45221-5_50

25. Varaiya, P.: Smart cars on smart roads: problems of control. IEEE Trans. Autom. Control **38**(2), 195–207 (1993)

26. Wellin, P.R., Gaylord, R.J., Kamin, S.N.: An Introduction to Programming with Mathematica®. Cambridge University Press, Cambridge (2005)

27. Zhong, Q.C., Hornik, T.: Control of Power Inverters in Renewable Energy and Smart Grid Integration, vol. 97. Wiley, Hoboken (2012)

Modular Verification of Vehicle Platooning with Respect to Decisions, Space and Time

Maryam Kamali[1], Sven Linker[2($\boxtimes$)], and Michael Fisher[2]

[1] Nominet, London, UK
maryam.kamali@nominet.uk
[2] University of Liverpool, Liverpool, UK
{s.linker,mfisher}@liverpool.ac.uk

Abstract. The spread of autonomous systems into safety-critical areas has increased the demand for their formal verification, not only due to stronger certification requirements but also to public uncertainty over these new technologies. However, the complex nature of such systems, for example, the intricate combination of discrete and continuous aspects, ensures that whole system verification is often infeasible. This motivates the need for novel analysis approaches that modularise the problem, allowing us to restrict our analysis to one particular aspect of the system while abstracting away from others. For instance, while verifying the real-time properties of an autonomous system we might hide the details of the internal decision-making components. In this paper we describe verification of a range of properties across distinct dimensions on a practical hybrid agent architecture. This allows us to verify the autonomous decision-making, real-time aspects, and spatial aspects of an autonomous vehicle platooning system. This modular approach also illustrates how both algorithmic and deductive verification techniques can be applied for the analysis of different system subcomponents.

Keywords: Modular verification · Hybrid agent architecture · Spatial reasoning

1 Introduction

Autonomous systems are increasingly being introduced into safety-critical areas, for example nuclear waste management [1], or transportation, in the form of unmanned aircraft, advanced driver assistance systems, and even driverless cars. Although autonomous cars are generally aimed at increasing the overall safety of traffic, vehicle *platooning* [16,27], shown in Fig. 1 in particular provides even more advantages over single vehicles: it potentially decreases both congestion on

Work supported EPSRC grants EP/N007565 (Science of Sensor Systems Software), EP/R026092 (FAIR-SPACE RAI Hub) and EP/L024845/1 (Verifiable Autonomy).

© Springer Nature Switzerland AG 2019
C. Artho and P. C. Ölveczky (Eds.): FTSCS 2018, CCIS 1008, pp. 18–36, 2019.
https://doi.org/10.1007/978-3-030-12988-0_2

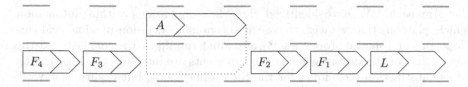

Fig. 1. Vehicle platooning—vehicle A joining interior of platoon

motorways, and fuel consumption, since the relative braking distance between vehicles should be smaller, and hence the vehicles can make use of slipstreams with reduced wind resistance. Here, vehicles are held in sequence on a highway, with distances and speeds controlled by the platoon rather than the individual vehicle. Platooning has recently gained more attention as it is considered as an eco-driving strategy especially for Heavy-Duty Vehicles (HDV) [2], for instance, the european truck platooning challenge[1] in 2016. Six automotive/truck commercial carriers drove semi-automated trucks in platoons aiming to prompt the real implementation of platooning in the roads. Besides, platooning is encouraged politically, for instance, by the Department of Transport of the UK.[2]

Autonomous vehicles within a platoon need to be verified to ensure the overall safety of the platoon. Specifically both autonomous decision-making concerning leaving/joining the platoon, and low-level interaction with its environment have to be analysed, in the best case by providing guarantees for reliable behaviour. Typically, simulations are used to support such guarantees [2,19]. However, these simulations are not performed in a way to gain any insight into the reasons why an agent performed a certain action. To certify high-level decisions of an individual autonomous system, the *rational agent* concept [29] is widely used, as it allows for an analysis of the *reasons* why a system chooses a certain action.

The physical interaction of a vehicle with the rest of the platoon of vehicles in its environment consists of several different dimensions. Two of the most important are *time* and *space*. Timing constraints are of major importance to the overall behaviour of a system. For example, if an unsafe situation is encountered, the vehicles have to react within a certain time frame to ensure safety during emergencies. But even for normal vehicle behaviour, such as joining or leaving a platoon, time constraints are eminently important [6]. Spatial aspects are vital for similar reasons. Ensuring that vehicles do not get too close, or can fit in the space they are trying to move in to, is clearly important.

So now we reach the key problem. A complex, autonomous system such as an automotive vehicle platoon, will incorporate a diverse range of properties and behaviours. If we wish to formally verify *all* of these dimensions then we will certainly hit complexity issues—multi-dimensional formalisation easily become *very* complex [5,12]. Two approaches are to use modular verification [18] or to use abstraction techniques [7] to separate out dimensions of concern.

---

[1] https://eutruckplatooning.com/.
[2] https://trl.co.uk/news/news/government-gives-green-light-first-operational-vehicle-platooning-trial.

Our Approach. We have identified three key dimensions within autonomous vehicle platoons that we wish to assess: autonomous decision-making, real-time properties, and spatial properties. We also aim to minimise the change to existing components of the system when new components are introduced. Consequently, we use abstraction techniques for the three dimensions, but ensure that verification results for parts of the system that are unchanged remain valid, and so the verification task is reduced to checking any new system components. We show the applicability of this approach by taking an existing autonomous vehicle platoon system whose decision-making and real-time properties have already been verified, in [17], and incorporating spatial aspects. A spatial controller is introduced to model the physical lane-changing behaviour of the vehicles using the logic introduced in [14] that guarantees the correctness of our spatial model. This was something that the original platoon verification did not consider [17]. We also show that not only does the high-level decision making (agent) code remain unchanged, but the new verification task is reduced to the analysis of the real-time requirements as the spatial aspects were shown to be correct [14].

Consequently, we show how this modular verification approach supports the flexibility of the underlying hybrid agent architecture, with any new components of the extended architecture still being relevant. The verification of such architectures remains feasible as long as we can apply appropriate abstractions to the system components. We do not consider malicious or faulty vehicles on the road. That is, the protocol we verify is a minimal requirement for vehicle platoons.

The paper is structured as follows. In Sect. 2, we present the hybrid agent architecture. Subsequently, we show how we instantiate this architecture for spatial and temporal aspects of vehicle platooning in Sect. 3, and present the verification results in Sect. 4. Following a discussion of related work in Sect. 5, Sect. 6 concludes the paper.

2   Hybrid Agent Architecture

Cyber-physical systems, such as autonomous vehicles, require a sophisticated architecture together with corresponding formalism. Practical systems combine continuous environmental interactions, through feedback control, together with discrete changes between these control regimes. In traditional hybrid systems, separating the high-level decision making from continuous control concerns is difficult. The other drawback of standard hybrid modelling approaches is that the representation of decision-making can become very complex and hard to distinguish. We instead utilise a *hybrid agent architecture* [20] where the decision-making aspect is separated into a distinguished 'agent' while the system still provides traditional feedback control systems. This approach provides a clear separation between these two concerns, and also the behaviour of each component is described in much more detail that can contribute to reasoning about their behaviours separately. Thus, the separation of high-level decision making and low-level controllers provides an infrastructure for modular verification.

In this paper, we use the hybrid agent architecture, proposed for autonomous vehicle platooning in [17], as shown in Fig. 2. A *Decision-Making Agent* instructs a *Physical and Continuous Engine* by passing instructions through an *Abstraction Agent*. The Abstraction Agent receives streams of continuous data from the Physical and Continuous Engines, extracts discrete information from this, and sends it to the decision-making agent. The Physical and Continuous engine manages the real-time continuous control of the vehicle through feedback controllers, implemented in MATLAB. We assumed that the dynamics of the vehicles are continuous, i.e., they may not arbitrarily change positions and velocities. An automotive simulator, TORCS[3], was used to implement the automotive environment and this environment is observed through the sensory input by the Physical and Continuous engine.

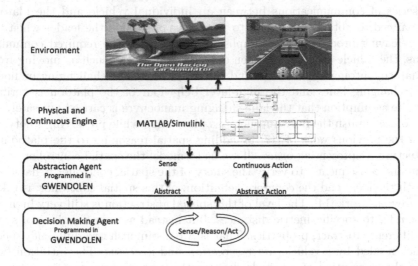

Fig. 2. Hybrid agent architecture [17]

The Decision-Making Agent is a *rational agent* [29] that not only makes decisions, but will have explicit reasons for making these decisions. This allows us to describe *what* the autonomous system chooses to do, and to reason about *why* it makes its choices. Our Decision-Making Agent is based on the BDI (*Belief-Desire-Intention*) paradigm. Here, *beliefs* represent the agent's views about the world, *desires* provide the long-term objectives to be accomplished, and *intentions* capture the set of goals currently being undertaken by the agent in order to achieve its desires.

The separation between the Decision-Making Agent and the Physical and Continuous Engine provides a way to verify the agent behaviour in isolation from the detail of feedback control. In this work we utilise *program model-checking* over the Decision-Making Agent. This allows us to formally verify the

---

[3] The Open Racing Car Simulator https://sourceforge.net/projects/torcs.

real agent code rather than a model of the agent behaviour. This formal verification of agent behaviour is carried out using the AJPF model checker [10] and the agent itself is implemented in the verifiable language GWENDOLEN [9]. The model-checking approach using AJPF is used to demonstrate that the BDI agent always behaves according to the platoon requirements and never intentionally chooses unsafe options. Unfortunately, model checking through AJPF is not only resource-heavy, but also lacks support for the formal verification of timed behaviours. As indicated above, timing will be a key principle of relevance to safety-critical behaviour and so, to tackle this problem, Kamali et al. [17] proposed a modular approach to the verification of automotive platoons constructed in this way.

We here consider two of the main platooning procedures involved in joining and leaving a platoon. Both the joining and leaving procedures are comprised of a series of communications between an individual vehicle and the platoon leader aimed to obtain permission to join/leave or update the leader when the joining/leaving procedure is accomplished. Apart from the required communications, the vehicle switches between different controllers, such as moving from 'manual' to 'automatic' for speed and steering. One of the challenging manoeuvres is changing lanes and the high-level behaviour of the platoon is verified under the assumption that the lane changing manoeuvre is carried out safely. In order to accomplish the fully autonomous platooning while preserving safety, we extend the previous work of [17] by adding spatial reasoning to the platooning architecture. Representing *space* allows us to model the spatial controller of the system and consequently to verify the safety of the spatial controller behaviours.

Both the idea, and the concrete definition, of this spatial controller, is taken from previous work [14]. The level of this spatial abstraction is still very high: we do not refer to specific/metric distances, but instead associate regions of space with different, abstract, properties. That is, we distinguish two different aspects of space needed by a vehicle: its *reservation* and its *claim*. The intuition here is that the reservation of a vehicle denotes the part of space that is *necessary* for the vehicle to operate safely. It comprises both the physical extent of the vehicle and the distance it needs to come to a standstill in case of an emergency. The claim, however, is not as restrictive. It is an additional way for the vehicles to communicate, similar to the turning signals common to road vehicles. That is, a vehicle sets a claim somewhere on the motorway to indicate its desire to occupy this part of the motorway in the (near) future. If the vehicle decides that changing to the new lane is safe, it mutates its existing claim into a reservation. Consequently, within our abstraction the vehicle is considered to be on both lanes at once, thus modelling the act of changing lanes. For example, in Fig. 1, the car A currently set a claim on the right lane, to join the platoon.

3 Methodology

In this section, we show how the hybrid agent architecture of Sect. 2 can be instantiated to verify vehicle platooning with respect to the agent's decisions, the continuous behaviour, and the spatial changes necessary to change lanes, e.g., while joining a platoon. To that end, we refine the instantiation of previous work [17] with a new controller responsible for the spatial aspects of traffic, which in turn is inspired by previous work of one of the authors [14]. Generally, our system consists of several controllers, which constrain the possible behaviour of the vehicles on the road. This implies that the behaviour of the parallel product of two components is a subset of the behaviour of each component. To show the correctness of our refinement, we prove a set of proof obligations including deadlock freedom and invariant preservation. We also show that the properties of autonomous vehicle platooning presented in [17] hold after the refinement step. Figure 3 shows both the original and refined architecture modelling an individual vehicle within a platoon. The centre of the architecture consists of the *agent program*, which makes autonomous decisions for the vehicle and may both communicate with other agents via some *communication channel*, and with both a *continuous controller* and an *environment* (cf. Fig. 3a). A main feature of our approach is a translation of the different components into simpler abstractions for verification purposes. That is, to verify the agent program, we can abstract from the timing aspects of the continuous controller. Thus we gain a simple (finite-state) untimed automaton as the abstraction of the continuous behaviour. Similarly, we can reduce the agent program to the few parts necessary for the communication with the continuous controller for the verification of the latter. In both cases, the state space is reduced significantly, making verification feasible, in the case of the agent program by using AJPF [10] and in the case of the continuous controller by using UPPAAL [4].

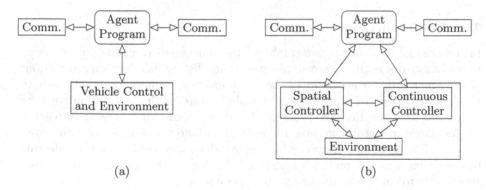

(a)   (b)

Fig. 3. Original and refined architecture

3.1   Agent

The BDI agent program in our architecture is written in GWENDOLEN [9], a prolog-style programming language that incorporates explicit representation of goals, beliefs, and plans. AJPF is a model checker that accepts GWENDOLEN code as an input model. It allows for the specification and verification of agent properties with respect to beliefs and intentions. Since the general interface between the underlying vehicle implementation and the agent is similar to [17], we could re-use that agent program with only minor changes. We distinguish between two agent programs: the *leader*, which manages all joining and leaving requests of vehicles within, or outside, the platoon, and the *follower*, which defines the functionality of vehicles within the platoon. We did not need to change the structure of the leader protocol, which is why we subsequently concentrate on the follower. The follower implements interactions for four main features:

1. joining a platoon;
2. leaving a platoon;
3. switching the steering control between manual and automatic; and
4. setting a new distance to the front vehicle.

A vehicle intending to join to a platoon initially sends a joining request to the leader and waits for confirmation from the leader. When it receives the confirmation, it instructs the vehicle to change lane and waits for the vehicle to send back a successful confirmation of changing lane. After receiving the confirmation the follower switches its speed controller to automatic. When the joining vehicle is close enough to the preceding follower within the platoon the agent instructs the vehicle to switch the steering controller to automatic. Finally, the joining vehicle confirms the procedure to the leader. When the joining vehicle receives a reply back from the leader, it deduces that the joining goal has been achieved. Leaving a platoon follows a similar protocol, except that the steering and speed control are switched to manual after the vehicle left the platoon.

3.2   Continuous Controller

In the original architecture, we combined the continuous controller and its environment into one entity. For example, we did not distinguish between interactions of the agent with the actuators of the autonomous system and interactions with the human driver. In both cases, the main feature of the interaction we were concerned with was the time taken for the controller or environment to react.

As shown in Fig. 3b, we now refine the continuous controller and the environment into three sub-components. We introduce two controllers, one referring to the timing aspects and the continuous behaviour of the vehicle, and the other specifically to control actuations with respect to space.

A part of the continuous controller automaton that has changed in our refinement step is shown in Fig. 4. In particular, the refinement extends the previous environment with a model of potential collision, which will be defined in the subsequent section. It removes the nondeterministic failure of changing lane from the continuous controller that implicitly modelled the existence of such a potential collision. In the figure, this failure was defined by the transition with the equality timer $== CH\_L\_T + CH\_L\_B$, defining that the controller silently assumes a failure, if the lane-changing manoeuvre takes more longer than the worst-case expectance. The synchronisation channels are changed from changing_lane to phy_changing_lane since the refined continuous controller is synchronised with the spatial controller, while previously, it was synchronised with the agent.

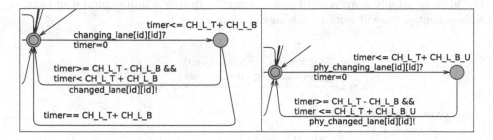

Fig. 4. Abstract and refined continuous controller automata

3.3 Introducing Space

In this section, we present an instantiation of the spatial controller, as well as the translation into timed and untimed automata for verification purposes. To that end, we formalise the ideas presented in Sect. 2 on the spatial model for platooning. We will not go into the details, but refer to previous work [14,21].

Recall that we distinguish between two types of space a car may need to reason about: its *reservation*, which should never overlap with the reservation of any other car, and its *claim*, which is similar to setting the turn signals. The intuitive idea of the controller is as follows. Whenever a change to a lane m is requested, the controller first claims the space on m it would occupy, if it was already driving there. Then it checks, whether this space overlaps with the reservation of any other car. If so, it removes its claim and aborts the manoeuvre. Otherwise, it changes the claim to a reservation and notifies the continuous controller to initiate the lateral lane change. After it receives an acknowledgment that the lane has been changed, it shrinks its reservation to only reside on m.

Formally, we fix a set of lanes $\mathbb{L} = \{1, \dots, n\}$ and for simplicity assume the motorway to be infinitely long. The dimension in the direction of the motorway, called the *extension*, is thus modelled by the real numbers $\mathbb{R}$. At any point in time, each vehicle c is then spatially characterised by its position $pos(c) \in \mathbb{R}$, its physical size $ps(c) \in \mathbb{R}$, its braking distance, i.e., the distance it needs to come to a standstill $bd(c) \in \mathbb{R}$, as well as the lanes it reserves $res(c) \subseteq \mathbb{L}$ and claims $clm(c) \subseteq \mathbb{L}$. These sets of lanes are subject to certain conditions (e.g., the set of claims has to be a singleton, etc.), which we will not expand upon. Each vehicle c can also perform certain *actions*, in particular

$c(c, n)$: create a claim on lane n
$r(c)$: change an existing claim into a reservation
$wdc(c)$: remove/withdraw an existing claim
$wdr(c, n)$: shrink its reservation to only be on lane n

We restrict the possible transitions such that after each transition a minimal amount of time greater than zero has to pass. This constraint enforces the permanency of spatial changes on the road, and thus prohibits zeno-behaviour in the form of infinite sequences of spatial changes during a finite amount of time. Subsequently, we will refer to this model of space as R.

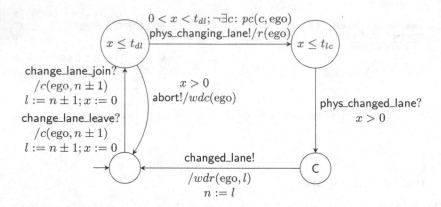

Fig. 5. Spatial controller for joining and leaving a platoon ($t_{dl} < t_{lc}$)

Using these abstract definitions as the semantics, we defined a dedicated specification logic [14]. However, in this work we will not require the full logic, and hence we only explain the necessary details. We employ two spatial atoms $re(c)$ and $cl(c)$, which denote that a part of a lane is fully occupied by the reservation (claim, respectively) of c. Furthermore, we use a single modality *somewhere* $\langle \varphi \rangle$, which denotes that the formula φ holds somewhere on the space under consideration. With these specific definitions, and standard first-order operators, we can express the following two formulas.

$$cc \equiv \neg \exists c \colon c \neq \text{ego} \wedge \langle re(\text{ego}) \wedge re(c) \rangle$$
$$pc(c, \text{ego}) \equiv c \neq \text{ego} \wedge \langle cl(\text{ego}) \wedge (re(c) \vee cl(c)) \rangle$$

Formula cc denotes the existence of a vehicle c whose reservation overlaps with the reservation of ego, which would amount to an unsafe situation. We term such situations as *collisions*. Formula $pc(c, \text{ego})$ denotes that the claim of ego overlaps with the claim of c or its reservation. This may result in an unsafe situation, if ego changed its claim into a reservation. Hence, $pc(c, \text{ego})$ allows us to identify potentially unsafe situations.

To model the spatial behaviour of a vehicle joining or leaving the platoon, we will use a type-amended timed automata called *automotive-controlling timed automata* (ACTA) [15]. These augment timed automata with the possibility to use spatial formulas as guards and invariants, as well as to use the spatial actions described above at the transitions. Figure 5 shows the controller in terms of an ACTA, where ego refers to the vehicle the controller is implemented in.

The actions change_lane_join, change_lane_leave, changed_lane, and abort are used to communicate with the decision making agent. The first two actions initiate the corresponding manoeuvre, while the spatial controller uses changed_lane and abort to indicate a successful and unsuccessful lane-change manoeuvre, respectively. The channel phys_changed_lane is a communication link with the continuous controller, indicating that steering onto the new lane was successful.

For the verification of the other components, we need to provide abstractions from this ACTA into both an untimed, and a standard timed automaton. To abstract from both the timing and spatial definitions, we only keep the discrete actions, maintaining the order of actions. In this way, we create a simple finite automaton which serves as the abstraction of the spatial controller that can be used during the verification of the agent programs. The translation into timed automata is slightly more involved. We employ a global set of identifiers for each vehicle. In fact, this set was already used to identify the different vehicles by parameterising the continuous controllers [17]. Hence, we replace each occurrence of ego with the parameter *id*. Furthermore, we introduce a global array c of Boolean values, where the identifiers serve as the indices, and each entry denotes whether the corresponding vehicle currently possesses a claim. Whether a vehicle is currently engaged in a lane-change manoeuvre and reserves two lanes at once, is indicated by a variable r, which is local to each controller.

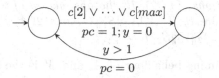

Fig. 6. Abstraction of spatial behaviour on the road

However, since claims and reservations are strongly tied together, we also need to define an abstraction of the road's behaviour. To that end, we use a very simple abstraction: a potential collision can only happen, if at least one vehicle currently holds a claim. Furthermore, a potential collision has to last a minimal amount of time before it can be resolved. This is a result of the assumption on the vehicles dynamics to be continuous and the necessary delays after the spatial transitions. Note that a potential collision can happen due to two reasons: either a spatial transition or the different velocities of two cars. In both cases, our model and its assumptions ensure that the situation persists for a minimal, non-zero, amount of time. We can formalise this with the following abstraction of the road's behaviour, as shown in Fig. 6. In this figure, y is a clock used to enforce the timing behaviour and the minimal delay is arbitrarily chosen to be 1. The timed abstraction of the spatial controller is as shown in Fig. 7.

Finally, we define how the agent program and the continuous controller can be abstracted for the verification of the spatial properties. The specification logic for the spatial properties does not contain modalities concerning timings

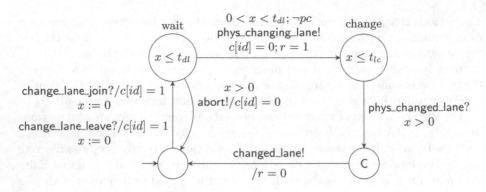

Fig. 7. Timed abstraction of spatial controller of Fig. 5 ($t_{dl} < t_{lc}$)

or decisions of the agent. That is, spatial properties may not refer to either time constraints or the internals of the agent. Hence, for spatial verification, we use the untimed abstractions of both the continuous controller and of the agent.

Lemma 1. *Let A_i, V_i and S_i be the agent program, continuous controller and spatial controller, respectively, of vehicle i, with $i \in \{1, 2\}$, and let $Comm12$ be the component modelling the communication of vehicle 1 and 2. Let S'_i and A'_i be corresponding abstractions (Fig. 7), R' the abstraction of the road (Fig. 6), and φ_t describe a time property. If $A'_1\|V_1\|S'_1\|Comms12\|A'_2\|V_2\|S'_2\|R' \models \varphi_t$ then $(A_1\|V_1\|S_1\|Comms12\|A_2\|V_2\|S_2\|R \models \varphi_t$.*

Proof (Sketch). The timing behaviour of A_i and A'_i is the same (cf. [17]). Furthermore, the timing constraints on S_i and S'_i are also the same. Now, after each spatial transition, in the original S_i, some time has to pass. In both S_i and its abstraction S'_i, every time a clock is reset the guards on the outgoing transitions of the target state s require the automaton to stay in s for some time. Finally, if the abstraction R flags a potential collision, then the original system possesses a trace containing at least one claim for a vehicle. Let us assume this claim is of vehicle 2. Then, all possible traces starting from this configuration are also possible in the abstraction R. Hence, whenever we can prove that the abstraction satisfies a timed formula φ_t, the original system also satisfies φ_t.   □

Lemma 2. *Let A_i, V_i and S_i be the agent program, continuous controller and spatial controller, respectively, of vehicle i, with $i \in \{1, 2\}$, and let $Comm12$ model the vehicles' communication. Let A'_i and V'_i be the abstractions without references to spatial properties. Then, if $A'_1\|V'_1\|S_1\|Comms12\|A'_2\|V'_2\|S_2\|R' \models \varphi_s$ then $A_1\|V_1\|S_1\|Comms12\|A_2\|V_2\|S_2\|R \models \varphi_s$.*

Proof (Sketch). This holds since the abstractions A'_i and V'_i allow for more behaviour than the original automata. Furthermore, spatial properties may neither refer to internals of the agent program, nor to time aspects of the system.   □

4   Verification of Vehicle Platooning

In this section, we explain the verification approach built on the methodology presented in Sect. 3.[4] On one hand, we did not have to re-run most of our verification methods from our previous work, particularly running AJPF, since we only refined non-agent parts of the system. In particular, we used the same topology, a chain of communicating entities, and similar numbers of vehicles. On the other hand, we needed to show that the refinement step was valid by proving proof obligations. In the following, we first identify a set of proof obligations that we proved to verify our refinement step. We then denote the spatial properties that we checked for our concrete vehicle platooning. We point out those parts of the system that remained unchanged and not re-verified. Finally, we prove that the spatial controller is a safe fragment of the space model in [14].

4.1   Proof Obligations

The refinement step allows us to introduce more details about the spatial properties of vehicle platooning. However, we need to ensure that the new details do not violate the system invariants, and do not introduce deadlocks. This needs to be checked for both verification of agent and timing behaviours. The untimed abstraction of the spatial controller only allows the same set of sequences of interactions with the agent. This means that we did not change the *structure* of the agent programs themselves; neither the leader nor the follower, i.e., the refinement step is correct wrt. agent behaviour. For the correctness of our refinement step wrt. temporal behaviour, we check four main proof obligations, shown in Table 1. The first three obligations are verified using UPPAAL, followed by a discussion of the correctness of the fourth obligation. We instantiated the agent timed automata, spatial, and continuous controllers for a platoon of four vehicles and one leader. We choose an arbitrary vehicle, for example vehicle 2, to denote our proof obligations and properties of interest, and described these with respect to this vehicle.[5] Note that $a2$ and $s2$ denote the follower agent program and lane-change controller implemented in vehicle 2, respectively.

We first ensured that our refinement step was not too restrictive by verifying deadlock freedom. The second proof obligation ensures that adding the spatial controller does not decrease the functionality of the platooning, and we checked whether joining and leaving procedures can occur. In the previous Uppaal model, we assumed that change lane could happen in $20 \pm CH\_L\_B$ where CH_L_B was reflecting the uncertainty of the changing lane. In our refinement, the lower bound remains the same, however, the upper bound splits to two waiting times for free space t_{dl} (cf. Fig. 5) and the uncertainty of the changing lane ($CH\_L\_B - t_{dl}$). Therefore, we could show that the time bound of joining and leaving are preserved (The third proof obligation in Table 1).

---

[4] The model and the verified properties can be found at https://github.com/ VerifiableAutonomy/AgentPlatooning.

[5] Since all following vehicles are defined similarly, this choice does not affect the verification.

Table 1. Proof obligations, with formalisation in timed temporal logic[7]

Deadlock freedom	$A\square$ *not deadlock*
Possible to join and leave	$E\Diamond$ *a2.join_completed*
	$E\Diamond$ *a2.leave_completed*
Time bound for joining and leaving	$A\square$ *a2.join_completed* **imply**
	$(a2.process\_time >= 50 \land a2.process\_time < 90)$
	$A\square$ *a2.leave_completed* **imply**
	$(a2.process\_time >= 30 \land a2.process\_time < 50)$
No new communication transaction	Changes were restricted to continuous and spatial controllers

We defined two new channels between the spatial and continuous controller, phy_changing_lane and phy_changed_lane. As these channels are not used in other parts of the system, we can guarantee that no new communication transition is added. In addition, we showed that our model does not inhibit zeno-behaviour. While most of the automata are not strongly non-zeno [28], their parallel product can be shown to be free of zeno-runs by checking it with *ZenoTool* [26].

4.2 Spatial Properties of Vehicle Platooning

We can verify that if a vehicle requested a lane-change, i.e., the spatial controller reaches the *wait* state (cf. Fig. 7), and still perceives a potential collision after the waiting time t_{dl}, then the manoeuvre in the agent program will fail.

$$(s2.wait \land pc \land s2.x == t_{ld}) \longrightarrow (a2.failed\_to\_join \lor a2.failed\_to\_leave)$$

In this formula $\longrightarrow$ denotes the "leads-to" operator of UPPAAL. Observe that we cannot identify whether the join manoeuvre or the leave manoeuvre failed, since the spatial controller acts similarly for both manoeuvres. However, identification of the manoeuvre can be easily implemented by adding a flag to the spatial controller. We can also show that, whenever the spatial controller chooses that a lane-change can be safely initiated, it does not perceive a potential collision on the road, and as long as it stays in this state, no potential collision can arise.

$$A\square\neg(s2.change \land pc)$$

This property shows that the space on the road as formalised in Fig. 6 is "well-behaved", since a potential collision can only happen, if a vehicle possesses a claim. However, if the controller of vehicle 2 is in state *change*, it already changed its claim to a new reservation. The time needed to verify these properties was similar to the time needed for the proof obligations. Details about time and space requirements to check deadlock freedom of the system are presented in Table 2. Since proving deadlock freedom requires a full exploration of the state space, the figure shows the worst-case requirements of our approach. In fact, the time and space necessary for the verification of the other properties was lower. We used a computer equipped with a 3.4 GHz Intel Core i5 CPU and 8 GB of memory, running UPPAAL on Mac OS. We conducted experiments for a platoon of four, five and six vehicles and compared to our previous analysis, lacking the spatial controller. The experiments with even six vehicles are feasible with a standard desktop machine, but require much more time and memory.

Table 2. Experimental statistics

Number of vehicles		4	5	6
Computation time (s)	Original model	0.58	4.6	43.9
	Extended model	3.7	57.4	885.7
Memory usage (MB)	Original model	11.5	46.3	349
	Extended model	34.8	402	4378

4.3 Spatial Safety Property

The main property that the spatial controller must ensure is that the space used by two different vehicles is disjoint. That is, it has to ensure that the formula cc as shown in Sect. 3.3 is an invariant of the system. To that end, we re-use a verification result [21] of a more general controller specification. Safety in this work means that $\forall e\colon \mathsf{safe}(e)$ is a global invariant, where $\mathsf{safe}(e)$ is defined by

$$\mathsf{safe}(e) \equiv \Box \neg \exists c\colon c \neq e \wedge \langle re(e) \wedge re(c) \rangle\,.$$

The modality $\Box$ quantifies over arbitrary transition sequences, but does not allow us to specify timing constraints. Then, the formula states that car e drives safely at all times: there is never a car c different from e, such that the reservations of e and c overlap. To prove this property to be invariant, we need two assumptions:

1. All vehicles keep their distance to the vehicles in their front and back.
2. All vehicles adhere to a certain protocol for changing lanes with respect to the platoon under consideration.

We do not elaborate on the first assumption. However, the second is that, the vehicle must not mutate its claim into a reservation, in case of a potential collision during the phase where a claim is held. Formally, we have the following constraint, where $\Box_{r(d)}$ quantifies over the transition where the vehicle d changes its claim into a reservation and c ranges only over the vehicles within the platoon.

$$\mathsf{LC} \equiv \forall d\colon \exists c\colon pc(c,d) \to \Box_{r(d)}\bot$$

For simplicity, assume that the platoon under consideration consists of two vehicles as in Sect. 3. That is, the platoon P consists of the following components.

$$P \equiv A_1 \| V_1 \| S_1 \| Comms12 \| A_2 \| V_2 \| S_2 \| R$$

Now, let $\llbracket S_1 \rrbracket$ and $\llbracket S_2 \rrbracket$ be the possible behaviours allowed by the controllers S_1 and S_2 as presented in Sect. 3.3. Since the only transition to change a claim into a reservation is guarded by the potential collision check, we have for $i \in \{1,2\}$,

$$\llbracket S_i \rrbracket \cap \{tr \mid tr \models \exists c \colon pc(c,i) \wedge \Diamond_{r(i)} \top\} = \emptyset$$

Since the behaviour of the parallel product of S_1 and S_2 is a subset of both $\llbracket S_1 \rrbracket$ and $\llbracket S_2 \rrbracket$, we get

$$\llbracket S_1 \| S_2 \rrbracket \cap \{tr \mid tr \models \exists c \colon pc(c,i) \wedge \Diamond_{r(i)} \top\} = \emptyset.$$

The other controllers only further restrict the possible behaviour. Hence

$$\llbracket P \rrbracket \cap \{tr \mid tr \models \exists c \colon pc(c,i) \wedge \Diamond_{r(i)} \top\} = \emptyset.$$

Due to our assumption on the behaviour of all other vehicles, we can infer that $\llbracket P \rrbracket$ does not contain any traces where other vehicles create a reservation during a potential collision. Hence, we can strengthen this property even further.

$$\llbracket P \rrbracket \cap \{tr \mid tr \models \exists c,d \colon pc(c,d) \wedge \Diamond_{r(d)} \top\} = \emptyset,$$

which in particular implies $\llbracket P \rrbracket \subseteq S$. This yields $\llbracket P \rrbracket \models \mathsf{LC}$, which has been shown to ensure that $P \models \forall e \colon \Box \mathsf{safe}(e)$. Hence, our controller is a refinement of the general case, which was shown to be safe.

5   Related Work

Lam and Katupitiya analysed platoons performing manoeuvres [19], where each vehicle is an agent with an associated dynamical model. Manoeuvres like overtaking a platoon are split into events, for example to change the lane, pass the platoon and change back into the original lane. That is, their notion of an event is a superset of the manoeuvres we considered. They simulated two platoons of three vehicles each, performing such manoeuvres, and identified deadlock situations. However, it is not obvious whether more potential deadlocks exist.

Our approach of a hierarchical structure of a vehicle is similar to the work of Hallé and Chaib-draa [13]. They split the model of a vehicle into three layers: Traffic control, management and guidance. While the traffic control consists of models or road-side infrastructure and further external components that we do not model, the different parts of our hierarchy can be mapped onto parts of the management and guidance layer. The management layer is split into a coordination and a planning component. The latter directly corresponds to the agent program of our approach. Within the guidance layer, they distinguish between the sensing component and the vehicle control. While the continuous controller is similar to the vehicle control, the spatial controller can be seen as a part of the sensing component, since it interprets raw sensor data and compiles it into more structured spatial properties. Hallé and Chaib-draa used their model to analyse the communication necessary for successful split and merge manoeuvres of platoons, which are similar to the leaving and joining manoeuvres of our work. However, their emphasis lies on the analysis of inter-vehicle distances with respect to different coordination strategies, while we focus on safety.

Müller et al. presented a technique to verify safety of hybrid systems [23] based on the identification of components. In their approach, they need to define and verify contracts for the behaviour of each component, which may simply assumed to be true during the verification of other components. In this manner, they can reduce the verification task for each component. Their systems need to be defined within a single formalism, differential dynamic logic [24], and are verified with the distinguished tool KeymaeraX [11]. In contrast, we can rather easily incorporate new formalisms into our approach, as evidenced by the introduction of the lane-change controller and the necessary spatial formalism. This is due to the minimised interaction between our controllers. In this way, we may use the verification techniques suitable for the corresponding subsystems, as long as we have a sensible abstraction and refinement results for each system.

Rashid et al. have presented an approach to formally verify controller strategies for platoons [25]. Their work differs from ours in several ways. While we abstract in our verification from the differential equations that make up the continuous behaviour, they explicitly model the connections between, for example, distance and velocity. Furthermore, they distinguish between *autonomous* controllers that only use inputs from the sensors of the vehicle they are implemented in, and *non-autonomous* controllers, which may use information from other vehicles via inter-vehicle communication. They verify the controllers with a theorem prover, while we use a combination of model-checking and theorem proving.

Within the context of unmanned aircraft systems, the ICAROUS architecture [3] provides a distinction of formally verified algorithms into separate modules: *monitors, resolvers, mission applications* and a *decision making layer*. The first three component types are responsible for receiving information, solving a potentially dangerous situation, and application specific algorithms, while the latter chooses the algorithms to run. This distinction has some similarities with our approach, namely the dedicated decision making component, but is not an exact match. For one, the decision making component of ICAROUS is implemented as finite automata, while we use a rational agent to allow for justified decisions. Furthermore, our low-level components incorporate functionality of monitors, resolvers and mission applications.

6   Concluding Remarks

We presented a verification technique for autonomous systems based on a hybrid agent architecture. The decomposition inherent in this architecture allows us to define different system aspects within different formalisms, tied together by the communication structure of the system and its timing constraints. For each formalisms we defined an abstraction compatible with the other formalisms. In this way, we can concentrate on each aspect in turn during verification, reducing the state space, and allowing us to use different techniques for each aspect.

Decomposition techniques often isolate the single components and replace the interaction with other components by assumptions, which are then shown to be guaranteed [22]. In contrast, in each step of the verification, we keep the general structure of the overall system. That is, we do not really *decompose* the system, but abstract from different parts. This eliminates the need to infer the behaviour of the single components, e.g., in the form of guarantees. Of course, this also means that large parts of the state space are retained during verification, in comparison to techniques which replace other components with their guarantees. However, we have shown that our approach is both feasible for autonomous systems, as well as that it scales well if new aspects are to be verified.

As future work, we have some clear extensions. For one, we intend formalise the additional manoeuvres necessary for a full working platoon [16]. This would of course increase the state space further, increasing the need for more abstraction techniques. It would be interesting to investigate, whether the models for different manoeuvres can be verified on their own, such that the safety of the combined system still follows. This would be orthogonal to the technique presented in this paper, and as such, would avoid further increases in the state space. Furthermore, since we only verified safety properties, we accept system implementations allowing for the starvation of vehicles intending to join a platoon. Hence, an analysis of liveness properties is a natural extension.

We assume that all vehicles adhere to the given protocol, that is, no malicious participants inhibit the execution of a manoeuvre. As a safety-critical system, a vehicle platoon has to be resilient against such threats as well. For example, it is necessary that the vehicle sending the joining request is actually the vehicle for which the platoon checks that necessary space is available. That is, we need to authenticate the identity of vehicles during a manoeuvre. This shows the need for verification techniques of security protocols in our approach [8].

References

1. Aitken, J., et al.: Autonomous nuclear waste management. Intell. Syst. (2018). https://doi.org/10.1109/MIS.2018.111144814
2. Amoozadeh, M., Deng, H., Chuah, C.N., Zhang, H.M., Ghosal, D.: Platoon management with cooperative adaptive cruise control enabled by vanet. Veh. Commun. **2**(2), 110–123 (2015)
3. Balachandran, S., Muñoz, C., Consiglio, M., Feliú, M., Patel, A.: Independent configurable architecture for reliable operation of unmanned systems with distributed on-board services. In: Proceedings of the 37th Digital Avionics Systems Conference (DASC 2018) (2018)
4. Behrmann, G., et al.: UPPAAL 4.0. In: Proceedings of International Conference on Quantitative Evaluation of Systems, pp. 125–126 (2006)
5. Blackburn, P., van Benthem, J., Wolter, F. (eds.): Handbook of Modal Logic. Elsevier, New York (2006)
6. Burns, A.: How to verify a safe real-time system: the application of model checking and timed automata to the production cell case study. Real-Time Syst. **24**(2), 135–151 (2003)

7. Clarke, E.M., Grumberg, O., Long, D.E.: Model checking and abstraction. ACM Trans. Program. Lang. Syst. **16**(5), 1512–1542 (1994)
8. Cortier, V.: Verification of security protocols. In: Jones, N.D., Müller-Olm, M. (eds.) VMCAI 2009. LNCS, vol. 5403, pp. 5–13. Springer, Heidelberg (2008). https://doi.org/10.1007/978-3-540-93900-9_5
9. Dennis, L.A., Farwer, B.: Gwendolen: a BDI language for verifiable agents. In: Proceedings of AISB 2008 Symposium Logic and the Simulation of Interaction and Reasoning, pp. 16–23 (2008)
10. Dennis, L.A., Fisher, M., Webster, M.P., Bordini, R.H.: Model checking agent programming languages. Autom. Softw. Eng. **19**(1), 5–63 (2012)
11. Fulton, N., Mitsch, S., Quesel, J.-D., Völp, M., Platzer, A.: KeYmaera X: an axiomatic tactical theorem prover for hybrid systems. In: Felty, A.P., Middeldorp, A. (eds.) CADE 2015. LNCS (LNAI), vol. 9195, pp. 527–538. Springer, Cham (2015). https://doi.org/10.1007/978-3-319-21401-6_36
12. Gabbay, D., Kurucz, A., Wolter, F., Zakharyaschev, M.: Many-Dimensional Modal Logics: Theory and Applications. Elsevier, New York (2003)
13. Hallé, S., Chaib-draa, B.: Collaborative driving system using teamwork for platoon formations. In: Applications of Agent Technology in Traffic and Transportation, pp. 133–151. Birkhäuser, Basel (2005)
14. Hilscher, M., Linker, S., Olderog, E.-R., Ravn, A.P.: An abstract model for proving safety of multi-lane traffic manoeuvres. In: Qin, S., Qiu, Z. (eds.) ICFEM 2011. LNCS, vol. 6991, pp. 404–419. Springer, Heidelberg (2011). https://doi.org/10.1007/978-3-642-24559-6_28
15. Hilscher, M., Schwammberger, M.: An abstract model for proving safety of autonomous urban traffic. In: Sampaio, A., Wang, F. (eds.) ICTAC 2016. LNCS, vol. 9965, pp. 274–292. Springer, Cham (2016). https://doi.org/10.1007/978-3-319-46750-4_16
16. Hsu, A., Eskafi, F., Sachs, S., Varaija, P.: Protocol design for an automated highway system. Discret. Event Dyn. Syst. **2**(1), 183–206 (1994)
17. Kamali, M., Dennis, L.A., McAree, O., Fisher, M., Veres, S.M.: Formal verification of autonomous vehicle platooning. Sci. Comput. Program. **148**, 88–106 (2017)
18. Konur, S., Fisher, M., Schewe, S.: Combined model checking for temporal, probabilistic, and real-time logics. Theor. Comput. Sci. **503**, 61–88 (2013)
19. Lam, S., Katupitiya, J.: Cooperative autonomous platoon maneuvers on highways. In: 2013 IEEE/ASME International Conference on Advanced Intelligent Mechatronics, pp. 1152–1157 (2013)
20. Lincoln, N., Veres, S.M., Dennis, L.A., Fisher, M., Lisitsa, A.: An agent based framework for adaptive control and decision making of autonomous vehicles. In: Proceedings of IFAC Workshop on Adaptation and Learning in Control and Signal Processing (ALCOSP) (2010)
21. Linker, S.: Spatial reasoning about motorway traffic safety with Isabelle/HOL. In: Polikarpova, N., Schneider, S. (eds.) IFM 2017. LNCS, vol. 10510, pp. 34–49. Springer, Cham (2017). https://doi.org/10.1007/978-3-319-66845-1_3
22. Misra, J., Chandy, K.M.: Proofs of networks of processes. IEEE Trans. Softw. Eng. **SE–7**(4), 417–426 (1981)
23. Müller, A., Mitsch, S., Retschitzegger, W., Schwinger, W., Platzer, A.: A component-based approach to hybrid systems safety verification. In: Ábrahám, E., Huisman, M. (eds.) IFM 2016. LNCS, vol. 9681, pp. 441–456. Springer, Cham (2016). https://doi.org/10.1007/978-3-319-33693-0_28

24. Platzer, A.: Logical Analysis of Hybrid Systems: Proving Theorems for Complex Dynamics. Springer, Heidelberg (2010). https://doi.org/10.1007/978-3-642-14509-4

25. Rashid, A., Siddique, U., Hasan, O.: Formal verification of platoon control strategies. In: Johnsen, E.B., Schaefer, I. (eds.) SEFM 2018. LNCS, vol. 10886, pp. 223–238. Springer, Cham (2018). https://doi.org/10.1007/978-3-319-92970-5_14

26. Rinast, J., Schupp, S.: Static detection of zeno runs in UPPAAL networks based on synchronization matrices and two data-variable heuristics. In: Jurdziński, M., Ničković, D. (eds.) FORMATS 2012. LNCS, vol. 7595, pp. 220–235. Springer, Heidelberg (2012). https://doi.org/10.1007/978-3-642-33365-1_16

27. Solyom, S., Coelingh, E.: Performance Limitations in vehicle platoon control. IEEE Intell. Transp. Syst. Mag. 5(4), 112–120 (2013)

28. Tripakis, S.: Verifying progress in timed systems. In: Katoen, J.-P. (ed.) ARTS 1999. LNCS, vol. 1601, pp. 299–314. Springer, Heidelberg (1999). https://doi.org/10.1007/3-540-48778-6_18

29. Wooldridge, M.J.: Reasoning about Rational Agents. MIT Press, Cambridge (2000)

Synthesizing and Optimizing FDIR Recovery Strategies from Fault Trees

Liana Mikaelyan[1] , Sascha Müller[1]([⊠]) , Andreas Gerndt[1] ,
and Thomas Noll[2]

[1] Software for Space Systems and Interactive Visualization,
DLR (German Aerospace Center), 38108 Braunschweig, Germany
{Liana.Mikaelyan,Sa.Mueller,Andreas.Gerndt}@dlr.de
[2] Software Modeling and Verification Group, RWTH Aachen University,
52056 Aachen, Germany
Noll@cs.rwth-aachen.de

Abstract. Redundancy concepts are an integral part of the design of space systems. Deciding when to activate which redundancy and which component should be replaced can be a difficult task. In this paper, we refine a methodology where recovery strategies are synthesized from a model of non-deterministic dynamic fault trees. The synthesis is performed by transforming non-deterministic dynamic fault trees into Markov Automata. From the optimized scheduler, an optimal recovery strategy can then be derived and represented by a model we call Recovery Automaton. We discuss techniques on how this Recovery Automaton can be further optimized to contain fewer states and transitions and show the effectiveness of our approach on two case studies.

Keywords: FDIR · Fault Tree Analysis · Synthesis · Formal methods

1 Introduction

Reliability engineering is an important discipline in the design of any safety critical system, in particular in the domain of aerospace systems and spacecraft. No matter how well designed a system is, it still has to deal with the presence of faults to some extent. Faults in this context can be events such as equipment failure, wrong sensor readings, external interferences and many more. To raise trust in handling system failures, reliability engineering tries to embed Failure Detection, Isolation and Recovery (FDIR) concepts. These concepts are derived using various tools and methodologies such as Fault Tree Analysis (FTA) [9].

FTA is a methodology commonly used in the industry for performing state-of-the-art failure analysis [13]. The resulting Fault Trees (FT) describe how faults propagate through components and subsystems of a system and eventually lead to a top-level system failure. Graphical representations of these trees are intuitive and easy to understand. On the one hand, FTs can be used to analyze the system qualitatively in terms of fault combinations that lead to system failure. On

C. Artho and P. C. Ölveczky (Eds.): FTSCS 2018, CCIS 1008, pp. 37–54, 2019.
https://doi.org/10.1007/978-3-030-12988-0_3

the other hand, they also enable quantitative analysis of important computable measures such as reliability. Dynamic Fault Trees (DFT) are an extension introducing temporal dependencies and new features to analyze redundancy concepts known as spare management. However, there are challenges arising from nondeterministic behavior of DFTs such as spare races. An example for such race behavior can be seen in a system of two operative memories together with a pool of two spare memories. If both operative memories fail at the same time it is unclear which backup memory takes over the role of which operational one.

To overcome this shortcoming, a new methodology was presented in [11]. It introduces a model of Non-deterministic Dynamic Fault Trees (NdDFT) as an extension to DFTs. In contrast to the latter, the new NdDFT does not impose a fixed, rigid order on the spares to be used. As next step, the methodology foresees transforming this NdDFT model into a Markov Automaton (MA) which is suitable for the computation of the aforementioned non-deterministic decisions on spare activations. By optimizing the scheduling of the MA model in terms of reliability of the system, a recovery strategy for the NdDFT can be synthesized. This recovery strategy defines which spare has to be used in which failure state of the system and can therefore guarantee an optimal reliability at all times.

The goal of the present paper is to refine the methodology presented in [11] by further developing an automata model that formalizes the decision process underlying a recovery strategy, a so-called Recovery Automaton (RA). We give its formal definition and show how it can be minimized in order to obtain an efficient implementation of recovery strategies for FDIR.

This paper is structured as follows. Section 2 of this paper summarizes the related work relevant to the topic of FTs, MA and synthesis of recovery strategies. Further background on the theory of FTs including their (nondeterministic) dynamic variants is given in Sect. 3. Section 4 describes the process of synthesizing recovery strategies from a given NdDFT as well as a model to represent such strategies, which is further optimized in Sect. 5. Section 6 then evaluates the technique on a use case example. Finally, the paper concludes in Sect. 7 and provides some outlook to future work.

2   Related Work

The goal of FDIR lies in keeping a system in a stable and operational state, even in the presence of faults. While some of the following steps may be omitted in some cases, performing FDIR generally means applying the following procedural approach [15]:

- Monitor the system to detect the occurrence of faults.
- Identify the fault and localize it within the system.
- Isolate the fault and prevent further propagation into other parts of the system.
- Perform recovery actions to reconfigure the system and return it into a stable state.

In order to derive how faults relate to each other and eventually lead to a system wide failure, failure analysis techniques such as FTA can be employed. One of the very basic types of FTs are Static Fault Trees (SFT). They employ Boolean algebra to combine various different failure events by AND and OR operations, often graphically represented as gates, until they sum up to the overall system failure. The failure events are usually related to faulty components of the system. Applying this methodology, statements such as "The system fails if component A and component B fail" can be modeled and refined to arbitrary levels of precision. The probability of the top-level failure after time t (reliability) can be computed from a given DFT for example by transforming a DFT into a Continuous-Time Markov Chain (CTMC) [5].

Markov Automata [6] are an extension to CTMCs. They are state-based transition systems with two types of transitions: They can contain continuous-time transitions (also called Markovian transitions) that are labeled with rates, that is, non-negative real values as well as immediate, non-deterministic transitions labeled by actions. In the latter case, transitions have to be chosen by a so-called scheduler. The computation of optimal schedulers for Markov Automata with respect to various quantitative objectives, such as state reachability, is discussed in [7].

Computing strategies for recovery purposes from a given fault model has been researched in other contexts. In [1], a similar approach is taken for repairable fault trees. The authors consider non-deterministic repair policies where the repair order is not fixed. Optimal repair policies are then computed by converting the repairable fault tree to a Markov decision process, a time-discrete version of Markov Automata. However, the authors do not consider DFT models. In [4], Dynamic Decision Networks (DDN) are employed and their inference capabilities are exploited to create autonomous on-board FDIR systems for spacecraft that can select reactive and preventive recovery actions during run-time. In [12], the authors propose creating the DDN from an extension of the DFT model. Timed Failure Propagation Graphs are used in [2] to synthesize FDIR components, namely monitors for the purpose of fault detection and recovery plans for every specified combination of fault and mode. Here, the recovery components are created using a planning based approach on predefined actions.

3   Fault Trees

FTs are graphs consisting of two types of nodes respectively representing events and gates. The root node, or top level event (TLE), usually represents the event of a system failure whereas the leaves of the tree model the event of individual components failing. The leaves are also called basic events (BE). They correspond to a Boolean variable where false represents the initial state of no failure. The variable is considered true in case of a failure event. We consider here only the case of permanent failure, i.e. once a BE has failed, it remains in a failed state for all future points in time. The branches of the trees are represented by the gates performing operations on the events. FTs are directed acyclic graphs starting from the BEs pointing over the gates towards the system failure event. In the following, basic events will be denoted by $b_1, b_2, \ldots$, sets of basic events by $B_1, B_2, \ldots$ and failure rates by $\lambda_1, \lambda_2, \ldots$.

3.1 Static Fault Trees

Figure 1 shows the gates and events used in the SFT notation. SFTs use Boolean operations represented by AND and OR gates. There also exist other gates such as the k-VOTE gate, which propagates if at least k inputs have failed. Observe that a 1-VOTE gate corresponds to an OR gate and a k-VOTE gate with k inputs to an AND gate. Implementation wise, all gates can therefore be considered as k-VOTE gates for some appropriate k. Some other extensions also introduce a NOT gate. However, this allows the construction of fault trees where the TLE can change from having failed to working again as new failures occur. These fault trees are known as non-coherent fault trees and have been dismissed as being a sign for modeling errors [14].

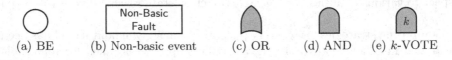

(a) BE   (b) Non-basic event   (c) OR   (d) AND   (e) k-VOTE

Fig. 1. Gates and events in a Static Fault Tree

3.2 Dynamic Fault Trees

Many extensions have been proposed to the formalism of FTs [13] to increase its expressiveness and enhance its features. A particular extension is the notion of Dynamic Fault Trees (DFT). It introduces temporal understanding and new features to analyze redundancy concepts known as spare management. In DFTs, a node can be either failed, active (operational) or dormant (operational). A node that is an unactivated spare is dormant. All other nodes are activated. Together with this state, failure rates for failing actively and failing dormantly can be defined for every BE.

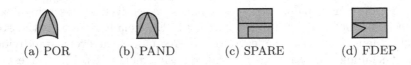

(a) POR   (b) PAND   (c) SPARE   (d) FDEP

Fig. 2. Standard dynamic gates

Figure 2 depicts the notation to extend SFTs to DFTs introducing new gates POR, PAND, SPARE and FDEP. The PAND (priority AND) gate propagates in case all inputs fail exactly in sequence from left to right. The POR (priority OR) gate propagates in case the leftmost input occurs before all other inputs.

The SPARE gate is connected to a primary event and a set of spare events. It propagates a failure if the primary input failed and all spares are either claimed or failed themselves. The spare events can be shared with another SPARE gate, therefore a spare can be claimed by either the one or the other SPARE gate. But there may be no shared elements between the primary input and any spare. The order in which such a spare is chosen is deterministic and defined at design time by the reliability engineer.

The FDEP (functional dependency) has a trigger event on the left hand side and any number of dependent events functionally dependent on the triggering event. When the trigger event occurs, the dependent events are set to fail as well. The output of an FDEP gate only indicates to which tree it belongs and has no further semantical meaning.

In the following, we give an example to illustrate the DFT notation. Figure 3 shows a system consisting of two memory components which are covered by two spare memories for failures. The two spares are shared among the two SPARE gates. According to DFT semantics, Memory3 will be used before Memory4 in case of a failure of Memory1 or Memory2. In addition, the system has two hot redundant, always active power sources, Power1 and Power2. Both primaries Memory1 and Memory2 are powered by Power1 and the redundancies Memory3 and Memory4 are powered by the second power source Power2. Using FDEPs, the failure of a power source is propagated to the respective memory components.

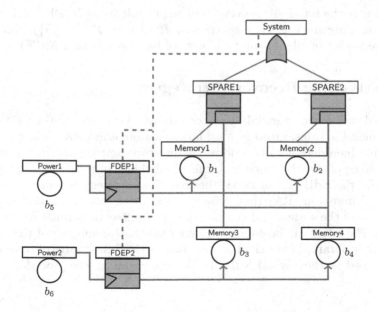

Fig. 3. Example DFT

In the figure, FDEP dependent events are marked by an arrow and dashed lines indicate the parent of an FDEP.

3.3 Non-deterministic Dynamic Fault Trees

As described before, DFTs require spares to be activated in a fixed and rigid order. This order cannot be adapted depending on faults that have previously occurred. Additionally, in cases of spare races it is not semantically clear which SPARE gate claims the actual redundancy. To relax on this semantical restriction of the DFT model, [11] introduces an inherently non-deterministic DFT model (NdDFT, following the naming in [1]). The syntax and notation of the NdDFT is completely adopted from the DFT. Semantically, the NdDFT drops the requirement that spares are always activated from left to right. Moreover, the new non-deterministic semantics allows for a SPARE gate to leave the spares available for more important SPARE gates by not claiming. Whenever BEs occur in an NdDFT, the new semantics allow to perform valid recovery actions of the following form:

Definition 1 (Recovery Action). *A recovery action r in an NdDFT T is an action of the form*

- *$[]$ (empty action) or*
- *$CLAIM(G, S)$ (spare gate G claims spare S, where S is a spare of G).*

We denote the set of all recovery actions possible in an NdDFT T by $R(T)$ and the set of recovery action sequences by $RS(T) := (R(T) \setminus \{[]\})^*$. Similarly we denote the set of all non-empty subsets of basic events by $BES(T)$.

4   Synthesizing Recovery Strategies

Here we describe the essential steps; details can be found in [11]. First, the NdDFT model is transformed into a Markov Automaton (MA) that represents all possible (non-deterministic) decisions on spare activations. By optimizing the scheduling of the MA model in terms of reliability of the system, a recovery strategy for the NdDFT can be synthesized. This strategy is represented by a Recovery Automaton (RA) that defines which spare has to be used in which failure state of the system and can therefore guarantee an optimal reliability at all times. The latter can be computed by a quantitative analysis of the Markov Chain that is obtained from the RA, enriched by the failure rates of basic events as determined by the original NdDFT. Figure 4 visualizes the procedure.

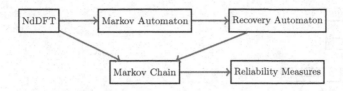

Fig. 4. Transformation road map

4.1 Recovery Strategies and Automata

In the NdDFT, the actual recovery action r that is applied is defined by a given recovery strategy. In the following, transitions of Recovery Automata are labeled by recovery action sequences. Given the observed basic events, a recovery strategy is then a mapping that returns the recovery action sequence that should be taken accordingly. The NdDFT considers recovery strategies that only have recovery actions as given in Definition 1. They are defined as follows:

Definition 2 (Recovery Strategy). *A recovery strategy for an NdDFT T is a mapping Recovery : $BES(T)^* \rightarrow RS(T)^*$ such that*

- *Recovery$(\varepsilon) = \varepsilon$ and*
- *Recovery$(B_1, \ldots, B_n) = $ Recovery$(B_1, \ldots, B_{n-1}), rs_n$ with $rs_n \in RS(T)$.*

As each basic event can occur at most once, the recovery strategy only needs to be defined for pairwise disjoint sets of basic events, i.e., $B_i \cap B_j = \emptyset$ for $i \neq j$. A finite automaton that represents a recovery strategy will be called Recovery Automaton.

Definition 3 (Recovery Automaton). *A Recovery Automaton (RA) $\mathcal{R}_T = (Q, \delta, q_0)$ of an NdDFT T is an automaton where*

- *Q is a finite set of states,*
- *$q_0 \in Q$ is an initial state, and*
- *$\delta \colon Q \times BES(T) \rightarrow Q \times RS(T)$ is a deterministic transition function that maps the current state and an observed set of faults to the successor state and a recovery action sequence.*

The recovery strategy induced by a Recovery Automaton $\mathcal{R}$ is denoted by *Recovery$_\mathcal{R}$*. An example of a Recovery Automaton for a simple Fault Tree consisting of a SPARE gate with a cold redundant spare is given in Fig. 5.

4.2 Non-deterministic Dynamic Fault Trees to Markov Automata

Transforming an NdDFT to a Markov Automaton can be done by adapting traditional algorithms for transforming DFTs to CTMCs. As base algorithm, we use the one given in [5]. The adapted algorithm operates by memorizing two sets of data in every of its states: First, the history of occurred basic event sets

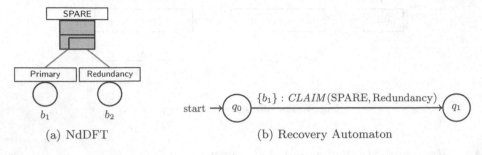

(a) NdDFT   (b) Recovery Automaton

Fig. 5. Example of (a) NdDFT and (b) RA

$(B_1, B_2, \ldots, B_n)$. Second, a mapping from spare gates to the currently claimed spare. The initial, empty history of the algorithm is denoted by (). Starting with this initial state, all active basic events, i.e. those that are not associated to an unactivated spare, are used to compute Markovian successors for each of them while extending the history accordingly.

The respective basic event set is obtained by taking the active basic event and computing all basic events that transitively fail due to FDEPs. The transitions are labeled with the respective failure rate of the basic event causing the transition. All transitions that would lead to a state that implies that the top-level event (system failure) has occurred, are connected to a special FAIL state instead. For each target state of a Markovian transition, the algorithm generates successors using non-deterministic transitions. Each non-deterministic transition is labeled by a valid recovery action.

4.3   Synthesizing Recovery Automata from Markov Automata

Using existing techniques for optimizing the scheduling of a Markov Automaton, the optimal non-deterministic transitions for maximizing the system reliability can be computed. The Recovery Automaton model is then used to represent the underlying decision process of the scheduler.

Extracting a Recovery Automaton from a scheduler for a Markov Automaton is achieved by replacing sequences of transitions for states $s_0, s_1, \ldots, s_n$ of the form $(s_0, B : \lambda, s_1), (s_1, r_1, s_2), \ldots, (s_{n-1}, r_n, s_n)$, where B is a basic event set, λ a failure rate and $r_1, \ldots, r_n$ recovery actions, by the transition $\delta(s_0, B) = (s_n, r_1 \ldots r_n)$ where empty recovery actions are ignored. This applies to all transitions where $s_1, \ldots, s_n$ are the successors computed by the optimized schedule of the Markov Automaton. All other non-deterministic transitions are then discarded. Finally, the algorithm discards all unreachable states.

5   Further Optimization of Recovery Automata

Complex systems usually exhibit a large number of faults that may occur. This means that NdDFTs describing such systems may be very large and correspondingly synthesized Recovery Automata may contain redundant states. In this section, we refine the given synthesis procedure by discussing some techniques for reducing the state space and the transition count of a synthesized Recovery Automaton. This leads to the task of finding an automaton with the same "behavior" that contains a smaller number of states. To capture this notion of having the same behavior, we introduce the concept of recovery equivalence between Recovery Automata as follows:

Definition 4 (RA Recovery Equivalence). *Let $\mathcal{R}_1 = (Q_1, \delta_1, q_{01})$ and $\mathcal{R}_2 = (Q_2, \delta_2, q_{02})$ be two RAs. We define a binary relation $\approx_R$ such that it holds true for any two RA that $\mathcal{R}_1 \approx_R \mathcal{R}_2$ iff for any sequence of sets of basic events $B_1, \ldots, B_n$ with $B_i \cap B_j = \emptyset$ for any $i \neq j$ it holds that:*

$$Recovery_{\mathcal{R}_1}(B_1, \ldots, B_n) = Recovery_{\mathcal{R}_2}(B_1, \ldots, B_n)$$

Given a Recovery Automaton as an input, the task of minimization involves obtaining an equivalent recovery automaton with as few states as possible. The standard problem of automata minimization is well-known and has been studied extensively. In this work, we apply the usual definition of trace equivalence and lift it to states of Recovery Automata:

Definition 5 (Trace Equivalence). *Let $\mathcal{R}_T = (Q, \delta, q_0)$ be an RA. A trace equivalence $\approx \subseteq Q \times Q$ is a maximal, binary relation such that it holds for any states $q_1, q_2 \in Q$ that $q_1 \approx q_2$ iff for any $B \in BES(T)$ it holds that:*

$$\delta(q_1, B) = (q_1', rs_1) \ \text{ and } \ \delta(q_2, B) = (q_2', rs_2) \ \text{ with } \ q_1' \approx q_2' \ \text{ and } \ rs_1 = rs_2$$

Equivalent states in automata can be computed using the Partition Refinement algorithm [8] and then a minimized automaton can be obtained by merging all equivalent states. In the setting of Recovery Automata, we can go even further and merge pairs of states that are not trace equivalent as long as the behavior of the automaton does not change. A simple example for a case where merging non-equivalent states yields a Recovery Automaton that induces an equivalent recovery strategy, can be seen in Fig. 6.

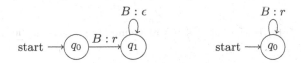

Fig. 6. (a) Initial RA; (b) minimized RA

In the following we present the main contribution of this work: Rules that allow to merge states that are not trace-equivalent, yet yield implementations of equivalent recovery strategies. We identified two cases where merging non-equivalent states does not change the induced recovery strategy.

- **Case 1: Merging Orthogonal States.**
- **Case 2: Merging the FAIL state to Predecessors.**

In both cases, the key to minimization that we exploit, is the fact that the inputs of the automaton are produced by an FT. Hence, basic events can only occur at most once. This leads to the effect that certain traces in the RA are not valid inputs for the correspondingly induced recovery strategy. Therefore it gives us additional freedom for merging states that do would not be allowed to be merged in a standard automaton model.

5.1   Merging Orthogonal States

In the first rule, the idea is to identify states that may have transitions with disagreeing outputs, but where we can guarantee for certain that those transitions can never be taken, as their necessary inputs can no longer be produced. As mentioned before, the key to this idea lies in the exploitation of the property that basic events can only occur at most once in an FT. This gives us the following observation: If a basic event occurs on every path leading to a state in an RA, then it is guaranteed that in the future no transition listing this basic event in its guards can be taken. Note that Recovery Automata are deterministic automata, meaning that unlike non-deterministic automata they always have a transition defined for every possible input. Figure 7 abstractly illustrates the application of this merging rule.

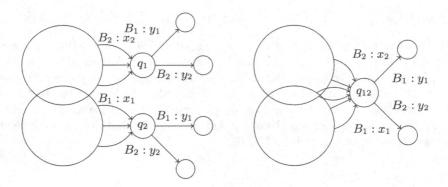

Fig. 7. (a) Initial RA; (b) RA after merging states q_1 and q_2

For the purpose of formalizing the intuitively given notion, we now introduce the concept of *orthogonal states*. To capture the basic event sets that can no longer be produced by an FT upon having reached a state in the RA, we define the set of guaranteed inputs of a state q as a function $GI \colon Q \to Q$ with:

$$GI(q) := \{B \in BES(\mathcal{T}) \mid \text{for all paths } q_0 B_0 : rs_0 \dots q_{n-1} B_{n-1} : rs_{n-1} q$$
$$\exists i : B_i \cap B \neq \emptyset\}$$

In order to compute the set of guaranteed inputs, we apply the work list algorithm [10] using the following transfer functions:

$$GI(q_0) := \emptyset$$

$$GI(q) := \bigcap_{(p,B) \in pred(q)} GI(p) \cup \{B\}$$

With $pred(q) := \{(p, B) \mid \delta(p, B) = (q, rs) \text{ for some } rs, p \neq q\}$ denoting the set of predecessor transitions of a state q. Having setup these preliminary definitions, the concept of orthogonality between states can now be formalized with the following definition:

Definition 6 (Orthogonal States). *Let $\mathcal{R}_T = (Q, \delta, q_0)$ be an RA. Let further $p, q \in Q$ be two non-initial distinct states and $B \in BES(T)$. Then p, q are orthogonal with respect to B iff*

$$B \in GI(p) \cup GI(q)$$

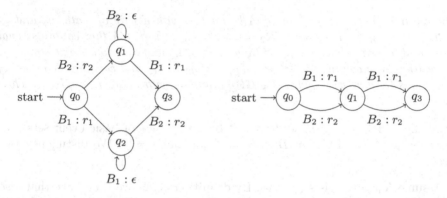

Fig. 8. (a) Initial RA $\mathcal{R}_1$; (b) RA $\mathcal{R}_2$ after merging states q_1 and q_2

To illustrate the definition of orthogonality, we consider as an example the Recovery Automaton depicted in Fig. 8. The RA we consider there reacts to two distinct basic event sets B_1 and B_2 and performs a corresponding recovery action r_1 or r_2 accordingly. An NdDFT that would produce such an RA would be for example a system consisting of two parallel spare gates running independently from each other, e.g. spare gates with no shared spare. For the guaranteed inputs we have:

- $GI(q_0) = \emptyset$,
- $GI(q_1) = GI(q_0) \cup \{B_2\} = \{B_2\}$,
- $GI(q_2) = GI(q_0) \cup \{B_1\} = \{B_1\}$ and
- $GI(q_3) = (GI(q_1) \cup \{B_1\}) \cap (GI(q_2) \cup \{B_2\}) = \{B_1, B_2\}$.

Thus, by Definition 6 it holds that q_1 and q_2 are orthogonal with respect to basic event sets B_1 and B_2. Observe that q_1 has an outgoing loop transition labeled with $B_2 : \epsilon$ that cannot occur. Similarly, q_2 has an outgoing loop transition labeled by $B_1 : \epsilon$ that cannot occur. In the merged RA, these transitions are eliminated and all the other incoming and outgoing transitions are redirected to start and end at the merged state respectively.

We are now ready to incorporate the orthogonality concept into an equivalence definition. We extend the basic trace equivalence definition as follows:

Definition 7 (RA State Recovery Equivalence). *Let $\mathcal{R}_T = (Q, \delta, q_0)$ be an RA. A state-based recovery equivalence $\approx_R \subseteq Q \times Q$ is a maximal relation such that it holds for any states $q_1, q_2 \in Q$ that $q_1 \approx_R q_2$ iff for any $B \in BES(T)$ it holds that either:*

- $\delta(q_1, B) = (q_1', rs_1)$ *and* $\delta(q_2, B) = (q_2', rs_2)$ *with* $q_1' \approx q_2'$ *and* $rs_1 = rs_2$ *or*
- q_1, q_2 *are orthogonal with respect to* B.

We now prove the correctness of our approach. The following theorem states that merging two recovery equivalent states yields a recovery equivalent RA.

Theorem 1. *Let $\mathcal{R}_1 = (Q_1, \delta_1, q_{01})$ be an RA with a pair of states q_1 and q_2 such that $q_1 \approx_R q_2$. Let further $\mathcal{R}_2 = (Q_2, \delta_2, q_{02})$ be an RA that contains equal states and transitions as $\mathcal{R}_1$, apart from merging q_1 and q_2 into a single state q_{12}, redirecting the incoming transitions of q_1 and q_2 to q_{12} and copying the outgoing transitions from q_1 with guard $B \notin GI(q_1)$ and q_2 with guard $B \notin GI(q_2)$. Then $\mathcal{R}_1 \approx_R \mathcal{R}_2$.*

Proof. Let $\beta := B_1, \ldots, B_n \in BES(T)^*$ be a sequence of basic event sets produced by an NdDFT. Then $B_i \cap B_j = \emptyset$ for any $i \neq j$. We distinguish two cases:

- Assume $\mathcal{R}_1$ never vists q_1 or q_2. By definition of $\mathcal{R}_2$ we then have that also $\mathcal{R}_2$ does not visit q_{12}. And by definition of $\mathcal{R}_2$ again we thus immediately have that $Recovery_{\mathcal{R}_1}(\beta) = Recovery_{\mathcal{R}_2}(\beta)$.
- Assume $\mathcal{R}_1$ visits q_1 (the case of visiting q_2 is analog) upon reading B_i for some $i < n$. Now consider B_{i+1}. Let q_1', q_{12}' and rs_1, rs_{12} be such that:

$$\delta_1(q_1, B_{i+1}) = (q_1', rs_1) \text{ and}$$
$$\delta_2(q_{12}, B_{i+1}) = (q_{12}', rs_{12}).$$

By Definition 7 this means that we have either:

- $rs_1 = rs_{12}$ and $q_1' \approx q_{12}'$. By correctness of merging trace equivalent states we hence obtain $Recovery_{\mathcal{R}_1}(\beta) = Recovery_{\mathcal{R}_2}(\beta)$.
- q_1, q_2 are orthogonal with respect to B_{i+1}. Then by Definition 6 it holds that:

$$B_{i+1} \in GI(q_1) \cup GI(q_2)$$

If $B_{i+1} \in GI(q_1)$ then there exists by construction of GI an index $j < i + 1$ such that $B_{i+1} \cap B_j \neq \emptyset$. Contradiction to the definition of β. Therefore we obtain conclude $B_{i+1} \in GI(q_2)$. By construction of $\mathcal{R}_2$ this implies that the transition of q_2 is not copied and the transition of q_1 is chosen instead. Thus, $rs_1 = rs_{12}$ and $q'_1 = q'_{12}$. Hence we can conclude $Recovery_{\mathcal{R}_1}(\beta) = Recovery_{\mathcal{R}_2}(\beta)$.

In all cases we have $Recovery_{\mathcal{R}_1}(\beta) = Recovery_{\mathcal{R}_2}(\beta)$ and thus $\mathcal{R}_1 \approx_R \mathcal{R}_2$ by Definition 4.

□

5.2   Merging the FAIL State to Predecessors

The idea of the second case is to identify FAIL states that do not contribute to new recovery actions sequences when a set of faults occurs. If a state only leads to a FAIL state, the transition can be turned into a self-loop. And should the FAIL state no longer be reachable, it can be eliminated. This rule is abstractly illustrated in Fig. 9. We further introduce the concept of a FAIL state.

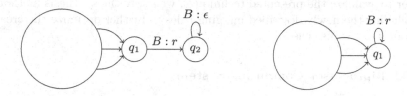

Fig. 9. (a) Initial RA; (b) RA after merging FAIL states to predecessors

Definition 8 (FAIL State). *Let $\mathcal{R}_T = (Q, \delta, q_0)$ be an RA and $q \in Q$ a state. Then q is a FAIL state iff for any $B \in BES(T)$, all transitions from q are of the form $\delta(q, B) = (q, \epsilon)$.*

The formalized merging rule can then be captured by the following theorem:

Theorem 2. *Let $\mathcal{R}_1 = (Q_1, \delta_1, q_{01})$ be an RA with a pair of states q_1 and q_2 such that q_2 is a FAIL state and all transitions of q_1 are ϵ-loops except for one transition being of the form $\delta_1(q_1, B) = (q_2, rs)$, such that $rs \neq \epsilon$. Let further $\mathcal{R}_2 = (Q_2, \delta_2, q_{02})$ be an RA with equal states and transitions as $\mathcal{R}_1$, except for turning outgoing transitions of q_1 into loop transitions. Then $\mathcal{R}_1 \approx_R \mathcal{R}_2$.*

Proof. Let $\beta := B_1, \ldots, B_n \in BES(T)^*$ be a sequence of basic event sets with $B_i \cap B_j = \emptyset$. We distinguish two cases:

– Assume $\mathcal{R}_1$ never visits q_1. Then by definition of $\mathcal{R}_2$, it also never visits q_1. As both automata are defined to be equal otherwise, we then immediately have that $Recovery_{\mathcal{R}_1}(\beta) = Recovery_{\mathcal{R}_2}(\beta)$.

– Assume $\mathcal{R}_1$ visits q_1 upon reading B_i for some $i < n$. Then by definition, $\mathcal{R}_2$ also visits q_1 upon reading B_i. Now consider B_{i+1}. By the construction of $\mathcal{R}_2$ it holds that $\delta_1(q_1, B_{i+1}) = (q_2, rs)$ and $\delta_2(q_1, B_{i+1}) = (q_1, rs)$. for some recovery action sequence rs. Since q_2 is a FAIL state we obtain from Definition 8 that $\delta_1(q_2, B_j) = (q_2, \epsilon)$ for any $j > i + 1$. Moreover, since also $B_j \cap B_{i+1} = \emptyset$ for any $j > i + 1$ we also have by definition of q_1 and $\mathcal{R}_2$ that $\delta_2(q_1, B_j) = (q_1, \epsilon)$. In total, we can therefore conclude that:

$$Recovery_{\mathcal{R}_1}(\beta) = Recovery_{\mathcal{R}_1}(B_1, \ldots, B_i, B_{i+1})$$
$$= Recovery_{\mathcal{R}_2}(B_1, \ldots, B_i, B_{i+1})$$
$$= Recovery_{\mathcal{R}_2}(\beta)$$

In all cases $Recovery_{\mathcal{R}_1}(\beta) = Recovery_{\mathcal{R}_2}(\beta)$. Hence, $\mathcal{R}_1 \approx_R \mathcal{R}_2$ by Definition 4.

□

6 Case Studies

In order to evaluate the presented techniques, we apply the synthesis methodology including the newly described merging rules to further optimize the created RA models to two use cases.

6.1 Multiprocessor Computing System

Target System. We consider the literature example of a Multiprocessor Computing System (MCS) based on the model given in [3]. The MCS consists of two main components: The Bus and the Computing Module (CM). The CM is hot redundant and consists of two further CMs CM_1 and CM_2. Each of these CMs requires a disk, a processor and a memory unit. Each CM has a warm redundant backup disk. Furthermore, a shared redundant memory unit MS is available to the entire CM in case that their own memory unit fails. Finally, both processors are powered by a common power source PS. The common power source itself is again hot redundant and consists of the two power units PS_1 and PS_2. Figure 10 shows a NdDFT that describes the MCS.

Experimental Results. The described synthesis algorithm was performed to obtain a Recovery Automaton from the described NdDFT. The RA was then optimized by merging trace-equivalent and recovery equivalent states and by eliminating redundant transitions.

Table 1 shows the results after minimizing the synthesized RA. Observe that initially the RA contained a large number of states and transitions. After performing the Partition Refinement algorithm based on the trace-equivalence definition, the number of states and transitions was significantly reduced. After performing the Partition Refinement and merging non-trace equivalent states

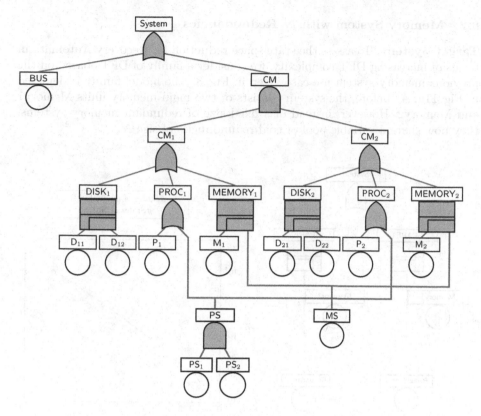

Fig. 10. NdDFT of the Multiprocessor Computing System

according to the described merging rules, it was observed that the number of states was further reduced by 95.86% and the number of transitions was further reduced by 95.05%. Thus, merging non-trace equivalent states additionally reduced the number of states obtained by merging trace-equivalent states by 38.81% and the number of transitions was reduced by 32.38%. This indicates the effectiveness of the proposed approach to consider cases when non-trace equivalent states can be merged to obtain an equivalent Recovery Automaton having the same behavior.

Table 1. Synthesizing and minimizing results.

Equivalence relation	#States	#Transitions	States removed	Transitions removed
–	991	7635	–	–
Trace equivalence	67	559	93.24%	92.68%
Recovery equivalence	41	378	95.86%	95.05%

6.2 Memory System with N Redundancies

Target System. To assess the state space reduction for Recovery Automata in terms of increasing DFT complexity, we consider a family of DFTs based on the previous memory system use case given in Fig. 3. The model family is depicted in Fig. 11a. As before, the system consists of two main memory units Memory1 and Memory2. However, instead of a fixed size of redundant memory systems, they now share a variable pool of cold redundancies of size N.

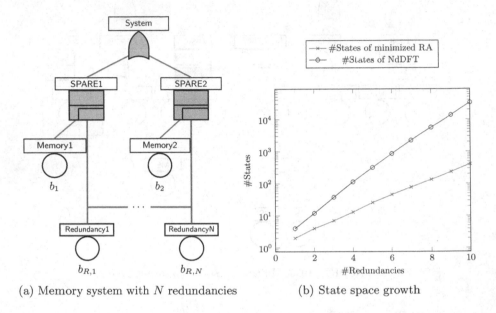

(a) Memory system with N redundancies   (b) State space growth

Fig. 11. State space growth of RA for memory system with N redundancies

Experimental Results. Figure 11b shows how the state space sizes increase with varying number of redundancies N for both the raw Markov Automaton of the NdDFT and the finally resulting minimized RA. Note that the y-axis is scaled logarithmically. It can be seen that the RA state space grows significantly slower, but still at an exponential pace. However, it can also be seen that the state space reduction remains consistent over the course of the increasing number of redundancies.

7   Conclusions and Future Work

In this paper, we investigated the problem of optimizing Recovery Automata that represent recovery strategies synthesized from NdDFTs. New algorithms to minimize an RA by additionally eliminating non trace-equivalent states and redundant transitions were provided. In particular, we extended the notion of recovery equivalence between states by introducing the notion of orthogonal states and a rule for merging them. In addition, we introduced the concept of fail states and a rule for merging them with predecessor states. A formal proof showing that an equivalent RA is produced for each case was given. A case study using the described approach was provided and the evaluated results showed that it allows to obtain a more efficient implementation of recovery strategies for FDIR than solely eliminating trace equivalent states.

In the future, we would like to extend the Recovery Automata model to deal with input of Fault Trees with transient and repairable faults and consider how the merging rules can be transferred.

References

1. Beccuti, M., Franceschinis, G., Codetta-Raiteri, D., Haddad, S.: Computing optimal repair strategies by means of NdRFT modeling and analysis. Comput. J. **57**(12), 1870–1892 (2014). https://doi.org/10.1093/comjnl/bxt134
2. Bittner, B., et al.: An integrated process for FDIR design in aerospace. In: Ortmeier, F., Rauzy, A. (eds.) IMBSA 2014. LNCS, vol. 8822, pp. 82–95. Springer, Cham (2014). https://doi.org/10.1007/978-3-319-12214-4_7
3. Bobbio, A., Portinale, L., Minichino, M., Ciancamerla, E.: Improving the analysis of dependable systems by mapping fault trees into Bayesian networks. Reliab. Eng. Syst. Saf. **71**(3), 249–260 (2001). https://doi.org/10.1016/S0951-8320(00)00077-6
4. Codetta-Raiteri, D., Portinale, L.: Dynamic Bayesian networks for fault detection, identification, and recovery in autonomous spacecraft. IEEE Trans. Syst. Man Cybern.: Syst. **45**(1), 13–24 (2015). https://doi.org/10.1109/TSMC.2014.2323212
5. Dugan, J.B., Bavuso, S.J., Boyd, M.A.: Dynamic fault-tree models for fault-tolerant computer systems. IEEE Trans. Reliab. **41**(3), 363–377 (1992). https://doi.org/10.1109/24.159800
6. Eisentraut, C., Hermanns, H., Zhang, L.: On probabilistic automata in continuous time. In: IEEE Symposium on Logic in Computer Science, pp. 342–351. IEEE (2010). https://doi.org/10.1109/LICS.2010.41
7. Guck, D., Hatefi, H., Hermanns, H., Katoen, J.-P., Timmer, M.: Modelling, reduction and analysis of Markov automata. In: Joshi, K., Siegle, M., Stoelinga, M., D'Argenio, P.R. (eds.) QEST 2013. LNCS, vol. 8054, pp. 55–71. Springer, Heidelberg (2013). https://doi.org/10.1007/978-3-642-40196-1_5
8. Hopcroft, J.: An n log n algorithm for minimizing states in a finite automaton. In: Theory of Machines and Computations, pp. 189–196. Elsevier (1971). https://doi.org/10.1016/B978-0-12-417750-5.50022-1
9. International Electrotechnical Commission, Geneva, Switzerland: Fault Tree Analysis (FTA) (2006)
10. Kildall, G.A.: A unified approach to global program optimization. In: Proceedings of the 1st Annual ACM SIGACT-SIGPLAN Symposium on Principles of Programming Languages, pp. 194–206. ACM (1973). https://doi.org/10.1145/512927.512945
11. Müller, S., Gerndt, A., Noll, T.: Synthesizing FDIR recovery strategies from non-deterministic dynamic fault trees. In: 2017 AIAA SPACE Forum, AIAA 2017-5163. American Institute of Aeronautics and Astronautics (2017). https://doi.org/10.2514/6.2017-5163

12. Raiteri, D.C., Portinale, L.: Arpha: an FDIR architecture for autonomous space-crafts based on dynamic probabilistic graphical models. Technical report TR-INF-2010-12-04-UNIPMN, Computer Science Institute, Università del Piemonte Orientale, Vercelli, Italy, December 2010. http://www.di.unipmn.it/TechnicalReports/TR-INF-2010-12-04-UNIPMN.pdf

13. Ruijters, E., Stoelinga, M.: Fault tree analysis: a survey of the state-of-the-art in modeling, analysis and tools. Comput. Sci. Rev. **15–16**, 29–62 (2015). https://doi.org/10.1016/j.cosrev.2015.03.001

14. Vesely, W.E., Goldberg, F.F., Roberts, N.H., Haasl, D.F.: Fault tree handbook. Technical report, Nuclear Regulatory Commission, Washington, DC (1981). https://www.osti.gov/biblio/5762464-fault-tree-handbook

15. Wander, A., Förstner, R.: Innovative fault detection, isolation and recovery strategies on-board spacecraft: state of the art and research challenges. In: Deutscher Luft- und Raumfahrtkongress 2012. German Society for Aeronautics and Astronautics - Lilienthal-Oberth e.V., Bonn, Germany, January 2013. https://www.dglr.de/publikationen/2013/281268.pdf

Formal Verification of Random Forests
in Safety-Critical Applications

John Törnblom[(✉)] and Simin Nadjm-Tehrani

Department of Computer and Information Science, Linköping University,
Linköping, Sweden
{john.tornblom,simin.nadjm-tehrani}@liu.se

Abstract. Recent advances in machine learning and artificial intelligence are now being applied in safety-critical autonomous systems where software defects may cause severe harm to humans and the environment. Design organizations in these domains are currently unable to provide convincing arguments that systems using complex software implemented using machine learning algorithms are safe and correct.

In this paper, we present an efficient method to extract equivalence classes from decision trees and random forests, and to formally verify that their input/output mappings comply with requirements. We implement the method in our tool VoRF (Verifier of Random Forests), and evaluate its scalability on two case studies found in the literature. We demonstrate that our method is practical for random forests trained on low-dimensional data with up to 25 decision trees, each with a tree depth of 20. Our work also demonstrates the limitations of the method with high-dimensional data and touches upon the trade-off between large number of trees and time taken for verification.

Keywords: Machine learning · Formal verification · Random forest · Decision tree

1 Introduction

In recent years, artificial intelligence utilizing machine learning algorithms has begun to outperform humans at several tasks, e.g. playing board games [21] and diagnosing skin cancer [8]. These advances are now being applied in safety-critical autonomous systems where software defects may cause severe harm to humans and the environment, e.g airborne collision avoidance systems [11].

Several researchers have raised concerns [4,13,18] regarding the lack of verification methods for these kinds of systems in which machine learning algorithms are used to train software deployed in the system. Machine learning models with large sets of parameters are hard to interpret. Humans are currently unable to provide convincing arguments that data used to test and train these models is sufficient, and exhaustive testing is generally intractable.

Instead, various formal methods have been suggested and evaluated. Most research is so far focused on the verification of neural networks, but there are

© Springer Nature Switzerland AG 2019
C. Artho and P. C. Ölveczky (Eds.): FTSCS 2018, CCIS 1008, pp. 55–71, 2019.
https://doi.org/10.1007/978-3-030-12988-0_4

other models that may be more appropriate when verifiability is important, e.g.
decision trees [2] and random forests [3]. Their structural simplicity makes them
easy to analyze systematically, but large (yet simple) models may still prove
hard to verify due to combinatorial explosion.

In this paper, we present a method to efficiently search for violations against
interesting properties in random forests. There may be many such properties,
some impacting system safety. We implement the method in our tool VoRF
(Verifier of Random Forests), and evaluate the tool on two case studies found in
the literature. The contributions of this paper are as follows.

– An efficient method to partition the input domain of decision trees into disjoint sets, and explore all path combinations in a random forest in such a way
  that counteracts combinatorial path explosions.
– A tool named VoRF to support the method.
– Application of the method to two case studies from earlier works.

The rest of this paper is structured as follows. Section 2 presents prelimi-
naries on decision trees, random forests, and a couple of interesting properties.
Section 3 discusses related works on formal methods and machine learning, and
Sect. 4 presents our method with our supporting tool VoRF to verify properties of decision trees and random forests. Section 5 presents applications of our
method on two case studies; a collision detection problem, and a digit recognition problem. Finally, Sect. 6 concludes the paper and summarizes the lessons
we learned.

2   Preliminaries

Government agencies from several countries have agreed upon guidelines [5, 10]
to help design organizations from different industries with assuring quality in
software with safety-critical applications. Several methods described in these
guidelines rely on human experts to analyze the software. However, manually
analyzing large and complex software authored by machine learning algorithms
is hard.

Recently, the avionics community published guidelines [6] describing how
design organizations may apply formal methods to the verification of safety-
critical software. Applying formal methods to complex and safety-critical software is a non-trivial task due to practical limitations in computing power, and
challenges in qualifying complex verification tools. These challenges are often
caused by a high expressiveness provided by the language in which the software
is defined in. In this paper, we address these challenges by selecting machine
learning models based on their simplicity rather than their expressiveness. Specifically, we develop a method with supporting tool to analyze decision trees and
random forests.

2.1   Decision Trees and Random Forests

A decision tree implements a function $t : X^n \rightarrow \mathbb{R}^m$ using a tree structure where each internal node is associated with a decision function, and the leaves define output values. The n-dimensional input domain X^n includes elements x as tuples where each element x_i captures some feature of the application as an input variable. In general, decision functions are defined by non-linear combinations of several input variables at each internal node. In this paper, we only consider binary trees with linear decision functions with one input variable, which Irsoy et al. call univariate hard decision trees [9].

The tree structure is evaluated in a top-down manner, where decision functions determine which path to take towards the leaves. When a leaf is hit, the output $y \in \mathbb{R}^m$ associated with the leaf is emitted. Assuming a perfectly balanced binary tree, the number of leaves in a tree is 2^d, where d is the tree depth. Figure 1 depicts a univariate hard decision tree with one decision function ($x \leq 0$) and two outputs (1 and 2).

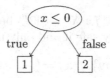

Fig. 1. A decision tree with two possible outputs, depending on the value of single variable x.

Decision trees are known to suffer from a phenomenon called overfitting. Models suffering from this phenomenon can be fitted so tightly to their training data that their performance on unseen data is reduced the more you train them. To counteract these effects in decision trees, Breiman [3] propose random forests.

Definition 1 (Random Forest). *A random forest $f : X^n \rightarrow \mathbb{R}^m$ is a collection of B decision trees that are combined by averaging the values emitted by each individual tree, i.e.*

$$f(x) = \frac{1}{B} \sum_{b=1}^{B} t_b(x)$$

where t_b is the b-th tree in the forest.

To reduce correlation between trees, each tree is trained on a random subset of the training data, using a random subset of the input variables.

Decision trees and random forests may also be used as classifiers. A classifier is a function that categorizes samples from an input domain into one or more classes. In this paper, we only consider one-class classifiers, i.e. functions that map each point from an input domain to exactly one class.

Definition 2 (Classifier). *Let $f(x) = (y_1, \ldots, y_m)$ be a model trained to predict the probability y_i of encountering a class i within disjoint regions in the input domain, where m is the number of classes. Then we would expect that $\forall i \in \{1, \ldots, m\}, 0 \leq y_i \leq 1,$ and $\sum_{i=1}^{m} y_i = 1$. A classifier $f_c(x)$ may then be defined as*

$$f_c(x) = \operatorname*{argmax}_i y_i.$$

2.2   Safety Properties

In this paper, we consider two properties commonly used in related works; global safety [17], and robustness against noise. Note that compliance with these two properties alone is generally not sufficient to ensure safety. Moreover, the notions used here as an illustration are from AI papers. System safety engineers typically define requirements on software functions that are richer than these properties alone. Hence, global safety may be a misnomer in that context, but we simply repeat it here to be consistent with the literature that we refer to.

Property 1 (Global safety). Let $f : X^n \to \mathbb{R}^m$ be the function subject to verification. The function is globally safe if and only if

$$\forall x \in X^n, \forall i \in \{1, \ldots, m\}, f(x) = (y_1, \ldots, y_m), \ \alpha_i \leq y_i \leq \beta_i.$$

for some $\alpha_i, \beta_i \in \mathbb{R}$.

In classification problems, the output tuple $(y_1, \ldots, y_m)$ contains probabilities, and thus $\alpha_i = 0$ and $\beta_i = 1$.

Property 2 (Robustness against noise). Let $f : X^n \to \mathbb{R}^m$ be the function subject to verification, $\epsilon \in \mathbb{R}_{\geq 0}$ a robustness margin, and $\Delta = \{\delta \in \mathbb{R} : -\epsilon < \delta < \epsilon\}$ noise. We denote by δ an n-tuple of elements drawn from Δ. The function is robust against noise iff

$$\forall x \in X^n, \ \forall \delta \in \Delta^n, f(x) = f(x + \delta).$$

Pulina and Tacchella [17] define a stability property that is similar to our notion of robustness here but use scalar noise.

3   Related Works

Due to the extreme progress made in the application of machine learning in artificial intelligence, awareness regarding its (lack of) security and safety have increased. Researchers from several fields are now addressing these problems in their own way, often in collaboration between fields [20].

There have been extensive research on formal verification of neural networks. Pulina and Tacchella [17] combine SMT solvers with an abstraction-refinement technique to analyze neural networks with non-linear activation functions. They conclude that formal verification of realistically sized networks is still an open challenge. Scheibler et al. [19] use bounded model checking to verify a non-linear neural network controlling an inverted pendulum. They encode the neural network and differential equations of the system as an SMT formula, and try to verify properties without success. These works [17,19] suggest that SMT solvers are currently unable to verify realistic non-linear neural networks.

Recent research focuses on piece-wise linear neural networks. Katz et al. [12] combine the simplex method with a SAT solver to verify properties of deep neural networks with piecewise linear activation functions. They successfully verify domain-specific safety properties of a prototype airborne collision avoidance system trained using reinforcement learning. The verified neural network contains a total of 300 nodes organized into 6 layers. Ehlers [7] combines an ILP solver with a modified SAT solver to verify neural networks. His method includes a technique to approximate the overall behavior of the network to reduce the search space for the SAT solver. The method is evaluated on two case studies; a collision detection problem, and a digit recognition problem. We reuse these two case studies in our work, and also provide a global approximation of the overall model (in our cases, random forests).

Mirman et al. [15] use abstract interpretation to verify robustness of neural networks with convolution and fully connected layers. They evaluate their method on four image classification problems (one of which we use in our work), and demonstrate promising performance. In our work, we address similar verification problems, but for random forests. Since decision trees and random forests are generally easier to analyze systematically than neural networks, we expect that formal verification methods scale better when applied to decision trees and random forest compared to neural networks. More importantly, the simplicity of our method allows implementations such as VoRF to be certified for online use in safety-critical applications.

The fact that decision trees may be easier to verify than neural networks is demonstrated by Bastani et al. [1]. They train a neural network to play the game Pong, then extract a decision tree policy from the trained neural network. The extracted tree is significantly easier to verify than the neural network, which they demonstrate by formally verifying properties within seconds using an of-the-shelf SMT solver. Our method provides even greater performance when verifying decision trees. However, our outlook is that decision trees per se may not be sufficient for problems in non-trivial settings and hence we address random forests which provides a counter-measure to overfitting.

4   Analyzing Random Forests

In this section, we define a process for verifying learning-based systems, and define a formal method capable of verifying properties of decision trees and random forests. We also describe VoRF (Verifier of Random Forests), our implementation of our method, and provide an example on how to define and verify the global safety property of random forest classifiers using VoRF.

4.1   Problem Definition

We formulate the software verification process for learning-based systems using the following problem definitions.

Problem 1 (Constraint Satisfaction). Let $f : X^n \to \mathbb{R}^m$ be a function that is known to implement some desirable behavior in a system, and a property $\mathbb{P}$ specifying additional constraints on the relationship between $\boldsymbol{x} \in X^n$ and $\boldsymbol{y} \in \mathbb{R}^m$. Verify that $\forall \boldsymbol{x} \in X^n$, the property $\mathbb{P}$ holds.

Since a random forest is a pure function and thus there is no state space to explore, this problem may be addressed by considering all combinations of paths through trees in the forest. Furthermore, by partitioning the input domain into equivalence classes, i.e. sets of points in the input domain that yield the same output, constraint satisfaction may be verified for regions in the input domain, rather than for individual points explicitly.

Problem 2 (Equivalence Class Partitioning). For each path combination p in a random forest $f : X^n \to \mathbb{R}^m$, determine the complete set of inputs $X_p \subseteq X^n$ that lead to traversing p, and the corresponding output $\boldsymbol{y}_p \in \mathbb{R}^m$. Then verify that $\forall \boldsymbol{x} \in X_p$, the property $\mathbb{P}$ holds.

Our method efficiently generates equivalence classes as pairs of $(X_p, \boldsymbol{y}_p)$, and automatically verifies the satisfaction of a property $\mathbb{P}$. Assuming that the trees in a random forest are of equal size, the number of path combinations in the random forest is $2^{d \cdot B}$. In practice, decisions made by the individual trees are influenced by a subset of features shared amongst several trees within the same forest, and thus several path combinations are infeasible and may be discarded from analysis.

Example 1 (Discarded Path Combination). Consider a random forest with the trees depicted in Fig. 2. There are four path combinations. However, x cannot be less than or equal to zero at the same time as being greater than five. Consequently, Tree 1 cannot emit 1 at the same time as Tree 2 emits 3, and thus one path combination may be discarded from analysis.

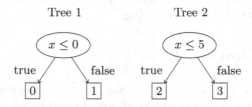

Fig. 2. Two decision trees that when combined into a random forest, contains three feasible path combinations and one discarded path combination.

We postulate that since several path combinations may be discarded from analysis, all equivalence classes in a random forest may be computed and enumerated within a reasonable amount of time for practical applications. To explore this idea, we developed the tool VoRF[1] which automates the computation, enumeration, and verification of equivalence classes.

4.2 Tool Overview

VoRF consists of two distinct components, VoRF Core and VoRF Property Checker. VoRF Core takes as input a random forest $f : X^n \to \mathbb{R}^m$, a hyperrectangle defining the input domain X^n (which may include $\pm\infty$), and emits all equivalence classes in f. These equivalence classes are then processed by VoRF Property Checker that checks if all input/output mappings captured by each equivalence class are valid according to a property $\mathbb{P}$, as illustrated by Fig. 3.

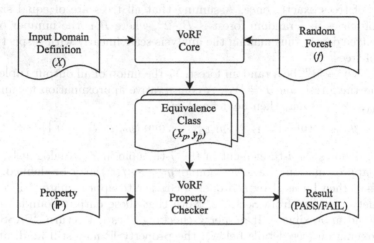

Fig. 3. Overview of VoRF.

4.3 Computing Equivalence Classes

There are three distinct tasks being carried out by VoRF Core while computing equivalence classes of a random forest:

- partitioning the input domain of decision trees into disjoint sets.
- exploring all feasible path combinations in the random forest.
- deriving output tuples from leaves.

---

[1] https://github.com/john-tornblom/vorf.

Path exploration is performed by simply walking the trees depth-first. When a leaf is hit, the output $\boldsymbol{y}_p$ for the traversed path combination p is incremented with the value associated with the leaf, and path exploration continues with the next tree. The set of inputs X_p is captured by a set of constraints derived from decision functions associated with internal nodes encountered while traversing p. When the final leaf in a path combination is hit, $\boldsymbol{y}_p$ is divided by the number of trees B (recall the definition of a random forest in Definition 1 which includes the same division). Finally, the VoRF Property Checker checks if the mappings from X_p to $\boldsymbol{y}_p$ comply with the property $\mathbb{P}$. If the property holds, the next available path combination is traversed, otherwise verification terminates with a "FAIL" and the most recent $(X_p, \boldsymbol{y}_p)$ mapping as a counterexample.

4.4   Approximating Output Bounds

The output of a random forest may be bounded by analyzing each leaf in the collection of trees exactly once. Assuming that all trees are of equal size, the number of leaves in a random forest is $B \cdot 2^d$, where B is the number of trees and d the tree depth, thus making the analysis scale linearly with respect to the number of trees.

Let $f : X^n \to \mathbb{R}^m$ be a random forest, Y_t the union of all output tuples from all trees in the forest, and $L = |Y_t|$. A conservative approximation for an upper bound $\boldsymbol{y}_{\max} \geq f(\boldsymbol{x})$ may then be defined as

$$\boldsymbol{y}_{\max} = (\max\{y_{1,1}, \ldots, y_{1,L}\}, \ldots, \max\{y_{m,1}, \ldots, y_{m,L}\}),$$

where $y_{i,j}$ denotes the i-th element in the j-th tuple in Y_t. Analogously, a conservative approximation of a lower bound $\boldsymbol{y}_{\min} \leq f(\boldsymbol{x})$ may be defined. These bounds may then be used by a property checker to approximate f in e.g. the global safety property from Sect. 2.2. Note that these output bounds are conservative and approximate. If property checking does not return "PASS" with the approximation (see details below), the property $\mathbb{P}$ may still hold, and further analysis of the forest is required, e.g. by computing all possible equivalence classes (which are precise).

4.5   Implementation

This section presents implementation details of VoRF Core and VoRF Property Checker, and aspects that impact accuracy in floating point computations.

VoRF Core. For efficiency, core features in VoRF are implemented as a library in C, and utilize a pipeline architecture as illustrated by Fig. 4 to compute and enumerate equivalence classes. The first processing element in the pipeline constructs an intermediate mapping from the entire input domain to an output tuple of zeros. The final processing element divides output tuples with the number of trees in the forest. In between, there is one refinery element for each tree that splits intermediate mappings into disjoint regions according to decision functions in the tree, and increments the output with values carried by the leaves.

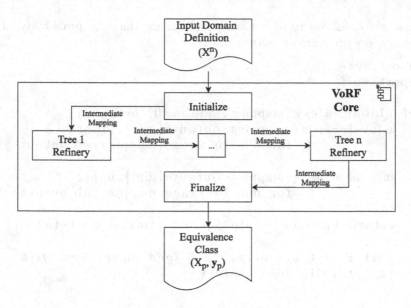

Fig. 4. Control flow of equivalence class partitioning in VoRF Core.

To decouple VoRF from any particular random forest training library, a random forest is loaded into memory by reading a JSON-formatted file from disk. VoRF includes a tool[2] to convert random forests trained by the library scikit-learn [16] to this file format.

VoRF Property Checker. VoRF includes two pre-defined property checkers which are parameterized and executed from a command line interface; the global safety property checker, and the robustness property checker.

The global safety property checker first uses the output bounds approximation to check for property violations, and resorts to equivalence class analysis only when a violation is detected when using the approximation.

The robustness property checker checks that all points X_r within a hypercube with sides ϵ, centered around a test point x_t, map to the same output. Note that selecting which test points to include in the verification may be problematic. In principle, all points in the input domain should be checked for robustness, but with random forest *classifiers*, there is always a hyperplane separating two classes from each other, and always points which violate the robustness property (adjacent to each side of the hyperplane). Hence, the property is only applicable to points at distances greater than ϵ from the classification boundary.

VoRF also includes Python bindings for easy prototyping of domain-specific property checkers. Example 2 depicts an implementation of the global safety property that uses these Python bindings to do sanity checking for a classifier's output.

---

[2] https://github.com/john-tornblom/vorf/blob/v0.1.0/support/train-sklearn.py.

Example 2 (Global Safety of a Classifier). Ensure that the probability of all classes in every prediction is within $[0,1]$.

```
import sys
import vorf

def global_safety(mapping, alpha=0, beta=1):
    minval = min([mapping.outputs[dim].lower
                for dim in range(mapping.nb_outputs)])

    maxval = max([mapping.outputs[dim].upper
                for dim in range(mapping.nb_outputs)])

    return (minval >= alpha) and (maxval <= beta)

f = vorf.Forest(sys.argv[1]) # load model from disk
assert f.forall(global_safety)
```

Computational Accuracy. Implementations of random forests normally approximate real values as floating point numbers, and thus may suffer from inaccurate computations. In general, VoRF and the software subject to verification must use the same precision on floating point numbers and averaging function as in Definition 1 to get a compatible property satisfaction. In this version of VoRF, we use the same representation so that the calculation errors are the same as in the machine learning library scikit-learn [16]. Specifically, we approximate real values as 32-bit floating point numbers, and implement the averaging function literally as presented in Definition 1, i.e. by first computing the sum of all individual trees, then dividing by the number of trees. Other machine learning libraries may use 64-bit floating point numbers, and may implement the averaging function differently, e.g.

$$f(x) = \sum_{b=1}^{B} \frac{t_b(x)}{B}.$$

This would be easily changeable in VoRF.

5   Case Studies

In this section, we present an evaluation of VoRF on two case studies found in the literature where neural networks have been analyzed for compliance with interesting properties. Each case study defines a training set and a test set, and we used scikit-learn [16] to train random forests of different sizes. All training parameters except the number of trees and maximum tree depth were kept constant and at their default values. We evaluated accuracy on each trained model against its test set, i.e. the percentage of samples from the test set where there are no misclassifications. We then implemented verification cases for the global safety and robustness against noise properties (from Sect. 2.2) using VoRF. The time spent on verification was recorded for each trained model as presented below. All experiments were conducted on an Intel Core i5 2500 K with 16 GB RAM, running Ubuntu 18.04.

5.1 Vehicle Collision Detection

In this case study, we verified properties of random forests trained to detect collisions between two moving vehicles traveling along curved trajectories at different speeds. Each verified random forest accepts six input variables, emits two output variables, and contains 10–25 trees with depths 10–20.

Dataset. We used a simulation tool from Ehlers [7] to generate 30,000 training samples and 3,000 test samples. Unlike neural networks which Ehlers used in his case study, the size of a random forest is limited by the amount of data available during training, hence we generated ten times more training data than Ehlers to ensure that sufficient data is available for the size and number of trees assessed in our case study. Each sample contains the relative distance between the two vehicles, the speed and starting direction of the second vehicle, and the rotation speed of both vehicles.

Robustness. We verified the robustness against noise for all trained models by defining input regions surrounding each sample in the test set with the robustness margin $\epsilon = 0.05$. Table 1 lists random forests included in the experiment with their maximum tree depth d, number of trees B, accuracy of the classifications (Accuracy), elapsed time T during verification, and the percentage of samples from the test set where there were no misclassifications within the robustness region (Robustness).

Table 1. Accuracy and robustness of random forests in the vehicle collision detection case study.

d	B	Accuracy (%)	T (s)	Robustness (%)
10	10	90.5	1	41.0
10	15	90.3	11	45.0
10	20	90.4	84	48.9
10	25	90.0	449	**50.3**
20	10	94.0	3	28.0
20	15	94.1	77	27.5
20	20	94.2	930	29.5
20	25	**94.5**	5499	29.6

Increasing the maximum depth of trees increased accuracy on the test set, but reduced the robustness against noise. This suggests that the models were over-fitted with noiseless examples during training, and thus adding noisy examples to the training set may improve robustness. Verifying the largest random forest with $B = 25$ trees and depth $d = 20$ took approximately 1.5 h. The significant drop in elapsed time between $\{d = 10, B = 25\}$ and $\{d = 20, B = 10\}$ may seem counter-intuitive at first. However, recall that the theoretical upper limit of the number of path combinations in a random forest is $2^{d \cdot B}$, and that $2^{20 \cdot 10} \ll 2^{10 \cdot 25}$.

Scalability. Next, we assessed the scalability of VoRF Core when the number of trees grows by verifying the trivial property $\mathbb{P} = true$ which accepts all input/output mappings. We implemented this trivial property in a verification case that also counts the number of equivalence classes emitted by VoRF Core. We then executed the verification case for all models with a tree depth of $d = 10$. The recoded number of equivalence classes C for different number of trees B is depicted in Fig. 5 on a logarithmic scale. The number of equivalence classes increased exponentially as more trees were added, but the magnitude of the growth decreased for each added tree. The number of equivalence classes for large number of trees are significantly smaller than the upper limit of $2^{d \cdot B}$ (which occurs when there are no shared features amongst trees, and thus each path combination yields a distinct equivalence class).

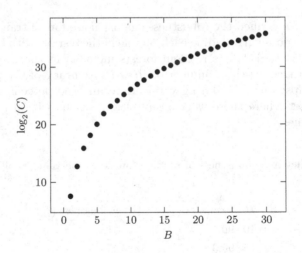

Fig. 5. Number of equivalent classes C on a logarithmic scale from the vehicle collision detection case study for different number of trees B with a depth $d = 10$.

Global Safety. Finally, we verified the global safety property (here ensuring that all predicted probabilities are in the range $[0, 1]$). All trained models passed the verification case within fractions of a second. This is expected since the output bound approximation algorithm implemented in the global safety property checker scales linearly with respect to the number of leaves in a forest, and thus there is no combinatorial explosion when the number of trees grows.

5.2 Digit Recognition

In this case study, we verified properties of random forests trained to recognize images of hand-written digits.

Dataset. The MNIST dataset [14] is a collection of hand-written digits commonly used to evaluate machine learning algorithms. The dataset contains 70,000 gray scale images with a resolution of 28×28 pixels at 8bpp. Each image was encoded as a tuple of 784 pixels, and the dataset was randomized and split into two subsets; a 85% training set, and a 15% test set (a similar split was used in [14]).

Robustness. We verified the robustness against noise for all trained models by defining input regions surrounding each sample in the test set with the robustness margin $\epsilon = 1$, which amounts to a 0.5% lightning change per pixel in a 8bpp gray-scaled image. Each input region contains 2^{784} noisy images, which would be too many for VoRF to handle within a reasonable amount of time. Consequently, we reduced the complexity of the problem significantly by only considering robustness against noise within a sliding window of 5×5 pixels. For a given sample from the test set, noise was added within the 5×5 window, yielding $2^{5.5}$ noisy images. This operation was then repeated on the original image, but with the window placed at an offset of 1px relative to its previous position. Applying this operation on an entire image yields $2^{5.5} \cdot (28 - 5)^2 \approx 2^{34}$ distinct noisy images per sample from the test set, and about 10^{14} noisy images when applied to the entire test set.

Table 2 lists random forests included in the experiment with their maximum tree depth d, number of trees B, accuracy on the test set (Accuracy), elapsed time T during verification, and the percentage of samples from the test set where there were no misclassifications within the robustness region (Robustness).

Table 2. Accuracy and robustness of random forests in the digit recognition case study.

d	B	Accuracy (%)	T (s)	Robustness (%)
10	10	93.0	245	65.8
10	15	93.6	824	68.8
10	20	93.8	2010	75.2
10	25	94.2	10787	74.8
20	10	94.9	482	70.4
20	15	95.8	1626	77.6
20	20	96.0	4101	82.3
20	25	**96.4**	17411	**83.7**

Increasing the complexity of a random forest slightly increased its accuracy, and significantly increased its robustness against noise. Verifying the largest random forest with $B = 25$ trees and depth $d = 20$ took approximately 5h.

Figure 6 depicts one of many examples from the MNIST dataset that were misclassified by the random forest with $B = 25$ and $d = 10$. Since the added noise is invisible to the naked eye, the noise (a single pixel) is highlighted in red.

Fig. 6. A missclassified noisy sample from the MNIST dataset. (Color figure online)

Scalability. Next, we assessed the scalability of VoRF Core when the number of trees grows by verifying the trivial property $\mathbb{P} = true$. This was done in a similar way as described in the vehicle collision detection use case presented in Sect. 5.1. We then executed the verification case for all models with a tree depth of $d = 10$. Enumerating all possible equivalence classes was intractable for random forests with more than $B = 4$ trees. We aborted the experiment after running the verification case with a random forest of $B = 5$ for 72 h. Figure 7 depicts the four data points we managed to acquire.

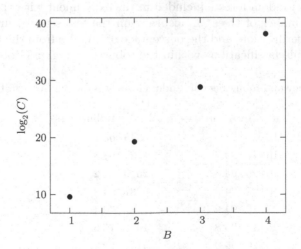

Fig. 7. Number of equivalent classes C on a logarithmic scale from the digit recognition case study for different number of trees B with a depth $d = 10$.

The number of equivalence classes increased exponentially as more trees were added, without demonstrating any signs of stagnation. The ability to discard infeasible path combinations in a random forest is an essential ingredient to our method. When random forests are trained on high-dimensional data, the number of features shared between trees is relatively low, so it is not surprising that our method experiences combinatorial path explosion. This shows that in non-trivial applications, transforming domain knowledge into reasonable constraints in the form of a property $\mathbb{P}$ is a useful means of addressing combinatorial problems in verification.

Global Safety. Finally, we verified the global safety property (again ensuring that that all predicted probabilities are in the range $[0, 1]$). All trained models passed the verification case within seconds. This is expected since the output bound approximation algorithm implemented in the global safety property checker scales linearly with respect to the number of leaves in a forest, and thus there is no combinatorial explosion when the number of trees grows.

6 Conclusions and Future Work

In this paper, we proposed a method to formally verify properties of random forests. Our method exploits the fact that several trees make decisions based on a shared subset of the input variables, and thus several path combinations in a random forest are infeasible. We implemented the method in a tool called VoRF, and demonstrated its scalability on two case studies.

In the first case study, a collision detection problem with six input variables, we demonstrated that problems with a low-dimensional input space can be verified using our method within a reasonable amount of time. In the second case study, a digit recognition problem with 784 input variables, we demonstrated that our method copes with high-dimensional input space when verifying robustness against noise. But it does so only if the systematically introduced noise does not attempt to exhaustively cover all possibilities. Since the number of shared input variables between trees is low, we observed a combinatorial explosion of paths in the forest. However, we successfully verified the global safety property in both case studies within seconds by using a fast approximation algorithm that scales linearly with respect to the number of trees in a random forest.

For future work, we plan to extend our method to include concepts from abstract interpretation to address the combinatorial path explosion observed when verifying the robustness property on high-dimensional data. Other directions of work include studying different search strategies, applying to use cases where control is involved (and not only sensing), and creating new properties that are meaningful in the context of the problem at hand, e.g. decisive classifications.

Acknowledgements. This work was partially supported by the Wallenberg AI, Autonomous Systems and Software Program (WASP) funded by the Knut and Alice Wallenberg Foundation.

References

1. Bastani, O., Pu, Y., Solar-Lezama, A.: Verifiable reinforcement learning via policy extraction. In: Advances in Neural Information Processing Systems (NIPS) (2018)
2. Breiman, L.: Classification and Regression Trees. Wadsworth International Group (1984)
3. Breiman, L.: Random forests. Mach. Learn. **45**(1), 5–32 (2001). https://doi.org/10.1023/A:1010933404324
4. Burton, S., Gauerhof, L., Heinzemann, C.: Making the case for safety of machine learning in highly automated driving. In: Tonetta, S., Schoitsch, E., Bitsch, F. (eds.) SAFECOMP 2017. LNCS, vol. 10489, pp. 5–16. Springer, Cham (2017). https://doi.org/10.1007/978-3-319-66284-8_1
5. DO-178C: Software Considerations in Airborne Systems and Equipment Certification. RTCA, Inc. (2012)
6. DO-333: Formal Methods Supplement to DO-178C and DO-278A. RTCA, Inc. (2012)
7. Ehlers, R.: Formal verification of piece-wise linear feed-forward neural networks. In: D'Souza, D., Narayan Kumar, K. (eds.) ATVA 2017. LNCS, vol. 10482, pp. 269–286. Springer, Cham (2017). https://doi.org/10.1007/978-3-319-68167-2_19
8. Esteva, A., et al.: Dermatologist-level classification of skin cancer with deep neural networks. Nature **542**(7639), 115 (2017). https://doi.org/10.1038/nature21056
9. Irsoy, O., Yildiz, O.T., Alpaydin, E.: Soft decision trees. In: International Conference on Pattern Recognition (ICPR) (2012)
10. ISO 26262: Road Vehicles - Functional Safety. International Organization for Standardization (2011)
11. Julian, K.D., Lopez, J., Brush, J.S., Owen, M.P., Kochenderfer, M.J.: Policy compression for aircraft collision avoidance systems. In: 2016 IEEE/AIAA 35th Digital Avionics Systems Conference (DASC), pp. 1–10. IEEE (2016). https://doi.org/10.1109/DASC.2016.7778091
12. Katz, G., Barrett, C., Dill, D.L., Julian, K., Kochenderfer, M.J.: Reluplex: an efficient SMT solver for verifying deep neural networks. In: Majumdar, R., Kunčak, V. (eds.) CAV 2017. LNCS, vol. 10426, pp. 97–117. Springer, Cham (2017). https://doi.org/10.1007/978-3-319-63387-9_5
13. Kurd, Z., Kelly, T., Austin, J.: Developing artificial neural networks for safety critical systems. Neural Comput. Appl. **16**(1), 11–19 (2007). https://doi.org/10.1007/s00521-006-0039-9
14. LeCun, Y., Bottou, L., Bengio, Y., Haffner, P.: Gradient-based learning applied to document recognition. Proc. IEEE **86**(11), 2278–2324 (1998). https://doi.org/10.1109/5.726791
15. Mirman, M., Gehr, T., Vechev, M.: Differentiable abstract interpretation for provably robust neural networks. In: International Conference on Machine Learning (ICML) (2018)
16. Pedregosa, F., et al.: Scikit-learn: machine learning in Python. J. Mach. Learn. Res. **12**(Oct), 2825–2830 (2011)
17. Pulina, L., Tacchella, A.: Challenging SMT solvers to verify neural networks. AI Commun. **25**(2), 117–135 (2012). https://doi.org/10.3233/AIC-2012-0525
18. Russell, S., Dewey, D., Tegmark, M.: Research priorities for robust and beneficial artificial intelligence. AI Mag. **36**(4), 105–114 (2015). https://doi.org/10.1609/aimag.v36i4.2577

19. Scheibler, K., Winterer, L., Wimmer, R., Becker, B.: Towards verification of artificial neural networks. In: Automatic Verification and Analysis of Complex Systems (MBMV), pp. 30–40 (2015)
20. Seshia, S.A., Zhu, X.J., Krause, A., Jha, S.: Machine learning and formal methods (Dagstuhl Seminar 17351). In: Dagstuhl Reports. Schloss Dagstuhl-Leibniz-Zentrum fuer Informatik (2018). https://doi.org/10.4230/DagRep.7.8.55
21. Silver, D., et al.: Mastering the game of go with deep neural networks and tree search. Nature **529**(7587), 484–489 (2016). https://doi.org/10.1038/nature16961

Analysis of Timed Systems

A Benchmark Library for Parametric Timed Model Checking

Étienne André[1,2,3]($\boxtimes$) (ID)

[1] Université Paris 13, LIPN, CNRS, UMR 7030, 93430 Villetaneuse, France
[2] JFLI, CNRS, Tokyo, Japan
[3] National Institute of Informatics, Tokyo, Japan
`eandre93430@lipn13.fr`

Abstract. Verification of real-time systems involving hard timing constraints and concurrency is of utmost importance. Parametric timed model checking allows for formal verification in the presence of unknown timing constants or uncertainty (e. g., imprecision for periods). With the recent development of several techniques and tools to improve the efficiency of parametric timed model checking, there is a growing need for proper benchmarks to test and compare fairly these tools. We present here a benchmark library for parametric timed model checking made of benchmarks accumulated over the years. Our benchmarks include academic benchmarks, industrial case studies and examples unsolvable using existing techniques.

Keywords: Case studies · Model checking · Parameter synthesis · Parametric timed automata

1 Introduction

Verification of real-time systems involving hard timing constraints and concurrency is of utmost importance, and is now recognized in standards such as the DO-178C, that allows formal methods without addressing specific process requirements. Model checking is a popular model-based technique that formally verifies whether a model satisfies a property. Parametric timed model checking significantly enhances model checking by allowing its application earlier in the design phase, when timing constants may not be known yet. In addition, it is possible to verify systems in the presence of uncertainty, e. g., when some periods are known with some limited precision. This is the case of Thales' FMTV[1] challenge 2014 where the system was characterized with uncertain but *constant* periods, that rules out the use of non-parametric timed model checking.

---

[1] "Formal Methods for Timing Verification Challenge", in the WATERS workshop: http://waters2015.inria.fr/.

This work is partially supported by the ANR national research program PACS (ANR-14-CE28-0002) and by ERATO HASUO Metamathematics for Systems Design Project (No. JPMJER1603), JST.

C. Artho and P. C. Ölveczky (Eds.): FTSCS 2018, CCIS 1008, pp. 75–83, 2019.
https://doi.org/10.1007/978-3-030-12988-0_5

Popular formalism for parametric timed model checking include parametric timed automata (PTAs) [3] and parametric time Petri nets [41].

Several tools support parameters, such as HyTech [26] (parametric hybrid automata), Romeo [34] (parametric time Petri nets), IMITATOR [9] (parametric timed automata), PSyHCoS [14] (parametric stateful timed CSP), or Symrob (robustness for timed automata) [38]. In addition, several tools support the larger class of *hybrid automata*, such as PHAVer [24] or SpaceEx [25] and, while not explicitly supporting parameters, can encode them.[1] Recently, a growing number of analyses and techniques were proposed to analyze parametric timed models (mainly PTAs) such as SMT-based techniques [31], integer hull abstractions [30], corner-point abstractions [15], distributed verification [8], NDFS-based synthesis [36], machine learning [13,33], etc. However, despite some case studies informally shared between these works, there is a lack of a common basis to compare new tools and techniques in a fair manner. Without a stable list of benchmarks publicly available, it is difficult to assess the efficiency of a new algorithm.

Contribution. We present here a library of benchmarks containing academic and industrial case studies collected in the past few years from academic papers and industrial collaborations. In addition, a focus is made on (possibly toy) examples known to be unsolvable using current state-of-the-art techniques, with the hope to encourage the development of new techniques to solve them. Benchmarks are available online in the IMITATOR input format, and distributed using the GNU General Public License.

Related Libraries. The library most related to ours is that by Chen *et al.*, that proposes a suite of benchmarks for hybrid systems [18]. However, it aims at analyzing hybrid systems, which are strictly more expressive than PTAs in theory, and incomparable in practice, as most hybrid systems do not feature timing parameters. In addition, that benchmark suite focuses only on reachability properties. Finally and most importantly, it does not focus on parameters, and the benchmarks are non-parametric. In contrast, our library focuses on parametric timed benchmarks, with various types of properties.

Another interesting library is that by Hoxha, Abbas, and Fainekos [27], that offers Matlab/Simulink models of automotive systems. However, it does not aim specifically at parametric timed model checking; two of our benchmarks originally partially come from the aforementioned library [27].

2   IMITATOR Parametric Timed Automata

Parametric timed automata extend finite-state automata with clocks, i. e., real-valued variables evolving at the same rate. Clocks can be reset along transitions, and can be compared to constants or parameters (integer- or rational-valued)

---

[1] In a hybrid automaton, a parameter is a variable that can evolve for an arbitrary amount of time at rate 1, and is then "frozen" (rate 0).

along transitions ("guards") or in locations ("invariants"). IMITATOR parametric timed automata extend PTAs [3] with some useful features such as synchronization between components, stopwatches (i.e., the ability to stop the elapsing of some clocks [17]), presence of parametric linear terms in guards, invariants and resets, shared global rational-valued variables, etc.

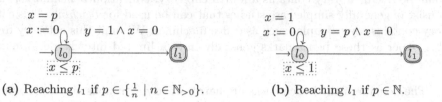

(a) Reaching l_1 if $p \in \{\frac{1}{n} \mid n \in \mathbb{N}_{>0}\}$.   (b) Reaching l_1 if $p \in \mathbb{N}$.

Fig. 1. Examples of PTAs.

Example 1. Consider the PTA in Fig. 1a, containing two locations l_0 and l_1, two clocks x and y, and one parameter p. The self-loop on l_0 can be taken whenever $x = p$ holds, and resets x, i.e., can be taken every p time units. In addition, initially, as $x = y = 0$ and clocks evolve at the same rate, the transition guarded by $y = 1 \wedge x = 0$ cannot be taken. Observe that, if $p = 1$, then the transition to l_1 can be taken after exactly one loop on l_0. If $p = \frac{1}{2}$, then the transition to l_1 can be taken after exactly two loops. In fact, the set of valuations for which l_1 is reachable is exactly $\{i \mid i = \frac{1}{n}, n > 0 \wedge n \in \mathbb{N}\}$.

L/U-PTAs. Lower-bound/upper-bound parametric timed automata (L/U-PTAs) [28] restrict the use of parameters: parameters must be partitioned between lower-bound parameters (always compared with clocks as lower bounds, i.e., $p \leq x$ or $p < x$) and upper-bound parameters. L/U-PTAs enjoy monotonicity properties and, while the full class of PTAs is highly undecidable [5], L/U-PTAs enjoy some decidability results [12,16,28]. U-PTAs [11,16] are L/U-PTAs with only upper-bound parameters.

3 The Benchmark Library

3.1 Categories

Our benchmarks are classified into three main categories:

1. academic benchmarks, studied in a range of papers: a typical example is the Fischer mutual exclusion protocol;
2. industrial case studies, which correspond to a concrete problem solved (or not) in an industrial environment;

3. examples famous for being unsolvable using state-of-the-art techniques; for some of them, a solution may be computed by hand, but existing automated techniques are not capable of computing it. This is the case of the PTA in Fig. 1a, as a human can very easily solve it, while (to the best of our knowledge) no tool is able to compute this result automatically.

Remark 1. Our library contains a fourth category: education benchmarks, that consist of generally simple case studies that can be used for *teaching*. This category contains toy examples such as coffee machines. We omit this category from this paper as these benchmarks generally have a limited interest performance wise.

The domain of the benchmarks are hardware asynchronous circuits, communication or mutual exclusion protocols, real-time systems ("RTS") and schedulability problems, parametric timed pattern matching ("PTPM"), train-gate-controllers models ("TGC"), etc.

In addition, we use the following classification criteria:

- number of variables: clocks, parameters, locations, automata;
- whether the benchmark (in the provided version) is easily *scalable*, i.e., whether one can generate a large number of instances; for example, protocols often depend on the number of participants, and can therefore be scaled accordingly;
- presence of shared rational-valued variables;
- presence of stopwatches;
- presence of location invariants, as some works (e.g., [3,11]) exclude them;
- whether the benchmark meets the L/U assumption.

3.2 Properties

We consider the three following main properties:

reachability/safety: synthesize parameter valuations for which a given state of the system (generally a location, but possibly a constraint on variables) must be reachable/avoided (see e.g., [30]).
optimal reachability: same as reachability, but with an optimization criterion: some parameters (or the time) should be minimized or maximized.
unavoidability: synthesize parameter valuations for which all runs must always eventually reach a given state (see e.g., [30]).
robustness: synthesize parameter valuations preserving the discrete behavior (untimed language) w.r.t. to a given valuation (see e.g., [7,38]).

In addition, we include some recent case studies of parametric timed pattern matching ("PTPM" hereafter), i.e., being able to decide for which part of a log and for which values of parameters does a parametric property holds on that log [10]. Finally, a few more case studies have *ad-hoc* properties (liveness, properties expressed using observers [2,4], etc.), denoted "Misc." later on.

3.3 Presentation

The benchmark library comes in the form of a Web page that classifies models and is available at https://www.imitator.fr/library.html.

The library is made of a list of a set of *benchmarks*. Each benchmark may have different *models*: for example, `Flip-flop` comes with three models, one with 2 parameters, one with 5, and one with 12 parameters. Similarly, some `Fischer` benchmarks come with several models, each of them corresponding to a different number of processes. Finally, each model comes with one or more *properties*. For example, for `Fischer`, one can either run safety synthesis, or evaluate the robustness of a given reference parameter valuation.

The first version of the library contains 34 benchmarks with 80 different models and 122 properties.

3.4 Performance

We present a selection of the library in Table 1. Not all benchmarks are given; in addition, most benchmarks come with several models and several properties, omitted here for space concern. We give from left to right the number of automata, of clocks, of parameters, of discrete variables, whether the model is an L/U-PTA, a U-PTA or a regular PTA, whether it features invariants and stopwatches, the kind of property, and a computation time on an Intel i7-7500U CPU @ 2.70 GHz with 8 GiB running Linux Mint 18.

"T.O." denotes time-out (after 300 s). "?" denotes unsolvable, because no such algorithm is implemented in existing tools. "HS" denotes time-out but human-solvable: e. g., for Fischer, one knows the correctness constraint independently of the number of processes, but tools may fail to compute it. This is also the case of the toy PTAs in Figs. 1a and 1b.

Despite time-out, some case studies come with a partial result: either because IMITATOR is running reachability-synthesis ("EFsynth" [30]) which can output a partial result when interrupted before completion, or because some other methods can output some valuations. For example, for `ProdCons`, IMITATOR is unable to synthesize a constraint; however, in the original work [31], some punctual valuations (non-symbolic) are given.

Robustness case studies are not part of Table 1, but are included in the online library.

4   Perspectives

Syntax. So far, all benchmarks use the IMITATOR input format; in addition, only if the benchmark comes from another model checker (e. g., a HYTECH or UPPAAL model), it also comes with its native syntax. In a near future, we plan to propose a translation to UPPAAL timed automata; however, some information will be lost as UPPAAL does not allow parameters, and supports stopwatches in a limited manner. A future work will be to propose other syntaxes, or a normalized syntax for parametric timed model checking benchmarks.

Table 1. A selection from the benchmark library

Benchmark	Ref	Domain	Scal.	$|\mathcal{A}|$	$|X|$	$|\mathbb{P}|$	$|V|$	L/U	Inv	SW	Prop.	Time
Academic												
And-Or	[20]	Circuit	×	4	4	12	0	–	√	×	Misc.	3.01
CSMA/CD	[32]	Protocol	√	3	3	3	0	–	√	×	Unavoid.	?
Fischer-AHV93	[3]	Protocol	√	3	2	4	0	L/U	×	×	Safety	0.04
Fischer-HRSV02:3	[28]	Protocol	√	3	3	4	1	L/U	√	×	Safety	HS
Flip-flop:2	[21]	Circuit	×	5	5	2	0	U	√	×	Misc.	0.04
Flip-flop:12	[21]	Circuit	×	5	5	12	0	U	√	×	Misc.	23.07
idle-time-sched:3	[35]	RTS	√	8	13	2	3	U	√	√	Safety	1.49
idle-time-sched:5	[35]	RTS	√	12	21	2	0	U	√	√	Safety	14.61
Jobshop:3-4	[1]	Sched	√	2	3	12	4	–	√	×	Opt. reach.	5.58
Jobshop:4-4	[1]	Sched	√	4	4	16	4	–	√	×	Opt. reach.	T.O.
NP-FPS-3tasks:50-0	[29]	RTS	×	4	6	2	0	–	√	×	Safety	1.03
NP-FPS-3tasks:100-2	[29]	RTS	×	4	6	2	0	–	√	×	Safety	65.23
SSLAF14-1	[37, 40]	RTS	×	7	16	2	2	–	√	√	Safety	0.33
SSLAF14-2	[40, 42]	RTS	×	6	14	2	4	–	√	√	Safety	T.O.
ProdCons:2-3	[31]	Prod.-cons	√	5	5	6	0	L/U	√	×	Reach.	T.O.
train-AHV93	[3]	TGC	×	3	3	6	0	L/U	×	×	Safety	0.01
WFAS	[15]	Protocol	×	3	4	2	0	–	√	×	Safety	T.O.
Industrial												
accel:1	[10, 27]	PTPM	√	2	2	3	0	–	√	×	PTPM	1.25
accel:10	[10, 27]	PTPM	√	2	2	3	0	–	√	×	PTPM	12.67
BRP	[23]	Protocol	×	6	7	2	12	–	√	×	Safety	248.35
FMTV:1A1	[39]	RTS	×	3	3	3	5	–	√	×	Opt. reach.	6.97
FMTV:1A3	[39]	RTS	×	3	3	3	7	–	√	×	Opt. reach.	87.39
FMTV:2	[39]	RTS	×	6	9	2	0	–	√	√	Opt. reach.	1.61
gear:1	[10, 27]	PTPM	√	2	2	3	0	–	√	×	PTPM	0.77
gear:10	[10, 27]	PTPM	√	2	2	3	0	–	√	×	PTPM	7.42
RCP	[22]	Protocol	×	5	6	5	6	L/U	√	×	Reach.	1.07
SIMOP:3	[6]	Automation	×	5	8	3	0	–	√	×	Reach.	T.O.
SPSMALL:2	[19]	Circuit	×	11	11	2	0	–	√	×	Reach.	0.96
SPSMALL:26	[19]	Circuit	×	11	11	26	0	–	√	×	Reach.	T.O.
Toy												
toy:n	Fig. 1b	Toy	×	1	2	1	0	–	√	×	Reach.	HS
toy:1/n	Fig. 1a	Toy	×	1	2	1	0	U	√	×	Reach.	HS

Contributions and Versioning. The library is aimed at being enriched with future benchmarks. Furthermore, it is collaborative, and is open to any willing contributor. A versioning system will be set up with the addition (or modification) of benchmarks in the future.

References

1. Abdeddaïm, Y., Maler, O.: Job-shop scheduling using timed automata. In: Berry, G., Comon, H., Finkel, A. (eds.) CAV 2001. LNCS, vol. 2102, pp. 478–492. Springer, Heidelberg (2001). https://doi.org/10.1007/3-540-44585-4_46

2. Aceto, L., Bouyer, P., Burgueño, A., Larsen, K.G.: The power of reachability testing for timed automata. In: Arvind, V., Ramanujam, S. (eds.) FSTTCS 1998. LNCS, vol. 1530, pp. 245–256. Springer, Heidelberg (1998). https://doi.org/10.1007/978-3-540-49382-2_22

3. Alur, R., Henzinger, T.A., Vardi, M.Y.: Parametric real-time reasoning. In: Kosaraju, S.R., Johnson, D.S., Aggarwal, A. (eds.) Proceedings of the Twenty-fifth Annual ACM Symposium on Theory of Computing, STOC 1993, pp. 592–601. ACM, New York (1993)

4. André, É.: Observer patterns for real-time systems. In: Liu, Y., Martin, A. (eds.) 18th IEEE International Conference on Engineering of Complex Computer Systems, ICECCS 2013, pp. 125–134. IEEE Computer Society, July 2013. https://doi.org/10.1109/ICECCS.2013.26

5. André, É.: What's decidable about parametric timed automata? Int. J. Softw. Tools Technol. Transf. (2018, to appear). https://doi.org/10.1007/s10009-017-0467-0

6. André, É., Chatain, Th., De Smet, O., Fribourg, L., Ruel, S.: Synthèse de contraintes temporisées pour une architecture d'automatisation en réseau. In: Lime, D., Roux, O.H. (eds.) Actes du 7ème colloque sur la modélisation des systèmes réactifs, MSR 2009. Journal Européen des Systèmes Automatisés, vol. 43, pp. 1049–1064. Hermès, November 2009

7. André, É., Chatain, T., Encrenaz, E., Fribourg, L.: An inverse method for parametric timed automata. Int. J. Found. Comput. Sci. 20(5), 819–836 (2009). https://doi.org/10.1142/S0129054109006905

8. André, É., Coti, C., Nguyen, H.G.: Enhanced distributed behavioral cartography of parametric timed automata. In: Butler, M., Conchon, S., Zaïdi, F. (eds.) ICFEM 2015. LNCS, vol. 9407, pp. 319–335. Springer, Cham (2015). https://doi.org/10.1007/978-3-319-25423-4_21

9. André, É., Fribourg, L., Kühne, U., Soulat, R.: IMITATOR 2.5: a tool for analyzing robustness in scheduling problems. In: Giannakopoulou, D., Méry, D. (eds.) FM 2012. LNCS, vol. 7436, pp. 33–36. Springer, Heidelberg (2012). https://doi.org/10.1007/978-3-642-32759-9_6

10. André, É., Hasuo, I., Waga, M.: Offline timed pattern matching under uncertainty. In: Lin, A.W., Sun, J. (eds.) Proceedings of the 23rd International Conference on Engineering of Complex Computer Systems, ICECCS 2018. IEEE (2018, to appear)

11. André, É., Lime, D., Ramparison, M.: TCTL model checking lower/upper-bound parametric timed automata without invariants. In: Jansen, D., Prabhakar, P. (eds.) FORMATS 2018. LNCS, vol. 11022. Springer, Cham (2018). https://doi.org/10.1007/978-3-030-00151-3_3

12. André, É., Lime, D., Ramparison, M.: Timed automata with parametric updates. In: Juhás, G., Chatain, T., Grosu, R. (eds.) Proceedings of the 18th International Conference on Application of Concurrency to System Design, ACSD 2018, pp. 21–29. IEEE (2018, to appear). https://doi.org/10.1109/ACSD.2018.000-2

13. André, É., Lin, S.-W.: Learning-based compositional parameter synthesis for event-recording automata. In: Bouajjani, A., Silva, A. (eds.) FORTE 2017. LNCS, vol. 10321, pp. 17–32. Springer, Cham (2017). https://doi.org/10.1007/978-3-319-60225-7_2

14. André, É., Liu, Y., Sun, J., Dong, J.S., Lin, S.-W.: PSyHCoS: parameter synthesis for hierarchical concurrent real-time systems. In: Sharygina, N., Veith, H. (eds.) CAV 2013. LNCS, vol. 8044, pp. 984–989. Springer, Heidelberg (2013). https://doi.org/10.1007/978-3-642-39799-8_70

15. Beneš, N., Bezděk, P., Larsen, K.G., Srba, J.: Language emptiness of continuous-time parametric timed automata. In: Halldórsson, M.M., Iwama, K., Kobayashi, N., Speckmann, B. (eds.) ICALP 2015. LNCS, vol. 9135, pp. 69–81. Springer, Heidelberg (2015). https://doi.org/10.1007/978-3-662-47666-6_6

16. Bozzelli, L., La Torre, S.: Decision problems for lower/upper bound parametric timed automata. Formal Methods Syst. Des. **35**(2), 121–151 (2009). https://doi.org/10.1007/s10703-009-0074-0

17. Cassez, F., Larsen, K.: The impressive power of stopwatches. In: Palamidessi, C. (ed.) CONCUR 2000. LNCS, vol. 1877, pp. 138–152. Springer, Heidelberg (2000). https://doi.org/10.1007/3-540-44618-4_12

18. Chen, X., Schupp, S., Makhlouf, I.B., Ábrahám, E., Frehse, G., Kowalewski, S.: A benchmark suite for hybrid systems reachability analysis. In: Havelund, K., Holzmann, G., Joshi, R. (eds.) NFM 2015. LNCS, vol. 9058, pp. 408–414. Springer, Cham (2015). https://doi.org/10.1007/978-3-319-17524-9_29

19. Chevallier, R., Encrenaz-Tiphène, E., Fribourg, L., Xu, W.: Timed verification of the generic architecture of a memory circuit using parametric timed automata. Formal Methods Syst. Des. **34**(1), 59–81 (2009). https://doi.org/10.1007/s10703-008-0061-x

20. Clarisó, R., Cortadella, J.: Verification of concurrent systems with parametric delays using octahedra. In: Proceedings of the Fifth International Conference on Application of Concurrency to System Design, ACSD 2005, pp. 122–131. IEEE Computer Society (2005). https://doi.org/10.1109/ACSD.2005.34

21. Clarisó, R., Cortadella, J.: The octahedron abstract domain. Sci. Comput. Program. **64**(1), 115–139 (2007). https://doi.org/10.1016/j.scico.2006.03.009

22. Collomb-Annichini, A., Sighireanu, M.: Parameterized reachability analysis of the IEEE 1394 root contention protocol using TReX. In: Proceedings of the Real-Time Tools Workshop, RT-TOOLS 2001 (2001)

23. D'Argenio, P.R., Katoen, J.-P., Ruys, T.C., Tretmans, J.: The bounded retransmission protocol must be on time!. In: Brinksma, E. (ed.) TACAS 1997. LNCS, vol. 1217, pp. 416–431. Springer, Heidelberg (1997). https://doi.org/10.1007/BFb0035403

24. Frehse, G.: PHAVer: algorithmic verification of hybrid systems past HyTech. Int. J. Softw. Tools Technol. Transf. **10**(3), 263–279 (2008). https://doi.org/10.1007/s10009-007-0062-x

25. Frehse, G., et al.: SpaceEx: scalable verification of hybrid systems. In: Gopalakrishnan, G., Qadeer, S. (eds.) CAV 2011. LNCS, vol. 6806, pp. 379–395. Springer, Heidelberg (2011). https://doi.org/10.1007/978-3-642-22110-1_30

26. Henzinger, T.A., Ho, P.-H., Wong-Toi, H.: A user guide to HyTech. In: Brinksma, E., Cleaveland, W.R., Larsen, K.G., Margaria, T., Steffen, B. (eds.) TACAS 1995. LNCS, vol. 1019, pp. 41–71. Springer, Heidelberg (1995). https://doi.org/10.1007/3-540-60630-0_3

27. Hoxha, B., Abbas, H., Fainekos, G.E.: Benchmarks for temporal logic requirements for automotive systems. In: Frehse, G., Althoff, M. (eds.) Proceedings of the 1st and 2nd International Workshops on Applied veRification for Continuous and Hybrid Systems, ARCH@CPSWeek 2014/ARCH@CPSWeek 2015. EPiC Series in Computing, vol. 34, pp. 25–30. EasyChair (2014). http://www.easychair.org/publications/paper/250954

28. Hune, T., Romijn, J., Stoelinga, M., Vaandrager, F.W.: Linear parametric model checking of timed automata. J. Logic Algebraic Program. **52–53**, 183–220 (2002). https://doi.org/10.1016/S1567-8326(02)00037-1

29. Jovanović, A., Lime, D., Roux, O.H.: Integer parameter synthesis for timed automata. In: Piterman, N., Smolka, S.A. (eds.) TACAS 2013. LNCS, vol. 7795, pp. 401–415. Springer, Heidelberg (2013). https://doi.org/10.1007/978-3-642-36742-7_28

30. Jovanović, A., Lime, D., Roux, O.H.: Integer parameter synthesis for timed automata. IEEE Trans. Softw. Eng. **41**(5), 445–461 (2015)

31. Knapik, M., Penczek, W.: Bounded model checking for parametric timed automata. In: Jensen, K., Donatelli, S., Kleijn, J. (eds.) Transactions on Petri Nets and Other Models of Concurrency V. LNCS, vol. 6900, pp. 141–159. Springer, Heidelberg (2012). https://doi.org/10.1007/978-3-642-29072-5_6

32. Kwiatkowska, M.Z., Norman, G., Sproston, J., Wang, F.: Symbolic model checking for probabilistic timed automata. Inf. Comput. **205**(7), 1027–1077 (2007)

33. Li, J., Sun, J., Gao, B., André, É.: Classification-based parameter synthesis for parametric timed automata. In: Duan, Z., Ong, L. (eds.) ICFEM 2017. LNCS, vol. 10610, pp. 243–261. Springer, Cham (2017). https://doi.org/10.1007/978-3-319-68690-5_15

34. Lime, D., Roux, O.H., Seidner, C., Traonouez, L.-M.: Romeo: a parametric model-checker for petri nets with stopwatches. In: Kowalewski, S., Philippou, A. (eds.) TACAS 2009. LNCS, vol. 5505, pp. 54–57. Springer, Heidelberg (2009). https://doi.org/10.1007/978-3-642-00768-2_6

35. Lipari, G., Sun, Y., André, É., Fribourg, L.: Toward parametric timed interfaces for real-time components. In: Andre, E., Frehse, G. (eds.) 1st International Workshop on Synthesis of Continuous Parameters, SynCoP 2014. Electronic Proceedings in Theoretical Computer Science, vol. 145, pp. 49–64, April 2014. https://doi.org/10.4204/EPTCS.145.6

36. Nguyen, H.G., Petrucci, L., van de Pol, J.: Layered and collecting NDFS with subsumption for parametric timed automata. In: Lin, A.W., Sun, J. (eds.) Proceedings of the 23rd International Conference on Engineering of Complex Computer Systems, ICECCS 2018. IEEE, December 2018 (to appear)

37. Palencia Gutiérrez, J.C., González Harbour, M.: Schedulability analysis for tasks with static and dynamic offsets. In: Proceedings of the 19th IEEE Real-Time Systems Symposium, RTSS 1998, pp. 26–37. IEEE Computer Society (1998). https://doi.org/10.1109/REAL.1998.739728

38. Sankur, O.: Symbolic quantitative robustness analysis of timed automata. In: Baier, C., Tinelli, C. (eds.) TACAS 2015. LNCS, vol. 9035, pp. 484–498. Springer, Heidelberg (2015). https://doi.org/10.1007/978-3-662-46681-0_48

39. Sun, Y., André, É., Lipari, G.: Verification of two real-time systems using parametric timed automata. In: Quinton, S., Vardanega, T. (eds.) Proceedings of the 6th International Workshop on Analysis Tools and Methodologies for Embedded and Real-time Systems, WATERS 2015, July 2015

40. Sun, Y., Soulat, R., Lipari, G., André, É., Fribourg, L.: Parametric schedulability analysis of fixed priority real-time distributed systems. In: Artho, C., Ölveczky, P.C. (eds.) FTSCS 2013. CCIS, vol. 419, pp. 212–228. Springer, Cham (2014). https://doi.org/10.1007/978-3-319-05416-2_14

41. Traonouez, L.M., Lime, D., Roux, O.H.: Parametric model-checking of stopwatch Petri nets. J. Univers. Comput. Sci. **15**(17), 3273–3304 (2009)

42. Wandeler, E., Thiele, L., Verhoef, M., Lieverse, P.: System architecture evaluation using modular performance analysis: a case study. Int. J. Softw. Tools Technol. Transf. **8**(6), 649–667 (2006). https://doi.org/10.1007/s10009-006-0019-5

Formal Timing Analysis of Digital Circuits

Qurat Ul Ain[(⊠)] and Osman Hasan

School of Electrical Engineering and Computer Science (SEECS),
National University of Sciences and Technology (NUST),
Islamabad, Pakistan
{qain.msee15seecs,osman.hasan}@seecs.nust.edu.pk

Abstract. Formal verification provides complete and sound analysis results and has widely been advocated for the functional verification of digital circuits. Besides the functional verification, a very important aspect of digital circuit design process is their timing analysis. However, despite its importance and critical nature, timing analysis is usually performed using traditional techniques, like gate-level simulation or static timing analysis, which provide approximate results due to their inexhaustive nature and thus may lead to an undesired functional behavior as well. To overcome these issues, we propose a generic framework to conduct the formal timing analysis using the Uppaal model checker in this paper. The first step in the proposed framework is to represent the timing characteristics of the given digital circuit using a state transition diagram in Uppaal. In this model, delays are integrated using the corresponding technology parameters and the information about timing paths is added using Quratus Prime Pro, which is used as a path extracting tool. The Uppaal timing model is then verified through TCTL properties to obtain timing related information, like maximum delay. For illustration purposes, we present the analysis of a number of real-world digital circuits, like Full Adder, 4-Bit Ripple Carry Adder, Shift Registers as well as C17, S27, S208, and S386 benchmark circuits.

Keywords: Timed automata · Uppaal · Formal verification ·
Timing analysis · Model checking

1 Introduction

Due to the gradual reduction in transistor sizing governed by the Moore's law and the continuous increase in integrated circuit complexity, modeling and analyzing timing characteristics of digital circuits has become a very challenging task. Timing analysis usually involves determining the timing delays associated with each component of the circuit based on the technology used and its fan-out while considering the circuit variations. The delays of individual components are then used to calculate the overall circuit delay using various analysis techniques, like gate-level simulation [25] or static timing analysis [16]. However, neither of

© Springer Nature Switzerland AG 2019
C. Artho and P. C. Ölveczky (Eds.): FTSCS 2018, CCIS 1008, pp. 84–100, 2019.
https://doi.org/10.1007/978-3-030-12988-0_6

these techniques can ensure an exhaustive analysis due to the complexity of the present-age digital circuits. This kind of an in-exhaustive analysis results in an incorrect timing analysis, which may in turn lead to a non-optimal design or a functional bug. Digital circuits are increasingly being used in designing safety-critical systems, like the ones used in health-care, transportation and defense related domains. Thus, a non-optimal design or a functional issue may lead to disastrous consequences, like financial losses or even the loss of human life in worst case scenarios.

Formal verification [14] is known to overcome the above-mentioned limitations of traditional analysis approaches, like simulation. It has been extensively used for the functional verification of digital circuits [4,9,15,27]. The main idea in formal verification based analysis is to construct a formal model of the given circuit and formally verify the desired behavior of this model using formal specifications. Model checking [7] is one of the most commonly used formal verification techniques for the functional verification of digital circuits due to its automatic verification and the ability to provide a counterexample in the case of a failing property. It mainly involves modeling the system as a state transition diagram and the verification is done by exhaustively exploring the state space in a push button manner.

Due to the dire need of accurate analysis in the domain of timing analysis, formal verification of timing analysis of digital circuits using model checking got some attention in recent years. The model checker Open-Kronos has been used for the timing analysis of combinational circuits [24]. An abstract model of the given circuit is developed by partitioning the circuit into smaller sub-circuits and reachability graphs are used to model timed automata. A major limitation of this approach is that it uses fixed delay values for all the gates, e.g., the delay of an inverter is assumed to be 0, and thus the technology parameters and process variations are completely ignored in the models. Similarly, Open-Kronos is also used for timing analysis with bi-bounded delay values in [8]. Formal timing verification of digital circuits, including their combinational and sequential components, is performed in [5]. The given circuit is modeled at the macroscopic level where a state transition graph (STG) is modeled as a configuration of inputs while excluding the multiple input transitions. The delays of the components are extracted from SPICE simulations. The timing behavior of the SPSMALL memory architecture is verified using a parametric timed automata based model [12]. This technique derives a set of linear constraints that ensure the correctness of the response times of the memory. Similarly, symbolic timing verification of concurrent systems is proposed in [13]. The complex polyhedra modeling approach is used as the abstraction to represent sets of timed states as a timed transition system. Each event in this model has a symbolic delay defined in an interval $[d_i, D_i]$ where d_i and D_i symbolize minimum and maximum delay values, respectively.

Formal timing analysis of digital circuits has also been done with various other motivations. For example, digital circuits have been formally modeled using propagational delays, which are assumed to take values in an interval $\delta[\tau_{min}, \tau_{max}]$ in the context of testing of circuits in [28]. The model is developed in Uppaal, where delay faults are intentionally inserted into the circuit to generate counterexamples. These counterexamples are then used for testing of circuits. Similarly, formal timing analysis of combinational circuits has been performed to detect the Hardware Trojans using side channel parameters, like delay and power, in [1]. The main idea in this work is to insert an intrusion in the circuit in the form of logic gates. After intrusion, formal timing verification is performed to generate a counterexample. In this technique, only combinational circuits are formally verified and no sequential circuit is analyzed. Moreover, various circuit paths are identified manually for delay calculations in a circuit in this work [1]. Based on the above-mentioned discussion, we identify the following limitations in the existing literature:

– **Incompleteness:** The existing timing analysis approaches do not consider all the gates and all their possible input transitions.
– **Limited Scope:** The delay models used in formal techniques are usually not based on real delay values.
– **Inviability:** The exhaustive analysis techniques have enormous verification times, which leads to their infeasibility for large circuits.

To overcome the deficiencies of the existing formal timing analysis approaches for digital circuits and thus making the formal timing analysis more accurate, we propose to use the Elmore delay model [30] to compute the delays of both combinational and sequential components of the given circuit. Moreover, instead of using bi-bounded delays, we propose to calculate the value of the delay at every possible input transition of every gate in the design. For example, in the case of a 2 input gate, delays are calculated for all the four possible transitions $\Gamma_{Delay} = [d_{00}, d_{01}, d_{10}, d_{11}]$. Moreover, instead of manually searching of timing paths within a circuit as is the case for all existing formal timing analysis approaches, we propose to use the Quartus Prime Pro software [21] for automatically extracting the paths of the given circuit. This choice allows us to not only automate the timing analysis flow but also reduces the risks of ignoring some timing paths in the design. While using the above-mentioned information, we develop a formal model of the given circuit in the Uppaal model checker and then verify its desired timing properties in Uppaal. To facilitate the modeling and verification process, we provide a generic framework in which by knowing delays of the basic circuit blocks, i.e., NAND, NOR, NOT and a Flip-Flop, we can verify the timing behavior of any digital circuit, such as the clock period of a circuit, the critical paths as well as setup and hold time constraints in a circuit. It is important to note that by using a model checking tool for the timing analysis, our results are based on a rigorous exploration of the state space of the circuit model and thus all the paths and input values are implicitly considered in the analysis.

The remainder of the paper is structured as follows: We present a brief introduction about the Uppaal model checker in Sect. 2. The proposed methodology is explained in detail in Sect. 3, followed by Sect. 4 where we describe case studies and verification results. Finally, Sect. 5 concludes the paper.

2   Uppaal Model Checker

Uppaal [6] is a free academic model checker for the formal verification of real-time systems. It is based on the timed automata theory [3] and its modeling language offers many additional features, such as bounded integer variables.

2.1   Timed Automata

A timed automaton (TA) is a tuple $TA = (S, s_o, T, \sigma, Y, \beta)$, where:

- S is a set of locations.
- $s_o \in S$ is an initial location.
- T is a set of clocks.
- σ is a set of all defined actions.
- $Y \subseteq S \times \sigma \times B(T) \times 2^T \times S$ is a set of edges between locations.
- $\beta : S \to B(T)$ assigns invariants to locations.

$B(T)$ is the set of conjunctions over simple conditions, i.e., $x - y \bowtie c$ or $x \bowtie c$, where $c \in \mathbb{N}$, $x, y \in T$ and $\bowtie \in \{=, \geq, \leq, >, <\}$. A clock valuation is a function $u : T \to \mathbb{R}_{\geq 0}$ from the set of clocks to the non-negative real values. Thus, writing $u \in \beta(s)$ means that u satisfies $\beta(s)$. Timed automata are finite state automata having states and transitions, enriched with built-in clocks, which evolve at a uniform rate and can be reset to their initial value.

A state is a pair $(S, \alpha$ where α is a valuation of clocks and variables in that particular state. A state (S, α) has a discrete transition t, and system moves to the next state (S', α') if the constraints on t, called guards, are satisfied. The interconnection between two timed automata can be obtained by using synchronization channels. The signal is emitted by one automaton in transition t and received by one or more automata.

2.2   Queries

Verification of a model using the required specifications is a crucial step in mode-checking. Similar to a model, properties must be expressed in a formal language. Uppaal uses a simplified version of TCTL (timed computational tree logic) properties. Various path formulae supported by Uppaal are:

- $\exists \Diamond \rho$ (Possibly): There exists a path along which query ρ eventually holds.
- $\exists \Box \rho$ (Potentially always): There exists a path where query ρ always satisfies.
- $\forall \Box \rho$ (Invariantly): For all paths, query ρ always satisfies.
- $\forall \Diamond \rho$ (Eventually): For all paths, query ρ eventually satisfies.
- $\rho \rightsquigarrow \xi$ (Leads-to): Whenever ρ satisfies, query ξ holds always eventually.

3   Proposed Methodology

In this section, we explain the proposed methodology, depicted in Fig. 1, for the formal timing analysis of a digital circuit. Our methodology is comprised of three major steps: delay calculation, path extraction and modeling and verification in the Uppaal model checker.

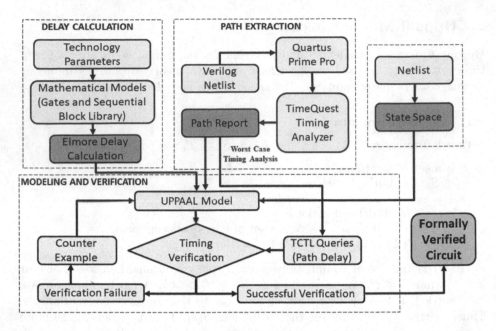

Fig. 1. Proposed methodology

3.1   Delay Calculation

The individual gate delays are estimated in the proposed methodology based on individual transitions at the gate inputs using the Elmore delay model [1], which computes the delay by representing each circuit in the form of an RC tree. Many timing analysis tools estimate the delay of the component based on the time difference between 50% of the input transition to the 50% of the output transition. However, the Elmore delay model considers the Resistor Capacitor relationships to compute the delay and hence provides a better estimate of the delay compared to the above-mentioned traditional approach. The delay is estimated by the model from a source node to one of the leaf nodes by accumulating the capacitances C_i on each node of the path, multiplied by the effective resistance R_{is} on the shared path from source node to the leaf node.

$$T_e = \sum_i C_i \times R_{is} \tag{1}$$

$$\tau_{delay} = T_e \times ln(2) \tag{2}$$

Using the basic technology parameters, we calculate the capacitance and resistance values for *PMOS* and *NMOS* transistors in an ON state. We propose to develop timing models for the basic circuit components, i.e., NAND, NOR, NOT and a Flip-Flop. These gates are then further used to model complex circuits. Gate capacitances for *PMOS* and *NMOS* [22] are given below:

$$C_{gatenMOS} = C_{gminN} \times fan - out \times WR_{nMOS} \tag{3}$$

$$C_{gatepMOS} = C_{gminP} \times fan-out \times WR_{pMOS} \tag{4}$$

Where C_{gmin} represents the minimum gate capacitance and WR represents the width ratio. C_L is the load capacitance calculated from the addition of gate capacitances of all the gates connected at the output of the considered component.

$$C_L = \sum_{k=1}^{a} C_{gatenMOSk} + \sum_{j=1}^{b} C_{gatepMOSj} \tag{5}$$

Diffusion capacitance C_{Diff} can be calculated from the drain capacitance [30]. The addition of load and diffusion capacitance leads to the total capacitance of a gate C_T, which is used for the calculation of delay.

$$C_T = C_L + C_{Diff} \tag{6}$$

Resistance of a *PMOS* or *NMOS* [23] can be calculated as follows:

$$R_{on} = \frac{1}{WL \times \mu \times Cox \times (V_{GS} - V_{TH})} \tag{7}$$

Using the values of corresponding resistances and capacitances, we can find out the Elmore delays for NAND, NOT, and NOR gates. Delay is calculated by considering all the possible input transitions of a gate. For example, the Elmore delay equations for the NAND gate are shown in Table 1.

Table 1. NAND gate delay equations

Input transition	Output	Delay equation
00	1	$ln(2) \times [(C_T \times R_p)/(2 \times WR_{pMOS})]$
01	1	$ln(2) \times [(C_T \times R_p)/WR_{pMOS}]$
10	1	$ln(2) \times [((C_T + C_{ST}) \times R_p)/WR_{pMOS}]$
11	0	$ln(2) \times [(C_T \times 2 \times R_n)/WR_{nMOS}]$

We have used the True Single-Phase Clocked (TSPC) Flip-Flop model [22] to capture the timing behavior of the Flip-Flop as this provides less complexity and less number of transistors to deal with [22]. Setup time, hold time, and clock to Q delay are the three most important timing constraints in a Flip-Flop. In the TSPC Flip-Flop model, the setup time is assigned a delay of one inverter, the hold time is considered to be less than one inverter delay and the propagational delay is considered to be equal to three inverter delays. Similarly, in our model, we consider the hold time to be equal to one inverter delay in the worst case. The delay equations used in our model for setup time, hold time and the clock to Q in a Flip-Flop are given in Table 2.

Table 2. Flip-Flop delay equations

Data input	Output	Delay equation
Setup time		
0	0	$ln(2) \times [(C_T \times R_p)/WR_{pMOS})]$
1	1	$ln(2) \times [(C_T \times R_n)/WR_{nMOS})]$
Hold time		
0	0	$ln(2) \times [(C_T \times R_p)/WR_{pMOS})]$
1	1	$ln(2) \times [(C_T \times R_n)/WR_{nMOS})]$
Clk2Q delay		
0	0	$ln(2) \times [(3 \times C_T \times R_p)/WR_{pMOS})]$
1	1	$ln(2) \times [(3 \times C_T \times R_n)/WR_{nMOS})]$

3.2 Path Extraction

Calculation of a delay in a circuit, which is composed of several gates and Flip-Flops, is done based on its various paths, i.e., from input to a Flip-Flop, between Flip-Flops and from a Flip-Flop to an output. The delay of a path is calculated by adding delays of logic elements present in that path. In the case of smaller circuits, we can manually analyze all the paths in a circuit and can calculate the delays of all the paths. But in case of large circuits, it is impossible to analyze the paths manually, therefore we propose to use a software that can provide all the valid paths in a circuit automatically from a given circuit netlist. We found Altera Quartus Prime Pro [21] to be the most relevant tool for this purpose. It not only provides all the possible paths from all input ports to all output ports but can also provide paths from the input port to a Flip-Flop, Flip-Flop to a Flip-Flop, or Flip-Flop to an output port.

In the path extraction phase of the proposed methodology, we have to provide the Verilog code of the circuit that needs to be analyzed. This Verilog file is first analyzed and synthesized. After compilation, we run the TimeQuest Timing Analyzer tool to get the information about the paths in the given circuit. Synopsys design constraint file and a timing netlist is thus created automatically by the Timing Analyzer. After this, we can analyze the paths that are reported by the TimeQuest Timing Analyzer.

3.3 Modeling and Verification in Uppaal Model Checker

Modeling and verification in Uppaal is the most important step in our approach for the timing verification of circuits. Firstly, the given netlist is translated to its corresponding state transition diagram. This state transition diagram along with the delay values of logic elements and path information from TimeQuest Timing Analyzer is used for this purpose in the Uppaal Model Checker. The TCTL properties of path delays have to be given to the Uppaal model checker as well. The state space model is then verified in Uppaal against the identified TCTL properties to judge the circuit performance. We mainly check that the delay in a circuit is less than the required maximum delay. If the delay of the circuit exceeds the maximum delay, then the Uppaal model checker returns a counterexample which provides us the exact trace that caused the timing violation. Thereafter, it can be investigated if the issues are due to a modeling error or its an actual timing violation.

In order to facilitate the modeling of digital circuits, we developed the formal models of the basic gates, i.e., NAND, NOR, NOT and a Flip-Flop, in Uppaal and these models can be built upon to formalize models of larger complex circuits.

For example, The TA of the NOT gate is shown in Fig. 2 where xin_not is the input and $xout\_not$ is the output. At the initial state, the selection expression $xin\_not: int[0, 1]$ allows to assign a boolean value 1 or 0 to the input xin_not. The fan-out fo_not is updated depending upon how many gates are connected at the output port of the gate. Based on the value of the input, internal resistances, internal capacitances, fan-out, and various technology parameters, the delay $delay\_not$ is calculated using the Elmore delay equation. The output gets its appropriate value, i.e., the negation of input $out\_not:= !(xin\_not)$, after the delay has elapsed. Similarly, the models of other basic gates have also been developed and they can be used to formalize any combinational gate-level circuit. Sequential circuits also contain Flip-Flops besides the basic logic gates and to formalize their behavior, we also formalized the Flip-Flop. The proposed Flip-Flop model along with the clock is shown in Fig. 3. The input signal is updated in the first state. Based on the value of the input, internal resistances, internal capacitances, fan-out, and various technology parameters, the setup time, hold time and clock to Q delay is calculated using the Elmore delay equations.

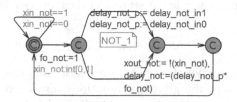

Fig. 2. Timed automaton of the NOT gate

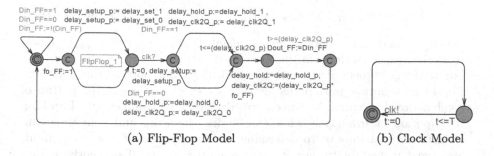

(a) Flip-Flop Model   (b) Clock Model

Fig. 3. Timed automata of a flip-flop and a clock

In the proposed methodology, we can develop the models of more complex circuits by interconnecting the basic gates and Flip-Flop models. Some simple circuits designed from the basic gates, i.e., NAND, NOT, and NOR, are shown in Fig. 4.

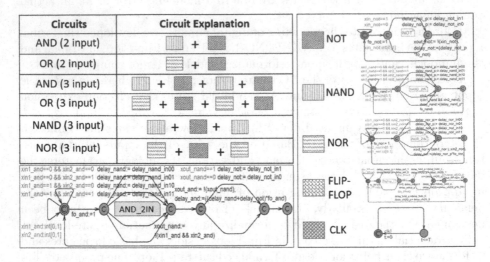

Fig. 4. Designing some simple circuits using basic gates

We propose to verify the following properties.

– Firstly, we check the deadlock property, which ensures that the timed automaton is not stuck at any particular state and thus moves ahead through all the states.

$$\forall \ \square \ not \ \ deadlock$$

– For verifying combinational circuits, we check that the delay, considering all the paths delay in the given combinational model, does not exceed the maximum delay value for the given circuit. If the delay exceeds the maximum value and the property fails then we get a counterexample.

$$\forall \ \square \ !((delay_{gate1} + delay_{gate2} + \cdots\cdots + delay_{gaten}) > D\max_{comb}))$$

Where $D\max_{comb} = \max(delay_{gate1}, delay_{gate2}, \cdots\cdots, delay_{gaten})$ represents the maximum delay in the considered path.

– For verifying sequential circuits, we check the input port to Flip-Flop and Flip-Flop to output port paths just like we check the timing properties of combinational circuits. Moreover, we also need to conduct the Flip-Flop to Flip-Flop path analysis while considering the setup and hold time constraints, which allows us to determine the clock period of the given circuit and avoid metastability. For example, consider a typical sequential circuit scenario, shown in Fig. 5, where we have an input port *IN*, two Flip-Flops

FF1 and *FF2* and an output port *OUT*. There are *i* gates between input and *FF1*, *n* gates between Flip-Flops, and *j* gates between *FF2* and output. We propose to verify the following properties in this case.

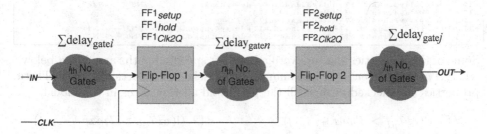

Fig. 5. A typical sequential circuit

$$\forall \;\; \Box \;\; ((delay_{gate1} + delay_{gate2} + \cdots + delay_{gatei}) \leq D \max_{INtoFF})$$
$$\forall \;\; \Box \;\; (T \geq (FF1_{clk2Q} + delay_{gate1} + delay_{gate2} + \cdots + delay_{gaten}) + FF2_{setup})$$
$$\forall \;\; \Box \;\; ((FF1_{clk2Q} + delay_{gate1} + delay_{gate2} + \cdots + delay_{gaten}) \geq FF2_{hold})$$
$$\forall \;\; \Box \;\; ((FF2_{clk2Q} + delay_{gate1} + delay_{gate2} + \cdots + delay_{gatej}) \leq D \max_{FFtoOUT})$$

4 Case Studies

For illustration purpose, we present the analysis of C17, and S27 benchmark circuits in this section. Due to the large size of transition diagrams, we only summarize path information and verified properties of these circuits in this section.

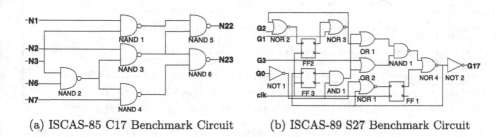

(a) ISCAS-85 C17 Benchmark Circuit   (b) ISCAS-89 S27 Benchmark Circuit

Fig. 6. Benchmark circuits

4.1 C17 Benchmark

C17, shown in Fig. 6(a), is one of the benchmarks from ISCAS-85 that consists of 5 input ports and 2 output ports. The path report of the C17 circuit generated from TimeQuest Timing Analyzer is modeled in Uppaal with the help of a single function in order to reduce the complexity in a state transition diagram.

```
c17_p1 = (delay1_nand_c17+delay5_nand_c17); //N1 --> N22
c17_p2 = (delay3_nand_c17+delay5_nand_c17); //N2 --> N22
c17_p3 = (delay3_nand_c17+delay6_nand_c17); //N2 -->N23
c17_p4 = (delay2_nand_c17+delay3_nand_c17+delay6_nand_c17); //N3 --> N23
c17_p5 = (delay2_nand_c17+delay3_nand_c17+delay5_nand_c17); //N3 --> N22
c17_p6 = (delay2_nand_c17+delay4_nand_c17+delay6_nand_c17); //N6 --> N23
c17_p7 = (delay2_nand_c17+delay4_nand_c17+delay5_nand_c17); //N6 --> N22
c17_p8 = (delay4_nand_c17+delay6_nand_c17); //N7 --> N23
c17_p9 = (delay1_nand_c17+delay5_nand_c17); //N3 --> N22
c17_p10 = (delay2_nand_c17+delay4_nand_c17+delay6_nand_c17); //N3 --> N23
c17_p11 = (delay2_nand_c17+delay3_nand_c17+delay6_nand_c17); //N6 --> N23
```

Some of the properties that are verified against specified paths are shown below, where $Tmax$ represents the maximum value of delay for a particular path. These properties are checked against all the paths and all the states in the model.

- $\forall \Box\ (!(c17_{p1} > Tmax_{c17-p1}))$ - $\forall \Box\ (!(c17_{p2} > Tmax_{c17-p2}))$

We also verified many other properties for this benchmark and the details can be found in [2].

4.2   S27 Benchmark

S27, shown in Fig. 6(b), is one of the sequential circuit benchmarks from ISCAS-89 that consists of 4 input ports and 1 output port. All the timing reports of S27, including the paths from input to Flip-Flops, between Flip-Flops, and from Flip-Flops to output, generated from TimeQuest Timing Analyzer, were modeled in Uppaal with the help of three functions, one function for each type, in order to reduce the complexity in the resulting state transition diagram.

```
delay_p1_in = (delay2_or+delay1_nand+delay4_nor); // G3--->FF3
delay_p2_in = (delay3_nor+delay1_or+delay1_nand+delay4_nor); // G1--->FF3
delay_p3_in = (delay1_not+delay2_or+delay1_and+delay1_nand+delay4_nor); // G0--->FF3
delay_p4_in = (delay1_not+delay1_or+delay1_and+delay1_nand+delay4_nor); // G0--->FF3
delay_p5_in = (delay2_nor); // G2--->FF2
delay_p6_in = (delay3_nor+delay2_nor); // G1--->FF2
delay_p7_in = (delay1_not+delay1_nor); // G0--->FF1
delay_p8_in = (delay1_not+delay1_or+delay1_and+delay1_nand+delay4_nor+
    delay1_nor); // G0--->FF1
delay_p9_in = (delay1_not+delay2_or+delay1_and+delay1_nand+delay4_nor+
    delay1_nor); // G0--->FF1

delay_p1_ff = (delay1_clk2Q+delay4_nor+delay3_setup); // FF1--->FF3
delay_p2_ff = (delay2_clk2Q+delay3_nor+delay1_or+delay1_nand+delay4_nor+
    delay3_setup); // FF2--->FF3
delay_p3_ff = (delay3_clk2Q+delay1_and+delay2_or+delay1_nand+delay4_nor+
    delay3_setup); // FF3--->FF3
delay_p4_ff = (delay3_clk2Q+delay1_and+delay1_or+delay1_nand+delay4_nor+
    delay3_setup); // FF3--->FF3
delay_p5_ff = (delay2_clk2Q+delay3_nor+delay2_nor+delay2_setup); // FF2--->FF2

delay_p1_h1 = (delay1_clk2Q+delay4_nor); // FF1--->FF3
delay_p2_h2 = (delay2_clk2Q+delay3_nor+delay1_or+delay1_nand+delay4_nor);// FF2--->FF3
delay_p4_h3 = (delay3_clk2Q+delay1_and+delay2_or+delay1_nand+delay4_nor);// FF3--->FF3
delay_p5_h4 = (delay3_clk2Q+delay1_and+delay1_or+delay1_nand+delay4_nor);// FF3--->FF3
delay_p6_h5 = (delay3_clk2Q+delay3_nor+delay2_nor); // FF2--->FF2

delay_p1_out = (delay2_clk2Q+delay3_nor+delay1_or+delay1_nand+delay4_nor+
    delay2_not); // FF2--->G17
delay_p2_out = (delay1_clk2Q+delay4_nor+delay1_or+delay2_not); // FF1--->G17
delay_p3_out = (delay3_clk2Q+delay1_and+delay2_or+delay1_nand+delay4_nor+
    delay2_not); // FF3--->G17
delay_p4_out = (delay3_clk2Q+delay1_and+delay1_or+delay1_nand+delay4_nor+
    delay2_not); // FF3--->G17
```

Some of the properties which are verified against each specified path are written below. We also verified many other properties for this benchmark and the details can be found in [2]. In these properties, the variable, $Tmax$, represents the maximum delay time and T_{clk}, represents the time period of a clock.

$- \forall \Box \ (delay_{p1-in} \leq Tmax_{p1-in})$ $- \forall \Box \ (delay_{p2-in} \leq Tmax_{p2-in})$

$- \forall \Box \ (T_{clk} \geq (delay_{p1-ff}))$ $- \forall \Box \ (T_{clk} \geq (delay_{p2-ff}))$

$- \forall \Box \ (delay_{p-h1} \geq (delay_{3-hold}))$ $- \forall \Box \ (delay_{p-h2} \geq (delay_{3-hold}))$

$- \forall \Box \ (delay_{p1-out} \leq (Tmax_{p1-out}))$ $- \forall \Box \ (delay_{p2-out} \leq (Tmax_{p2-out}))$

4.3 Verification Results

The considered combinational circuits and their verification statistics are summarized in Table 3 using the information about the total number of gates in the given circuit, its verification time and the memory utilization during the verification phase of corresponding circuit. Modeling and verification details of sequential circuits are summarized in Table 4 using the total number of gates and Flip-Flops in the given circuit, its verification time, and the memory utilization. We noticed that the number of explored states during the verification significantly increases with an increase in the number of inputs of basic gates,

Table 3. Result of combinational circuits

Circuits	Number of gates			Verification	
	NAND	NOR	NOT	Time (s)	Memory (MB)
C17 [11]	6	-	-	0.014	7.34
C17 [29]	7	-	-	0.021	7.35
C17 [19]	9	1	2	0.033	11.78
Full Adder [20]	11	-	-	0.032	8.82
Full Adder [17]	10	3	1	0.074	16.06
Full Adder [1]	14	3	1	0.91	18.06
4-bit RCA [17]	40	12	4	63.31	2684

Table 4. Result of sequential circuits

Circuits	Number of gates			Number of Flip-Flops	Verification	
	NAND	NOR	NOT		Time (s)	Memory (MB)
Flip-Flop [22]	-	-	-	1	0.019	7.85
16-bit SIPO shift register [18]	-	-	-	16	0.031	10.38
64-bit SISO shift register [18]	-	-	-	64	0.047	16.80
64-bit Ring counter [26]	-	-	-	64	0.090	21.19
64-bit Johnson counter [26]	-	-	1	64	0.100	27.29
S27 [10]	2	6	5	3	2.46	43.96
S208 [10]	39	37	90	8	316	8820
S386 [10]	151	36	228	6	3306	29745

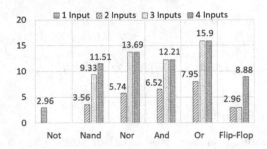

Fig. 7. Maximum delays of basic gates

such as NOT, NAND, NOR, AND and OR. For example, the total number of explored states in the 4-bit RCA is 16316416 whereas 105735463 states were explored while analyzing the S368 circuit.

We calculated the maximum delays of basic gates, such as NOT, NAND, NOR, AND and OR as shown in Fig. 7. In case of NOT, AND and OR, the maximum delay for 3 input and 4 input is same since the type and number of logic elements are same in a path. The maximum delays in case of the considered combinational circuits is shown in Fig. 8(a), whereas the maximum time periods of the clock in case of sequential circuits is shown Fig. 8(b).

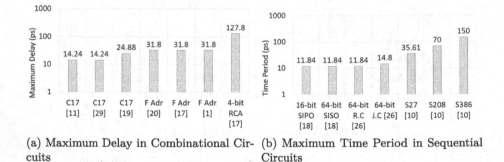

(a) Maximum Delay in Combinational Circuits

(b) Maximum Time Period in Sequential Circuits

Fig. 8. Timing analysis results

In comparison with an existing technique, presented in [1], which uses the nuXmv model checker for verifying combinational circuits, we find our results to be acquired in a much faster manner as shown in Fig. 9(a). This result is based on the maximum time utilized by the model checker for the property verification. For example, the verification time in [1] and the proposed technique in case of the C17 circuit is 1530 s and 0.014 s, respectively. In [1], real numbers are used for modeling and delay calculations, which causes an enormous increase in the state space. We propose to overcome these limitations by performing major real number calculations manually and then use the final delay values in an integral form in the model checker in order to minimize the state explosion problem. In comparison with the existing techniques, we also verify circuits with larger number of gates and Flip-Flops, i.e., upto 415 gates and 64 Flip-Flops, as shown in Fig. 9(b).

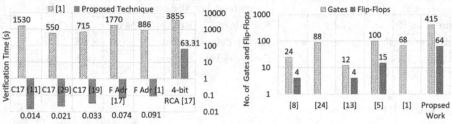

(a) Comparison of Verification Time of [1] and the Proposed Technique

(b) Number of Logic Elements Analyzed by Existing and Proposed Techniques

Fig. 9. Comparison with existing techniques

A summary of comparison of the proposed approach with some existing techniques is shown in Table 5. The comparative analysis is mainly based on seven parameters. The first two parameters show the type of a circuit, which is analyzed, i.e, combinational or sequential circuit. Automatic path extraction, depicts whether the existing techniques perform path analysis automatically or not. Next two parameters refer to delay modeling techniques and the model checker used for the formal verification. Finally, the last two parameters show the maximum gates and Flip-Flops verified by the corresponding technique. Our technique is found to be better than existing techniques in the following ways:

- Unlike some existing techniques [1,24], we perform timing verification of the combinational as well as sequential circuits.
- In order to perform more realistic modeling and verification, we proposed to use the Elmore delay modeling technique [1] instead of assumed delay model as used in [8,13,24,28].
- We proposed to extract the path information automatically using Quartus Prime Pro [21].
- We verify circuits with comparatively larger number of gates and Flip-Flops compared to all the existing formal timing analysis works.

Table 5. Comparison with existing techniques

Related work	Comb cct	Seq cct	Auto. Path	Delay model	Tool	Max gates	Max FF
Bozga et al. [8]	✓	✓	x	Assumed delay	Open-Kronos	24	4
Salah et al. [24]	✓	x	x	Assumed delay	Open-Kronos	88	x
Clariso et al. [13]	✓	✓	x	Symbolic delay	Abstract Algorithm	12	4
Bara et al. [5]	✓	✓	x	Spice delay	Kronos/Uppaal	100	15
Abbasi et al. [1]	✓	x	x	Elmore delay	nuXmv	68	x
Proposed work	✓	✓	✓	Elmore delay	Uppaal	415	64

5 Conclusions

This paper presented a model checking based approach for the formal timing analysis of digital circuits. The main idea behind this approach is to use timed automata as a state transitions diagram for formal modeling of the digital circuits and TCTL queries for the formal verification of their timing properties using the Uppaal model checker. We have developed a generic framework to facilitate the formal timing analysis by developing the models of the basic components of a digital circuit, i.e., logic gates and Flip-Flops, that can be built upon for the formal modeling of more complex circuits. Moreover, the proposed approach supports the automatic path extraction using Quartus Prime Pro along with the modeling and verification in Uppaal. The proposed approach can be used to formally verify various timing characteristics, such as finding the clock period of a circuit, finding the critical path and the setup and hold time constraints in a circuit. For illustration purposes, we used the proposed approach to conduct the formal timing analysis of a number of real-world digital circuits, such as Adders, Shift Registers, C17, S27, S208, and S386 circuits. In the future, we plan to incorporate routing delays and clock skew in a circuit so that we have a more accurate and realistic timing model.

References

1. Abbasi, I.H., Lodhi, F.K., Kamboh, A.M., Hasan, O.: Formal verification of gate-level multiple side channel parameters to detect hardware Trojans. In: Artho, C., Ölveczky, P.C. (eds.) FTSCS 2016. CCIS, vol. 694, pp. 75–92. Springer, Cham (2017). https://doi.org/10.1007/978-3-319-53946-1_5
2. Ul Ain, Q.: Formal Timing Analysis of Digital Circuits (2018). http://save.seecs.nust.edu.pk/projects/ftadc/
3. Alur, R., Courcoubetis, C., Dill, D.: Model-checking for real-time systems. In: Logic in Computer Science, pp. 414–425. IEEE (1990)
4. Andraus, Z.S., Sakallah, K.A.: Automatic abstraction and verification of verilog models. In: Proceedings of 41st Design Automation Conference, pp. 218–223 (2004)
5. Bara, A., Bazargan-Sabet, P., Chevallier, R., Ledu, D., Encrenaz, E., Renault, P.: Formal verification of timed VHDL programs. In: Forum on Specification Design Languages, pp. 80–85. IET (2010)

6. Behrmann, G., David, A., Larsen, K.G.: A tutorial on Uppaal 4.0 (2006)
7. Bérard, B., et al.: Systems and Software Verification: Model-Checking Techniques and Tools. Springer, Heidelberg (2013). https://doi.org/10.1007/978-3-662-04558-9
8. Bozga, M., Jianmin, H., Maler, O., Yovine, S.: Verification of asynchronous circuits using timed automata. Electron. Notes Theor. Comput. Sci. **65**(6), 47–59 (2002)
9. Braibant, T.: Coquet: a Coq library for verifying hardware. In: Jouannaud, J.-P., Shao, Z. (eds.) CPP 2011. LNCS, vol. 7086, pp. 330–345. Springer, Heidelberg (2011). https://doi.org/10.1007/978-3-642-25379-9_24
10. Brglez, F., Bryan, D., Kozminski, K.: Notes on the ISCAS 1989 benchmark circuits. North-Carolina State University (1989)
11. Bryan, D.: The ISCAS 1985 benchmark circuits and netlist format. North Carolina State University, vol. 25 (1985)
12. Chevallier, R., Encrenaz-Tiphene, E., Fribourg, L., Xu, W.: Timed verification of the generic architecture of a memory circuit using parametric timed automata. Form. Methods Syst. Des. **34**(1), 59–81 (2009)
13. Clarisó, R., Cortadella, J.: Verification of timed circuits with symbolic delays. In: Asia and South Pacific Design Automation Conference, pp. 628–633. IEEE (2004)
14. Hasan, O., Tahar, S.: Formal verification methods. In: Encyclopedia of Information Science and Technology, Third Edition, pp. 7162–7170. IGI Global (2015)
15. Irfan, A., Cimatti, A., Griggio, A., Roveri, M., Sebastiani, R.: Verilog2SMV: a tool for word-level verification. In: Design Automation Test in Europe Conference Exhibition, pp. 1156–1159 (2016)
16. Kilts, S.: Static Timing Analysis. Advanced FPGA Design: Architecture, Implementation, and Optimization, pp. 269–278 (2007)
17. Mano, M.M., Kime, C.R.: Logic and Computer Design Fundamentals, vol. 3. Prentice Hall, Upper Saddle River (2008)
18. Maxfield, C.: Bebop to the Boolean Boogie: An Unconventional Guide to Electronics. Newnes, Oxford (2008)
19. Mukhopadhyay, D., Chakraborty, R.S.: Hardware Security: Design, Threats, and Safeguards. Chapman and Hall/CRC, Boca Raton (2014)
20. Patterson, D.A., Hennessy, J.L.: Computer Organization and Design. zadnje izdanje (1994)
21. Quartus prime standard edition handbook (2015)
22. Rabaey, J.M., Chandrakasan, A.P., Nikolic, B.: Digital Integrated Circuits, vol. 2. Prentice hall Englewood Cliffs, New Jersey (2002)
23. Razavi, B.: Design of Analog CMOS Integrated Circuits. Tata McGraw-Hill Education, New York City (2002)
24. Salah, R.B., Bozga, M., Maler, O.: On timing analysis of combinational circuits. In: Larsen, K.G., Niebert, P. (eds.) FORMATS 2003. LNCS, vol. 2791, pp. 204–218. Springer, Heidelberg (2004). https://doi.org/10.1007/978-3-540-40903-8_17
25. Saleh, R., Jou, S.J., Newton, A.R.: Gate-level simulation. In: Saleh, R., Jou, S.J., Newton, A.R. (eds.) Mixed-Mode Simulation and Analog Multilevel Simulation, pp. 123–152. Springer, Heidelberg (1994). https://doi.org/10.1007/978-1-4757-5854-2_5
26. Shift Registers and Counters (2014). https://computing.ece.vt.edu/Li-aB/Microelectronic%20Systems/Lectures/Digital%20Logic/pdf/Shift%20register-s.pdf
27. Shiraz, S., Hasan, O.: A library for combinational circuit verification using the hol theorem prover. IEEE Trans. Comput.-Aided Des. Integr. Circ. Syst. **37**(2), 512–516 (2018)

28. Takan, S., Guler, B., Ayav, T.: Model checker-based delay fault testing of sequential circuits. In: Architecture of Computing Systems, pp. 1–7. VDE (2015)
29. Wei, S., Meguerdichian, S., Potkonjak, M.: Malicious circuitry detection using thermal conditioning. IEEE Trans. Inf. Forensics Secur. **6**(3), 1136–1145 (2011)
30. Weste, N.H., Harris, D.: CMOS VLSI Design: A Circuits and Systems Perspective. Pearson Education, London (2015)

Embedding CCSL into Dynamic Logic: A Logical Approach for the Verification of CCSL Specifications

Yuanrui Zhang[1], Hengyang Wu[1], Yixiang Chen[1], and Frédéric Mallet[2]($\boxtimes$)

[1] MoE Engineering Research Center for Software/Hardware Co-design Technology
and Application, East China Normal University, Shanghai 200062, China
[2] Université Cote d'Azur, I3S, CNRS, Inria, 06900 Sophia Antipolis, France
`frederic.mallet@inria.fr`

Abstract. The Clock Constraint Specification Language (CCSL) is a
clock-based specification language for capturing causal and chronometric
constraints between events in Real-Time Embedded Systems (RTESs).
Due to the limitations of the existing verification approaches, CCSL lacks
a full verification support for 'unsafe CCSL specifications' and a unified
proof framework. In this paper, we propose a novel verification approach based on theorem proving and SMT-checking. We firstly build a
logic called CCSL Dynamic Logic (CDL), which extends the traditional
dynamic logic with 'signals' and 'clock relations' as primitives, and with
synchronous execution mechanism for modelling RTESs. Then we propose a sound and relatively complete proof system for CDL to provide
the verification support. We show how CDL can be used to capture RTES
and verify CCSL specifications by analyzing a simple case study.

1 Introduction

UML/MARTE [1] is an extension of UML dedicated to the modelling and analysis of Real-Time Embedded Systems (RTESs). Its time model relies on so-called
clocks to identify control and observation points in the UML model. These clocks
can be used to specify how the system behaves. The Clock Constraint Specification Language (CCSL) [2,3] is a formal declarative language defined in an annex
of MARTE to specify the expected behaviour of the model. Given a system
model (or a concrete implementation) and a CCSL specification, the question
to answer is whether the system can only perform behaviors that are accepted
by the CCSL specification [4]. When a CCSL specification can be encoded as a
finite transition system, it is called 'safe' [5], then the verification task mainly
consists in making reachability analysis on the product of the system and the
CCSL specification. Most recently SMT encoding of CCSL [6] proved to be a
promising way to verify unsafe CCSL specification, however, there is no proof
environment available so far for reasoning on general specifications.

F. Mallet—This work was partly funded by the French Government, through program
#ANR-11-LABX-0031-01.

In this paper, we propose a novel approach for the verification of CCSL, which is based on the combination of theorem proving and SMT-checking. To capture both the system model and the CCSL specification, we choose dynamic logic [7], since it contains both dynamic program and static logic as its primitives. We propose a variation of dynamic logic, called 'CCSL Dynamic Logic' (CDL), which extends the traditional First-Order Dynamic Logic (FODL) [8] with 'signal' and 'CCSL clock relations' as primitives in its syntax. CDL also supports synchronous events in order to capture synchronous system models [9]. We propose a sound and relatively complete proof system for CDL in order to verify CDL formulas in a modular way.

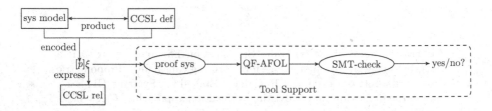

Fig. 1. Verification framework of CDL

Our approach for verification of CCSL specifications can be illustrated in a verification framework given in Fig. 1. The verification task can be captured as a CDL formula of the form $[p]\xi$, where part of the CCSL specification, called 'clock relations' (will be introduced in Sect. 2), are expressed by a formula ξ, and the product of the system model and 'clock definitions' (the other part of the CCSL specification) can be captured by a program of CDL p. In CDL, a formula $[p]\xi$ can be transformed into Quantifier-Free, Arithmetical First-Order Logic (QF-AFOL) formulas through a deduction procedure in the proof system of CDL. Then the validity of these formulas can be handled by an SMT-checking procedure in an efficient way [10], and according to which the verification result is obtained. With CDL, CCSL specifications can be verified in a unified proof framework, provided with strong tool support, e.g. Isabelle [11] and Coq [12].

The rest of this paper is organized as follows: Sect. 2 gives a general introduction to CCSL and FODL. Section 3 introduces the syntax and semantics of CDL. In Sect. 4, we propose the proof system for CDL. In Sect. 5, we give a simple case study to show how CDL can express and verify CCSL verification problems. Section 6 introduces the related works, and Sect. 7 concludes this paper and discusses about future work.

2   Preliminaries of CCSL and FODL

We present the syntax and semantics of CCSL based on [4,13]. In CCSL, a logical clock actually models a sequence of occurrences of a signal in synchronous models [14]. A logical clock c is defined as an infinite sequence of instants $(c^i)_{i \in \mathbb{N}^+}$, where each c^i can be 'tick' or 'idle', representing that the signal associated to c occurs or not at a discrete time i. $\mathbb{N}^+$ is the set of natural numbers. Clock relations describe binary relationships between clocks. The syntax of clock relations is defined by:

$$Rel ::= c_1 \subseteq c_2 \mid c_1 \# c_2 \mid c_1 \prec c_2 \mid c_1 \preceq c_2,$$

where c_1, c_2 are arbitrary clocks. We use $\mathcal{C}$ to denote a finite set of clocks. A schedule $\sigma : \mathbb{N} \to \mathcal{P}(\mathcal{C})$ is a finite or infinite sequence of clock ticks, $\mathbb{N} = \mathbb{N}^+ \cup \{0\}$. It gives a global view of how each clock ticks at each instant. For any $i \in \mathbb{N}^+$, $\sigma(i) = \{c \mid c \in \mathcal{C} \wedge c^i = tick\}$. $\sigma(0) = \emptyset$ indicates the beginning of the sequence where no clock ticks. $\mathcal{X}_\sigma : \mathcal{C} \times \mathbb{N}^+ \to \mathbb{N}$ keeps track of the number of ticks for each clock. $\mathcal{X}_\sigma(c, i) = |\{j \mid j \in \mathbb{N}^+, j \leq i, c \in \sigma(j)\}|$ is called a configuration of clock c at time i. The semantics of clock relations is defined as items 1–4 in Table 1. 'Subclock' says that c_1 can only tick if c_2 ticks; 'Exclusion' means that c_1, c_2 can not tick at the same instant; 'Precedence' means that c_1 always ticks faster than c_2; 'Causality' expresses that c_1 ticks not slower than c_2.

For example, the leftmost figure of Fig. 2 shows a possible schedule σ for clock relation $c_1 \prec c_2$, where clock

$$b = tick\ tick\ tick\ tick\ tick\ tick\ tick\ tick\ tick\ tick\ tick\ tick\ \ldots,$$
$$c_1 = tick\ idle\ tick\ tick\ idle\ idle\ tick\ idle\ idle\ tick\ idle\ idle\ \ldots,$$
$$c_2 = idle\ tick\ idle\ tick\ idle\ idle\ tick\ tick\ idle\ idle\ tick\ idle\ \ldots.$$

b is a based clock representing the minimal granularity of time. Schedule

$$\sigma = \emptyset\{c_1\}\{c_2\}\{c_1\}\{c_1, c_2\}\emptyset\emptyset\{c_1, c_2\}\{c_2\}\emptyset\{c_1\}\{c_2\}\emptyset\ldots.$$
$$\mathcal{X}_\sigma(c_1, 1) = 1,\ \mathcal{X}_\sigma(c_1, 2) = 1,\ \mathcal{X}_\sigma(c_1, 3) = 2.\ \mathcal{X}_\sigma(c_2, 1) = 0,\ \mathcal{X}_\sigma(c_2, 2) = 1.$$

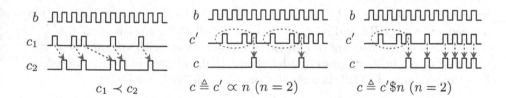

$$c_1 \prec c_2 \qquad\qquad c \triangleq c' \propto n\ (n = 2) \qquad\qquad c \triangleq c'\$n\ (n = 2)$$

Fig. 2. A possible schedule for selected clock constraints

Clock definition enhances the expressiveness of CCSL by allowing new clocks to be defined using different clock expressions. A clock definition is of the form: $Cdf ::= c \triangleq E$ where E is a clock expression defined by the following grammar:

$$E ::= c_1 + c_2 \mid c_1 * c_2 \mid c_1 \blacktriangleright c_2 \mid c_1 \triangleright c_2 \mid c_1 \curvearrowright c_2 \mid c \propto n \mid c\$n \mid c_1 \vee c_2 \mid c_1 \wedge c_2.$$

c_1, c_2 are arbitary clocks. $n \geq 1$. The semantics of clock definitions are defined as items 5–13 in Table 1. 'Union' defines the clock that ticks iff either c_1 or c_2 ticks; 'Intersection' defines the clock that ticks whenever both c_1 and c_2 tick; '(Strict) Sample' defines the clock that (strictly) samples c_1 based on c_2; 'Interruption' defines the clock that ticks as c_1 until c_2 ticks; 'Periodicity' defines the clock that ticks every n ticks of clock c'; 'Delay' defines the clock that ticks when c' ticks but is delayed for n ticks of c'. 'Infimum' ('Supremum') defines the slowest (fastest) clock that is faster (slower) than both c_1 and c_2.

e.g., Fig. 2 shows a possible schedule of clock definitions $c \triangleq c' \propto n$ and $c \triangleq c'\$n$ (when $n = 2$), which are used in the case study we give in Sect. 5.

Table 1. Semantics of CCSL

1. $\sigma \vDash_{ccsl} c_1 \subseteq c_2$	iff $\forall i \in \mathbb{N}^+.c_1 \in \sigma(n) \to c_2 \in \sigma(n)$	(Subclock)
2. $\sigma \vDash_{ccsl} c_1 \# c_2$	iff $\forall i \in \mathbb{N}^+.c_1 \notin \sigma(i) \lor c_2 \notin \sigma(i)$	(Exclusion)
3. $\sigma \vDash_{ccsl} c_1 \prec c_2$	iff $\forall i \in \mathbb{N}^+.(\mathcal{X}_\sigma(c_1, i) = 0 \land \mathcal{X}_\sigma(c_2, i) = 0) \lor \mathcal{X}_\sigma(c_1, i) > \mathcal{X}_\sigma(c_2, i))$	(Precedence)
4. $\sigma \vDash_{ccsl} c_1 \preceq c_2$	iff $\forall i \in \mathbb{N}^+.\mathcal{X}_\sigma(c_1, i) \geq \mathcal{X}_\sigma(c_2, i)$	(Causality)
5. $\sigma \vDash_{ccsl} c \triangleq c_1 + c_2$	iff $\forall i \in \mathbb{N}^+.c \in \sigma(i) \leftrightarrow (c_1 \in \sigma(i) \lor c_2 \in \sigma(i))$	(Union)
6. $\sigma \vDash_{ccsl} c \triangleq c_1 * c_2$	iff $\forall i \in \mathbb{N}^+.c \in \sigma(i) \leftrightarrow (c_1 \in \sigma(i) \land c_2 \in \sigma(i))$	(Intersection)
7. $\sigma \vDash_{ccsl} c \triangleq c_1 \blacktriangleright c_2$ iff	$\forall i \in \mathbb{N}^+.c \in \sigma(i) \leftrightarrow (c_2 \in \sigma(i) \land$ $(\exists 0 < j < i)(\forall j \leq k < i).c_1 \in \sigma(j) \land c_2 \notin \sigma(k))$	(Strict Sample)
8. $\sigma \vDash_{ccsl} c \triangleq c_1 \triangleright c_2$ iff	$\forall i \in \mathbb{N}^+.c \in \sigma(i) \leftrightarrow (c_2 \in \sigma(i) \land$ $(\exists 0 < j \leq i)(\forall j \leq k < i).c_1 \in \sigma(j) \land c_2 \notin \sigma(k))$	(Sample)
9. $\sigma \vDash_{ccsl} c \triangleq c_1 \curvearrowright c_2$	iff $\forall i \in \mathbb{N}^+.c \in \sigma(i) \leftrightarrow (c_1 \in \sigma(i) \land (\forall 0 < j \leq i).c_2 \notin \sigma(j))$	(Interruption)
10. $\sigma \vDash_{ccsl} c \triangleq c' \propto n$	iff $\forall i \in \mathbb{N}^+.c \in \sigma(i) \leftrightarrow (c' \in \sigma(i) \land \exists m \in \mathbb{N}^+.\mathcal{X}_\sigma(c', i) = m \cdot (n+1))$	(Periodicity)
11. $\sigma \vDash_{ccsl} c \triangleq c'\$n$	iff $\forall i \in \mathbb{N}^+.\mathcal{X}_\sigma(c, i) = max(\mathcal{X}_\sigma(c', i) - n, 0)$	(Delay)
12. $\sigma \vDash_{ccsl} c \triangleq c_1 \land c_2$	iff $\forall i \in \mathbb{N}^+.\mathcal{X}_\sigma(c, i) = max(\mathcal{X}_\sigma(c_1, i), \mathcal{X}_\sigma(c_2, i))$	(Infimum)
13. $\sigma \vDash_{ccsl} c \triangleq c_1 \lor c_2$	iff $\forall i \in \mathbb{N}^+.\mathcal{X}_\sigma(c, i) = min(\mathcal{X}_\sigma(c_1, i), \mathcal{X}_\sigma(c_2, i))$	(Supremum)

A CCSL specification is a conjunction of clock relations and clock definitions, denoted as a triple $SP ::= \langle \mathcal{C}, \widetilde{Cdf}, \widetilde{Rel} \rangle$, where $\mathcal{C}$ is the set of clocks. $\widetilde{Cdf}$ is a set of clock definitions and $\widetilde{Rel}$ is a set of clock relations. $\sigma \vDash_{ccsl} \langle \mathcal{C}, \widetilde{Cdf}, \widetilde{Rel} \rangle$ is defined s.t. $\sigma \vDash_{ccsl} Rel$ and $\sigma \vDash_{ccsl} Cdf$ hold for all $Rel \in \widetilde{Rel}$ and $Cdf \in \widetilde{Cdf}$.

FODL is an extension of propositional dynamic logic with assignment $x := e$ and testing $P?$ in its program model. The FODL we present here is based on [7]. The program of FODL is a regular program, defined as follows:

$$p ::= x := e \mid P? \mid p; p \mid p \cup p \mid p^*,$$

where e is an arithmetical expression. $P?$ means at current state, P is true. $p; q$ means the program first executes p, and after p terminates, it executes q. $p \cup q$ means the program either executes p, or executes q, it is a non-deterministic choice. p^* means the program executes p for a finite number of times. An FODL formula is defined as follows:

$$\phi ::= tt \mid e \leq e \mid [p]\phi \mid \neg\phi \mid \phi \land \phi \mid \forall x.\phi,$$

where tt is the boolean true, $\leq$ represents the 'less than' relation in number theory. $[p]\phi$ is the dynamic formula, meaning after all executions of program p, formula ϕ holds.

The semantics of FODL is based on Kripke structure [7]. A Kripke structure is a pair (S, val) where S is a set of states, val is a function that interprets a logic to data structures on S.

In FODL, val interprets a regular program as a set of state pairs (s, s') and interprets a formula as a set of states. Intuitively, each pair $(s, s') \in val(p)$ means that starting from state s, after execution of p, the program may terminate at state s'. Each state $s \in val([p]\phi)$ means that for all pairs $(s, s') \in val(p)$, s' satisfies ϕ. For a formal definition of the semantics of FODL, refer to [7].

The deductive system for FODL is sound and relatively complete. Except for the rule for atomic program '$x := e$', all rules can be found in Tables 3 and 4 below, as a part of CDL proof system. Refer to [7] for more details.

3   Syntax and Semantics of CDL

CDL enriches the traditional FODL with a synchronous program model that contains 'signal' as a primitive, and 'clock relation' as an ingredient of logic formulas. We first give the syntax of the CDL program model and the CDL formula, and then define their semantics.

3.1   The Syntax of CDL

Syntax of Synchronous Event Programs. CCSL essentially describes the logical and chronometrical constraints between signals in synchronous models, where the time model is discrete and at each time, several signals can be triggered simultaneously. To capture CCSL constraints in dynamic logic, we need to introduce the synchronous execution mechanism in the regular program of FODL. Synchronous systems often involve infinite executions, thus to support it we also import 'infinite loop'. The program after enriched turns out to be an 'omega program', with the support of synchronous mechanism. We call it 'Synchronous Event Program' (SEP).

Definition 1 (Syntax of SEP). *The syntax of SEP is based on the regular program of FODL, defined as follows:*

$$p ::= \varepsilon \mid \alpha \mid P?\alpha \mid p; p \mid p \cup p \mid p^* \mid p^\omega,$$

where α is a combinational event, defined as:

$$\alpha ::= \epsilon \mid Cmb,$$
$$Cmb ::= c \mid x := e \mid (Cmb|Cmb).$$

Arithmetical expression e, testing condition P are defined as follows:

$$e ::= x \mid n \mid e + e \mid e - e \mid n \cdot e \mid e/n,$$
$$P ::= tt \mid e \leq e \mid \neg P \mid P \wedge P.$$

ε represent an 'empty program', it does nothing nor consumes time. A combinational event α consumes a unit of time, it consists of an 'idle event' ϵ, or several signals or assignments that occur simultaneously. An idle event ϵ does nothing but waits for a unit of time. Several signals and assignments can be composed by operator '$|$'. A signal[1] c in an SEP represents that its corresponding clock (with the same name c) ticks at current time. Since CCSL constraints only captures the logical relationships between signals which are not related to the value of signals, we only consider 'pure signals' (signals without values) in SEP. e is a Presburger arithmetic expression. In e, $n \in \mathbb{Z}$ is an integer number, $+, -, \cdot, /$ are the addition, subtraction, multiplication and division signs respectively.

$P?\alpha$ is a testing event, it means that if condition P is true, event α proceeds, otherwise the program causes a deadlock. In SEP, testing $P?$ must combines with an event α, because $P?$ does not consume time. P can be expressed with a QF-AFOL formula, where tt represents the boolean true, $\leq$ represents the 'less than' relation between two integers. Operator $;, \cup, *$ are defined just as in FODL [7]. ω represents the infinite loop. p^ω means that program p executes for infinite number of times and never terminates.

e.g., program $f = 1?\alpha_2; p^*$ where $p ::= n = 0 \wedge f = 0?\alpha_3 \cup n > 0 \wedge f = 0?\alpha_4$ firstly executes α_2 if $f = 1$ holds, then it executes program p for finite number of times. In p, it either executes α_3 (if $n = 0 \wedge f = 0$ holds), or executes α_4 (if $n > 0 \wedge f = 0$ holds).

The precedence of operators are listed as follows from the highest to the lowest: $\omega, *, ;, \cup$. We stipulate that $;$ is right-associative, $\cup$ is left-associative. e.g., program $\alpha_1 \cup p_1; p_2; p_3^\bullet \cup P_1?\alpha_2^\bullet \cup P_2?\alpha_3$ means $(((\alpha_1 \cup p_1; (p_2; p_3^\bullet)) \cup P_1?\alpha_2^\bullet) \cup P_2?\alpha_3)$.

As in synchronous models (e.g., Esterel [14]), we do not allow two signals with the same name triggered at the same time. e.g. event $(c|c)$. For simplification, we also do not allow two assignments with the same target variable executing simultaneously, e.g. event $(x := 5|x := y + 1)$.

Syntax of CDL. In CDL formula, we need to introduce a special kind of variable which is related to clock. These variables help record the 'information' of each clock at current time, just as the roles the schedule σ and the configuration $\mathcal{X}_\sigma$ play in CCSL.

Definition 2 (Clock Related Variables). *For each clock $c \in \mathcal{C}$, we define two variables related to it: c^n, c^s. Variable c^n is of type $\mathbb{N}$, it records the number of times the clock has ticked at current time. Variable c^s is of type $\{0, 1\}$, and it records the status of the clock (1 for present and 0 for absent) at current time.*

Given a clock set $\mathcal{C}$, we denote the set of variables related to $\mathcal{C}$ as $Var(\mathcal{C})$.

---

[1] In SEP, for convenience, we use the same name 'c' to represent the signal corresponding to clock c, which should not cause any ambiguities. Sometimes we also say a signal c in p 'a clock c in p'.

Definition 3 (Syntax of CDL Formula). *The CDL formula ϕ is defined as:*

$$\phi ::= tt \mid E \le E \mid [p]\xi \mid [p]\phi \mid \neg\phi \mid \phi \wedge \phi \mid \forall x.\phi$$

where

$$\xi ::= Rel \mid \curlywedge (Rel_1, \ldots, Rel_n),$$
$$E ::= x \mid c^n \mid c^s \mid n \mid E + E \mid E \cdot E.$$

$E \le E$ is an atomic AFOL formula. E is an integer arithmetic expression. Different from e, it also includes clock-related variable c^n, c^s, and multiplication between variables. $x \in Var$. $[p]\xi$ is a dynamic formula, where p is an SEP. $[p]\xi$ is the dynamic formula special in CDL, it means that all execution paths of program p satisfies ξ. $\curlywedge(Rel_1, \ldots, Rel_n)$ represents the conjunction of clock relations $Rel_1, \ldots, Rel_n$, we define $\sigma \vDash_{ccsl} \curlywedge(Rel_1, \ldots, Rel_n)$ iff $\sigma \vDash_{ccsl} Rel_1, \ldots, \sigma \vDash_{ccsl} Rel_n$. In order to express the negation of $[p]\xi$ in CDL, we also import the negation $\sim$ and the disjunction $\curlyvee$ of clock relations: (i) $\sigma \vDash_{ccsl} \sim cr$ iff $\sigma \nvDash_{ccsl} cr$, (ii) $\sigma \vDash_{ccsl} \curlyvee(cr_1, \ldots, cr_n)$ iff $\sigma \vDash_{ccsl} \sim \curlywedge(\sim cr_1, \ldots, \sim cr_n)$, where $cr, cr_i \in \{Rel_i, \sim Rel_i\}(1 \le i \le n)$. $[p]\phi$ is the dynamic formula in FODL, meaning that after all executions of p, formula ϕ is satisfied.

We often call ξ or $\sim \xi$ "path formulas", denoted by π. Other arithmetic expressions, relations, and logic expressions, e.g., $E - E$, E/E, $E = E$, $E < E$, $f\!f$, $\langle p \rangle \sim \xi$, $\langle p \rangle \phi$, $\phi \vee \phi$, $\phi \to \phi$, $\exists x.\phi$, etc., can be expressed using the formulas given above. e.g., $\langle p \rangle \sim \xi$ can be expressed as $\neg[p]\xi$, $E_1 - E_2$, E_1/E_2 can be expressed as $\exists x.(E_2 + x = E_1)$, $\exists x.(x \cdot E_2 = E_1)$ respectively.

In FODL, given a formula ϕ, a variable whose value changes with the execution of a program is called a 'dynamic variable' [7] of the formula ϕ. Here in CDL, for convenience sake, any clock-related variable c^s, c^n is defined as a dynamic variable. As we will see in Definition 5(ii), they can be seen 'changed' after the execution of any event at current time. Any general variable that appears on the left side of an assignment is defined as a dynamic variable as well. Variables which are not dynamic variables are called 'static variables'. e.g., the set of dynamic variables of formula $z = 5 \to [(c_1|x := y + 1); c_2]c_1 \preceq c_3$ is $\{x, c_1^n, c_1^s, c_2^n, c_2^s, c_3^n, c_3^s\}$, where c_3^n, c_3^s can be seen as 'changed' after the set of static variables is $\{y, z\}$.

Like in FODL, we say a variable x is 'bound' in ϕ iff: 1. x is in the scope of the effect of some quantifier $\forall x$, or 2. x is in the scope of the effect of some event α which has x on the left side of an assignment of the form $x := e$. A variable is not bound in ϕ is called 'free'. e.g., in formula $\phi ::= (x = 1 \wedge z = 2 \wedge \exists z.x = z) \to [(x := z + 1|c|y := 1); x := y + 1]x > z$, the first and second variable x is free, while the third one (in expression '$x > z$') is bounded by the assignment '$x := y + 1$'.

Given a formula ϕ, a substitution $\phi[E/x]$ in CDL replaces all the free occurrences of variable x with expression E (of the same type). Given a formula multiset Γ, $\Gamma[E/x]$ means to carry out the substitution $\phi[E/x]$ for each formula ϕ in Γ. Given two vectors $(E_1, \ldots, E_n), (x_1, \ldots, x_n)$, $\phi[E_1, \ldots, E_n/x_1, \ldots, x_n]$ is the shorthand of $\phi[E_1/x_1][E_2/x_2]\ldots[E_n/x_n]$. A substitution is admissible with respect to a formula ϕ if there are no variables x, y such that y is in E, and after the replacement $\phi[E/x]$, y is bound in ϕ. e.g., in the formula ϕ given above, $\phi[z + 1/z] = (x = 1 \land z + 1 = 2 \land \exists z.x = z) \rightarrow [(x := (z + 1) + 1|c|y := 1); x := y + 1]x > z + 1$ is admissible, while $\phi[x + 1/z] = (x = 1 \land x + 1 = 2 \land \exists z.x = z) \rightarrow [(x := (x + 1) + 1|c|y := 1); x := y + 1]x > x + 1$ is not admissible. Intuitively, in $\phi[x + 1/z]$, it is about to prove $x > x + 1$ which is generally not true. In the rest of paper, unless we specially point out, all substitutions we discuss are admissible.

3.2   The Semantics of CDL

The semantics of CDL is based on Kripke structure (introduced in Sect. 2). In the Kripke structure (S, val) of CDL, val interprets a program as a set of traces on S and a logic formula as a set of states. A trace tr is a finite or infinite sequence of states. Given a finite trace $tr_1 = s_1 s_2 \ldots s_n$ and a (possibly infinite) trace $tr_2 = u_1 u_2 \ldots u_n \ldots$, we define: $tr_1 \cdot tr_2 ::= s_1 s_2 \ldots s_n u_2 u_3 \ldots$ if $s_n = u_1$. Given any tr_1, tr_2, we define $tr_1 \circ tr_2 ::= \begin{cases} tr_1 \cdot tr_2, \text{ if } tr_1 \text{ is finite} \\ tr_1, \qquad \text{otherwise} \end{cases}$. Given two sets of traces S_1, S_2, $S_1 \circ S_2$ is defined as $\{tr_1 \circ tr_2 \mid tr_1 \in S_1, tr_2 \in S_2\}$. Let $tr(i)$ denotes the ith element of trace tr, $i \geq 0$; tr_b denotes the first element of trace tr, $tr_b = tr(0)$. Let tr_e denotes the last element of trace tr, provided that tr is a finite trace.

In CDL, we assume an interpretation which interprets arithmetical operators '$+, -, \cdot, /$' and relation '$\leq$' as their usual meanings in the traditional number theory, and interprets relations '$\subseteq, \prec, \preceq, \#$' as their corresponding clock relations in CCSL. Next we first define the concept of 'state' and 'evaluation' in CDL.

Definition 4 (State and Evaluation in CDL). *A state s in CDL is a total function defined as follows:*

(i) s maps each variable c^n in $Var(\mathcal{C})$ to a value in domain $\mathbb{N}$.
(ii) s maps each variable c^s in $Var(\mathcal{C})$ to a value in domain $\{0, 1\}$.
(iii) s maps each variable x in Var to a value in domain $\mathbb{Z}$.

Given an expression E and a state s, an evaluation $Eval_s(E)$ is defined as:

(i) If $E = a$, where $a \in \{x, c^n, c^s\}$, then $Eval_s(a) ::= s(a)$.
(ii) If $E = n$, then $Eval_s(n) ::= n$.
(iii) If $E = f(E_1, E_2)$, where $f \in \{+, \cdot\}$, then $Eval_s(E) ::= f(Eval_s(E_1), Eval_s(E_2))$.

e.g., given a state $s ::= \{x \mapsto 9, c^n \mapsto 2, (c')^s \mapsto 0, \ldots\}$, there is $Eval_s(2) = 2$, $Eval_s(x) = 9$, $Eval_s(x + c^n) = Eval_s(x) + Eval_s(c^n) = 11$.

Semantics of SEP. Different from traditional FODL, the semantics of SEP is based on traces, since our CDL contains a path formula π which is satisfied by a program trace.

Definition 5 (Semantics of SEP). *Given a Kripke structure (S, val), for any SEP p, let $\mathcal{C}$ be a finite set of clocks, the semantics of SEP is given as follows:*

(i) $val(\varepsilon) := S$, S *is the set of all traces of length 1.*
   $val(\alpha) := \{ss' \mid s, s' \in S;$ *for each clock* $c \in \alpha, s'(c^s) = 1 \wedge s'(c^n) = s(c^n) + 1;$

(ii) *for other clock* $d \in \mathcal{C}, s'(d^n) = s(d^n) \wedge s'(d^s) = 0;$ *for each* $x := e$ *in* α,
   $s'(x) = Eval_s(e);$ *for other* $x \in Var, s'(x) = s(x)\}.$

(iii) $val(P?\alpha) ::= \{ss' \mid s \in val(P), ss' \in val(\alpha)\}.$

(iv) $val(p; q) ::= val(p) \circ val(q).$

(v) $val(p \cup q) ::= val(p) \cup val(q).$

(vi) $val(p^*) ::= \bigcup_{n \geq 0} val^n(p),$ *where* $val^n(p) = \underbrace{val(p) \circ \ldots \circ val(p)}_{n}, val^0(p) = S.$

(vii) $val(p^\omega) ::= \underbrace{val(p) \circ val(p) \circ \ldots}_{\infty}.$

Note that ε defines a set of traces of length 1, so $val(p; \varepsilon) = val(\varepsilon; p) = val(p)$, which means that ε can be taken as a unit element of operator ;. Event α defines a transition from a state s to a state s'. In s', for each clock c in α, the variable c^n that records the number of ticks is added by 1 and the variable c^s is set to 1, indicating at current time, clock c is emitted. For each clock d not in α, its variable d^n in s' is kept the same while d^s is set to 0. For any assignment $x := e$ in α, the value of x in s' is set to the value of expression e in state s, while other variables in both s and s' are kept the same. Traces satisfying $P?\alpha$ are exactly those traces satisfying p adding that their beginning states must satisfy P.

e.g., let $\alpha = (c|x := x+1), P = x > 1, \mathcal{C} = \{c, c'\}, Var = \{x, y\},$ if $s = \{x \mapsto 0, y \mapsto 0, c^n \mapsto 0, c^s \mapsto 0, c'^n \mapsto 0, c'^s \mapsto 0\}, s' = \{x \mapsto 1, y \mapsto 0, c^n \mapsto 1, c^s \mapsto 1, c'^n \mapsto 0, c'^s \mapsto 0\},$ then trace $ss' \in val(\alpha)$. If $u = \{x \mapsto 2, y \mapsto 0, c^n \mapsto 1, c^s \mapsto 1, c'^n \mapsto 0, c'^s \mapsto 1\}, u' = \{x \mapsto 3, y \mapsto 0, c^n \mapsto 2, c^s \mapsto 1, c'^n \mapsto 0, c'^s \mapsto 0\},$ then trace $uu' \in val(P?\alpha)$.

The semantics of $p; q, p \cup q, p^*$ are directly inherited from the traditional FODL [7]. The traces of program p^ω consists of all infinite traces of the form $tr_1 \circ tr_2 \ldots$ where each $tr_i \in val(p)$ is finite $(i \in \mathbb{N}^+)$, or of the form $tr_1 \circ tr_2 \circ \ldots \circ tr_n,$ where $n \geq 1, tr_1, \ldots, tr_{n-1} \in val(p)$ is finite, but $tr_n \in val(p)$ is infinite. e.g., suppose $val(p) = \{s_1 s_2\}, val(q) = \{u_1 u_2, t_1 t_2\}$ where $s_2 = u_1, s_2 \neq t_1,$ then $val(p; q) = \{s_1 s_2 u_2\}, val(p \cup q) = \{s_1 s_2, u_1 u_2, t_1 t_2\}, val(p^*) = \{\varepsilon, s_1 s_2, s_1 s_2 s_1 s_2, \ldots, \underbrace{s_1 s_2 s_1 s_2 \ldots s_1 s_2}_{2n}, \ldots\}$ $(n \geq 1), val(p^\omega) = val(p^*) \cup \{\underbrace{s_1 s_2 s_1 s_2 \ldots s_1 s_2 \ldots}_{\infty}\}.$

Semantics of CDL. For each trace tr, we can actually build a corresponding schedule σ^{tr} s.t. for all clock $c \in \mathcal{C}$ and $i \in \mathbb{N}^+$, there is: 1. $tr(i)(c^n) = \mathcal{X}_\sigma(c, i)$. 2. $tr(i)(c^s) = 1$ iff $c \in \sigma^{tr}(i)$. In this way, we can actually define $tr \vDash_{ccsl} X$ given a clock relation or definition X: $tr \vDash_{ccsl} X$ iff $\sigma^{tr} \vDash_{ccsl} X$. Note that we do not require any relationships between $tr(0)$ and $\sigma(0)$.

e.g., consider the trace ss' discussed above, we have a schedule $\sigma^{ss'}$ defined as: $\sigma^{ss'} ::= \emptyset\{c\}$. So $\mathcal{X}_{\sigma^{ss'}}(c,0) = \mathcal{X}_{\sigma^{ss'}}(c',0) = 0$, $\mathcal{X}_{\sigma^{ss'}}(c,1) = 1$, $\mathcal{X}_{\sigma^{ss'}}(c',1) = 0$.

Definition 6 (Semantics of CDL Formula). *Given a Kripke structure* (S, val), *the semantics of CDL formula is given as follows:*

(i) $val(tt) ::= S$.
(ii) $val(E \leq E') ::= \{s \mid Eval_s(E) \leq Eval_s(E')\}$.
(iii) $val([p]\xi) ::= \{s \mid$ *for all* tr *s.t.* $s = tr_b$ *and* $tr \in val(p), tr \vDash_{ccsl} \xi\}$.
(iv) $val([p]\phi) ::= \{s \mid$ *for all finite* $tr \in val(p)$ *s.t.* $tr_b = s, tr_e \in val(\phi)\}$.
(v) $val(\neg\phi) ::= \{s \mid s \notin val(\phi)\}$.
(vi) $val(\phi \wedge \varphi) ::= val(\phi) \cap val(\varphi)$.
(vii) $val(\forall x.\phi) ::= \{s \mid$ *for any* $v_0 \in \mathbb{Z}, s \in val(\phi[v_0/x])\}$.

The semantics of CDL formula is based on states. In (iii), a trace satisfying a clock relation is from the second state of the trace due to the definition of $\vDash_{ccsl}$ in Sect. 2. So state s itself is unrelated to ξ. (iv)-(vii) are similar to the definition in FODL [7], except that the semantics of SEP is based on traces. (iv) requires the trace must be finite, indicating that it only matters whether ϕ holds on those states on which program p terminates.

The first two figures in Fig. 3 give an illustration of $[p]\phi$ and $[p]\xi$, where the 'snake arrow' indicates an execution path (could be infinite) of program. Some states are tagged with a formula aside that they satisfy. States and paths are colored red to stress that they satisfy the corresponding formulas (ϕ, ξ).

At last we define the satisfaction relation of the CDL logic. Given a state s and any CDL formula ϕ, the satisfaction relation $s \vDash_{cdl} \phi$ is defined as: $s \vDash_{cdl} \phi$ iff $s \in val(\phi)$. If for all state s, $s \vDash_{cdl} \phi$ holds, then we say ϕ is valid, denoted as $\vDash_{cdl} \phi$.

4 Proof System of CDL

In this section we propose a proof system, which forms the foundation of the verification of CDL. The proof system provides a modular way of transforming a CDL formula into a QF-AFOL formula. Our proof system is based on that of FODL, which is only for regular program model [7].

A sequent [15] is defined as follows: $\Gamma \Rightarrow \Delta ::= \bigwedge_{\phi \in \Gamma} \phi \rightarrow \bigvee_{\varphi \in \Delta} \varphi$, where Γ, Δ are two finite *multi-sets* of logic formulas. It means that every formula in Γ holds can conclude that at least one of formulas in Δ holds. The conditions when either (both) Σ or (and) Δ is (are) empty set(s) is (are) expressed as follows: 1. $\cdot \Rightarrow \Delta ::= tt \rightarrow \bigvee_{\varphi \in \Delta} \varphi$, 2. $\Gamma \Rightarrow \cdot ::= \bigwedge_{\phi \in \Gamma} \phi \rightarrow ff$, 3. $\cdot \Rightarrow \cdot ::= tt \rightarrow ff$, where we use $\cdot$ to indicate Γ or Δ is empty. A rule in sequent calculus is of the form: $\frac{\Gamma_1 \Rightarrow \Delta_1 ... \Gamma_n \Rightarrow \Delta_n}{\Gamma \Rightarrow \Delta}$, which means that if $\Gamma_1 \Rightarrow \Delta_1, ..., \Gamma_n \Rightarrow \Delta_n$ are all valid, then $\Gamma \Rightarrow \Delta$ is valid. Each $\Gamma_i \Rightarrow \Delta_i$ in the upper part is called a 'premise', while $\Gamma \Rightarrow \Delta$ in the lower part is called 'conclusion'. We use $\frac{\Gamma \Rightarrow \varphi \Rightarrow \Delta}{\Gamma \Rightarrow \phi \Rightarrow \Delta}$ to represent a pair of sequent rules: $\frac{\Gamma, \varphi \Rightarrow \Delta}{\Gamma, \phi \Rightarrow \Delta}$ and $\frac{\Gamma \Rightarrow \varphi, \Delta}{\Gamma \Rightarrow \phi, \Delta}$, i.e., ϕ, φ can be on both side of the sequent. Sometimes we write $\frac{\varphi}{\phi}$ to represent $\frac{\Gamma \Rightarrow \varphi \Rightarrow \Delta}{\Gamma \Rightarrow \phi \Rightarrow \Delta}$ if Γ, Δ can be neglected. We call Γ, Δ the context of formula ϕ in sequent $\Gamma \Rightarrow \phi, \Delta$ or $\Gamma, \phi \Rightarrow \Delta$.

4.1   Proof Rules for CDL

The proof rules of CDL we present are divided into three categories: rules for path formulas π (in Table 2), rules for non-path formulas (in Table 3) and rules of First-Order Logic (FOL) (in Table 4).

In Table 2, rule (π) is for a single event, where we set $\alpha = (c|x := e)$ as an example of combinational events.

Table 2. Rules for path formulas

$$\Gamma[V'/V], c^n = (c^n)' + 1, c^s = 1, x = e[V'/V],$$
$$(d_1^n, ..., d_n^n) = ((d_1^n)', ..., (d_n^n)'), (d_1^s, ..., d_n^s) = \underbrace{(0, ..., 0)}_{n} \Rightarrow$$

$$\frac{\hbar(\xi) \Rightarrow \Delta[V'/V]}{\Gamma \Rightarrow [\alpha]\xi \Rightarrow \Delta} \quad (\pi)$$

where $\alpha = (c|x := e)$, $\{d_1, ..., d_n\} = \mathcal{C} - \mathcal{C}(\alpha)$, $V = \mathcal{V}(\alpha)$,
V' is the set of new variables (w.r.t. $\Gamma, [\alpha]\xi, \Delta,$) corresponding to V.

$$\frac{P \to [\alpha]A}{[P?\alpha]A} \ (P?)$$
where $A \in \{\xi, \phi\}$

$$\frac{tt}{[\varepsilon]\xi} \ (\pi\varepsilon) \qquad \frac{[p^*]\xi}{[p^\omega]\xi} \ (\pi[\omega]) \qquad \frac{[p]\xi \wedge [p][q]\xi}{[p;q]\xi} \ (\pi[;])$$

$$\frac{[p]\xi \wedge [q]\xi}{[p \cup q]\xi} \ (\pi[\cup]) \qquad \frac{[p; p^*]\xi}{[p^*]\xi} \ (\pi[*]u) \qquad \frac{[p^*][p]\xi}{[p^*]\xi} \ (\pi[*]i)$$

The rule says that for any state s, the conclusion holds at state s, iff there exists a state s' with $ss' \in val((c|x := e))$, s.t. the premise holds at s'. The vector equation $(x_1, \ldots, x_n) = (e_1, \ldots, e_n)$ is the shorthand of $x_1 = e_1, \ldots, x_n = e_n$. $d_1, \ldots, d_n$ are all clocks not appeared in α. Given a CDL formula ϕ (or an SEP p), let $\mathcal{C}(\phi)$ ($\mathcal{C}(p)$) returns all clocks appeared in ϕ (p), $\mathcal{V}(\phi)$ ($\mathcal{V}(p)$) returns all dynamic variables appeared in ϕ (p). V' is the set of new variables corresponding to V, for each variable $x \in V$, there is a new variable x' with respect to $\Gamma, [\alpha]\xi, \Delta$ corresponding to it. Function $\hbar(\xi)$ maps each relations to an AFOL formula which should hold at state s'. It is defined as follows: for any c_1, c_2, (i) $\hbar(c_1 \subseteq c_2) ::= c_1^s = 1 \to c_2^s = 1$. (ii) $\hbar(c_1 \# c_2) ::= c_1^s = 0 \vee c_2^s = 0$. (iii) $\hbar(c_1 \prec c_2) ::= (c_1^n = 0 \wedge c_2^n = 0) \vee (c_1^n > c_2^n)$. (iv) $\hbar(c_1 \preceq c_2) ::= c_1^n \geq c_2^n$. (v) $\hbar(\lambda(Rel_1, \ldots, Rel_n)) ::= \bigwedge_{1 \leq i \leq n} \hbar(Rel_i)$.

($P?$) is a rule for both path-formulas and non-path formulas. Rule ($P?$) says that the conclusion at a state is true, iff if P is true, then $[\alpha]A$ is true. In rule ($\pi\varepsilon$), $tr \vDash_{ccsl} \xi$ always holds for trace tr of length 1. Rule ($\pi\omega$) is based on two facts about clock relation ξ and SEP traces: (i) For any infinite trace $tr \in val(p^\omega)$ and any state s in tr, there exists a finite trace $tr' \in val(p^*)$ that contains s. (ii) For any relation ξ and trace tr, $tr \vDash_{ccsl} \xi$ iff $tr(i) \vDash_{cdl} \hbar(\xi)$ for any $i \in \mathbb{N}^+$. These two facts can be easily obtained according to Definition 5 and the definition of

$\vDash_{ccsl}$ in Table 1. With them not hard to see the premise and conclusion of rule $(\pi\omega)$ are logical equivalent. With rule $(\pi\omega)$ we can reduce the proof case of $[p^\omega]\xi$ to the proof case of $[p^*]\xi$.

$(\pi[;])$, $(\pi[\cup])$, $(\pi[*]u)$, $(\pi[*]i)$ are structure rules for path formulas. $(\pi[;])$ means every trace of $p;q$ satisfies ξ iff every trace of p satisfies ξ, and after p every trace of q satisfies ξ. $(\pi[\cup])$ says every trace of $p \cup q$ satisfies ξ iff every trace of p and q satisfies ξ. Rule $(\pi[*]u)$ unwinds the star operator $*$. It is due to the fact that every trace (whose length ≥ 2) of p^* are the trace of $p;p^*$. $(\pi[*]i)$ states that ξ holds along all paths of any times of repetitions of p, iff after any times of repetitions p, ξ holds along all paths of p. Figure 3 gives a graphical illustration of rule (π), $(\pi[;])$, $(\pi[\cup])$, $(\pi[*]u)$, $(\pi[*]i)$.

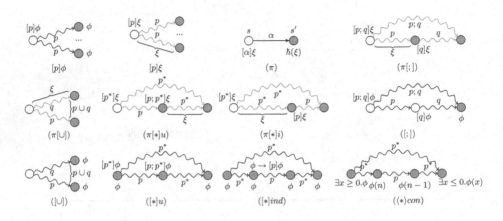

Fig. 3. Graphical illustrations of $[p]\phi$, $[p]\xi$ and some proof rules (Color figure online)

All non-path formula rules in Table 3 except for (ϕ), (ε), (ω) are based on the corresponding structure rules of FODL in [7]. (ϕ) is similar to (π), except that ϕ is kept unchanged in the premise. (ε) is obvious because the traces of ε all have length 1. Rule $([;])$ describes that ϕ holds after $p;q$ iff $[q]\phi$ holds after p. Rule $([\cup])$ says ϕ holds after $p \cup q$ iff ϕ holds after p, and also holds after q. $([*]u)$ means that ϕ holds after any times of repetitions of p, iff ϕ holds at current state, and ϕ holds after $p;p^*$.

$([]gen)$, $(\langle\rangle gen)$ strengthen the conclusions by extending the proposition $\phi \to \varphi$ into dynamic situations. $([]gen)$ $((\langle\rangle gen))$ expresses that if $\phi \to \varphi$ holds under all context of Γ, Δ, after any (some) executions of p, ϕ implies φ. $([*]ind)$ is the mathematical induction by the number of repetitions of program p: to prove ϕ holds after any repetitions (including 0), we need to prove that under any context of Γ, Δ, if ϕ holds, then it also holds after p. $(\langle*\rangle con)$ is from the Harel's convergence rule in [7] where integer x indicates the existing number of repetitions of p. $([*]i)$ and $(\langle*\rangle i)$ are rules for eliminating the star operator $*$ in practical verification. They can be derived by $([*]ind)$, $(\langle*\rangle con)$ with generalisation $([]gen)$, $(\langle\rangle gen)$ (see [7,16]). φ is the loop invariant of p. $([*]i)$ says that to prove ϕ holds after any repetitions of p, we need to prove that there exists an invariant φ such that: (i) φ holds at the beginning. (ii) Under any context of Γ, Δ if φ holds, then φ holds after p as well. (iii) Under any context of Γ, Δ, φ implies ϕ. Figure 3 gives a graphical illustration of rule $([\cup])$, $([;])$, $([*]u)$, $([*]ind)$, $(\langle*\rangle con)$.

Table 3. Rules for non-path formulas

$$\Gamma[V'/V], c^n = (c^n)' + 1, c^s = 1, x = e[V'/V],$$
$$(d_1^n, ..., d_n^n) = ((d_1^n)', ..., (d_n^n)'), (d_1^s, ..., d_n^s) = \underbrace{(0, ..., 0)}_{n} \Rightarrow$$

$$\frac{\phi \Rightarrow \Delta[V'/V]}{\Gamma \Rightarrow [\alpha]\phi \Rightarrow \Delta} \ (\phi)$$

where $\alpha = (c|x := e)$, $\{d_1, ..., d_n\} = \mathcal{C} - \mathcal{C}(\alpha)$, $V = \mathcal{V}(\alpha)$,

V' is the set of new variables (w.r.t. $\Gamma, [\alpha]\phi, \Delta,$) corresponding to V.

$$\frac{\phi}{[\varepsilon]\phi} \ (\varepsilon) \qquad \frac{tt}{[p^\omega]\phi} \ (\omega) \qquad \frac{[p][q]\phi}{[p;q]\phi} \ ([;]) \qquad \frac{[p]\phi \wedge [q]\phi}{[p \cup q]\phi} \ ([\cup]) \qquad \frac{\phi \wedge [p; p^*]\phi}{[p^*]\phi} \ ([*]u)$$

$$\frac{\cdot \Rightarrow \phi \to \varphi}{\Gamma \Rightarrow [p]\phi \to [p]\varphi, \Delta} \ ([]gen) \qquad \frac{\cdot \Rightarrow \phi \to \varphi}{\Gamma \Rightarrow \langle p \rangle \phi \to \langle p \rangle \varphi, \Delta} \ (\langle\rangle gen) \qquad \frac{\cdot \Rightarrow \phi \to [p]\phi}{\Gamma \Rightarrow \phi \to [p^*]\phi, \Delta} \ ([*]ind)$$

$$\frac{\cdot \Rightarrow \forall x > 0.(\phi(x) \to \langle p \rangle \phi(x - 1))}{\Gamma \Rightarrow \exists x \geq 0.\phi(x) \to \exists x \leq 0.\langle p^* \rangle \phi(x), \Delta} \ (\langle*\rangle con)$$

$$\frac{\Gamma \Rightarrow \varphi, \Delta \quad \cdot \Rightarrow \varphi \to [p]\varphi \quad \cdot \Rightarrow \varphi \to \phi}{\Gamma \Rightarrow [p^*]\phi, \Delta} \ ([*]i)$$

$$\frac{\Gamma \Rightarrow \exists x \geq 0.\varphi(x), \Delta \quad \cdot \Rightarrow \forall x > 0.(\varphi(x) \to \langle p \rangle \varphi(x - 1))}{\cdot \Rightarrow \exists x \leq 0.\varphi(x) \to \phi}{\Gamma \Rightarrow \langle p^* \rangle \phi, \Delta} \ (\langle*\rangle i)$$

Other FOL rules are listed in Table 4. As indicated in Sect. 1, after a QF-AFOL formula is obtained we can adopt SMT-checking procedure to check the validation of it. Since the SMT-checking procedure is independent from the CDL proof system, we propose an 'oracle' rule (o) in our proof system to indicate the termination of the proof. We assume that the validity of this QF-AFOL formula can be SMT-checked in a 'black box', through this oracle rule. Other rules comes from the traditional FOL and we omit the details of them.

Now we define the deduction relation of CDL. For any CDL formula ϕ and a formula multi-sets Φ, $\Phi \vdash_{cdl} \phi$ iff the sequent $\Phi \Rightarrow \phi$ can be derived according to rules in Tables 2, 3 and 4. If Φ is empty, we also write $\vdash_{cdl} \phi$. As a variation of dynamic logic, the soundness and relative completeness of proof system $\vdash_{cdl}$ can be analyzed in a similar way as those of FODL in [7,8]. For the soundness, above we have explained the intuitive meaning of each rule and their relations to the corresponding rules in FODL. For the relative completeness, intuitively, to prove it we show that each formula of form $[p]\xi$ can be transformed into an AFOL formula by applying the rules of the CDL proof system, which is similar for the formula $[p]\phi$ in FODL. Due to space limit, we omit the complete proof.

Table 4. Rules of first order logic

$$\frac{\models_{cdl} \bigwedge_{\phi \in \Gamma} \phi \to \bigvee_{\varphi \in \Delta} \varphi}{\Gamma \Rightarrow \Delta} \ (o) \qquad \frac{}{\Gamma, \phi \Rightarrow \phi, \Delta} \ (ax) \qquad \frac{\Gamma \Rightarrow \phi, \Delta \quad \Gamma, \phi \Rightarrow \Delta}{\Gamma \Rightarrow \Delta} \ (cut)$$

$$\frac{\Gamma, \neg\phi \Rightarrow \Delta}{\Gamma \Rightarrow \phi, \Delta} \ (\neg r) \qquad \frac{\Gamma \Rightarrow \neg\phi, \Delta}{\Gamma, \phi \Rightarrow \Delta} \ (\neg l) \qquad \frac{\Gamma \Rightarrow \phi, \Delta \quad \Gamma \Rightarrow \varphi, \Delta}{\Gamma \Rightarrow \phi \wedge \varphi, \Delta} \ (\wedge r)$$

$$\frac{\Gamma, \phi, \varphi \Rightarrow \Delta}{\Gamma, \phi \wedge \varphi \Rightarrow \Delta} \ (\wedge l) \qquad \frac{\Gamma \Rightarrow \phi[x'/x], \Delta}{\Gamma \Rightarrow \forall x.\phi, \Delta} \ (\forall r) \qquad \frac{\Gamma, \forall x.\phi, \phi[tn/x] \Rightarrow \Delta}{\Gamma, \forall x.\phi \Rightarrow \Delta} \ (\forall l)$$

$$\frac{\Gamma \Rightarrow \phi, \varphi, \Delta}{\Gamma \Rightarrow \phi \vee \varphi, \Delta} \ (\vee r) \qquad \frac{\Gamma, \phi \Rightarrow \Delta \quad \Gamma, \varphi \Rightarrow \Delta}{\Gamma, \phi \vee \varphi \Rightarrow \Delta} \ (\vee l) \qquad \frac{\Gamma, \phi \Rightarrow \varphi, \Delta}{\Gamma \Rightarrow \phi \to \varphi, \Delta} \ (\to r)$$

$$\frac{\Gamma \Rightarrow \phi, \Delta \quad \Gamma, \varphi \Rightarrow \Delta}{\Gamma, \phi \to \varphi \Rightarrow \Delta} \ (\to l) \qquad \frac{\Gamma \Rightarrow \phi[tn/x], \Delta}{\Gamma \Rightarrow \exists x.\phi, \Delta} \ (\exists r) \qquad \frac{\Gamma, \exists x.\phi, \phi[x'/x] \Rightarrow \Delta}{\Gamma, \exists x.\phi \Rightarrow \Delta} \ (\exists l)$$

where Γ, Δ are multi-sets of QF-AFOL formulas.
x' is a new variable w.r.t. Γ, ϕ, Δ, $\phi[tn/x]$ is admissible.

5   A Case Study

In this section, we illustrate how our proposed CDL can be used to capture RTES models and verify CCSL specifications, by analyzing a simple RTES—the Digital Filter (DF) system. The DF system we analyze here is based on [17].

As Fig. 4 shows, the DF is used in a video system, it reads image pixels from a memory, filters them and sends the result out to a video device. The explicit structure of DF is shown in the right figure of Fig. 4. The DF consists of two modules: a Feeder and a Filter. They interact with each other and with their environment through ports p, r and o. Ports are the only way for different modules to communicate in synchronous models. They can be modelled as signal c_p, c_r and c_o in SEP. The behaviour of the DF, as a whole system of two modules, is as follows: the Filter sends a 'Ready' message to the Feeder through port r, to tell it 'I am ready for the pixels'. The Feeder receives this message and the next time it begins feeding pixels towards the Filter, one pixel per unit of time. After the Filter gathers 4 pixels, it runs the computation (instantly) and outputs the result through port o. Then the next time it sends 'Ready' message to the Feeder again....

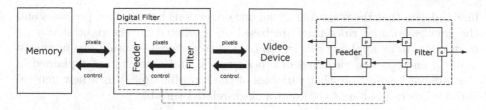

Fig. 4. The Digital Filter system

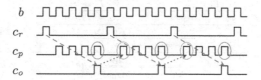

Fig. 5. The schedule of the Digital Filter (Color figure online)

The behaviour of the DF can be described by an SEP as follows:

$$DF ::= \alpha_1; (f = 1?\alpha_2; (n = 0 \wedge f = 0?\alpha_3 \cup n > 0 \wedge f = 0?\alpha_4)^*)^\omega,$$

where $\alpha_1 = (c_r | n := 4 | f := 1)$, $\alpha_2 = (c_r | f := 0)$, $\alpha_3 = (c_o | f := 1 | n := 4)$, $\alpha_4 = (c_p | n := n - 1)$. n is for counting the number of pixels the Filter has received. f is a flag, indicating the end of the loop '$(\ldots)^*$'. Figure 5 shows the schedule of the DF, where clock b is a basic clock. For this DF model we may be interested in two CCSL specifications as follows:

$$SP_1 ::= \langle \{c_r, c_o\}, \emptyset, \{c_r \prec c_o\} \rangle,$$
$$SP_2 ::= \langle \{c_p, c_o, c_{p'}, c_{p''}\}, \{c_{p'} \triangleq c_p \$1, c_{p''} \triangleq c_{p'} \propto 3\}, \{c_o \prec c_{p''}\} \rangle.$$

SP_1 expresses the property that 'the result can be obtained only after the "Ready" message is sent', i.e., clock c_r ticks strictly before c_o. SP_2 says that 'only after the last result is computed, the new pixels can be received'. SP_2 contains two clock definitions. $c_{p'}$, $c_{p''}$ are generated clocks not appeared in program DF. Two specifications are indicated by red and blue arrows in Fig. 5 respectively. The ticks of clock $c_{p'}$, $c_{p''}$ are indicated by green and yellow circles respectively.

For SP_1, the verification problem can be captured by a CDL formula:

$$I \rightarrow [DF]c_r \prec c_o,$$

where $I = \bigwedge_{c \in \{c_r, c_p, c_o\}} (c^n = 0 \wedge c^s = 0)$ represents the initial environment of the program. The deduction procedure of this formula is illustrated in Fig. 6. Starting from the root node (node ①), the procedure answers 'yes' iff every leave node of the proof tree returns a valid QF-AFOL formula, which can be checked through an SMT-checking procedure. Inference rules with a 'double line' indicate that there are more than one deductions between the premises and the conclusion, and rules they are based on are listed on the right side. e.g., from node ②, by applying rule $(\pi[;])$, $(\wedge r)$ in sequence, we obtain two premises: node ③ and ④. The meanings of other symbols and contexts are explained in the table of Fig. 6. Note that variables of the form like '$(c_r^n)^1$' is a new general variable (corresponding to c_r^n), not a clock-related variable.

$$\frac{⑨\ \bigwedge_{\varphi\in\Gamma_4}\varphi\to\varphi_2}{\Gamma_4\Rightarrow\varphi_2}\,(o)\qquad \frac{\Gamma_4\Rightarrow\varphi_2}{\varphi_2\Rightarrow[P_1?\alpha_3]\varphi_2}\,(P?,\to r,\phi)$$

$$\frac{\bigwedge_{\varphi\in\Gamma_5}\varphi\to\varphi_2}{\Gamma_5\Rightarrow\varphi_2}\,(o)\qquad \frac{\Gamma_5\Rightarrow\varphi_2}{\varphi_2\Rightarrow[P_2?\alpha_4]\varphi_2}\,(P?,\to r,\phi)$$

$$\frac{\varphi_2\Rightarrow[P_1?\alpha_3]\varphi_2\qquad \varphi_2\Rightarrow[P_2?\alpha_4]\varphi_2}{\varphi_2\Rightarrow[P_1?\alpha_3\cup P_2?\alpha_4]\varphi_2}\,([\cup],\wedge r)\qquad \frac{\varphi_2\Rightarrow[P_1?\alpha_3\cup P_2?\alpha_4]\varphi_2}{\cdot\Rightarrow\varphi_2\to[p_2]\varphi_2}\,(\to r)$$

$$\frac{\models_{cdl}\bigwedge_{\varphi\in\Gamma_3}\varphi\to\varphi_2}{\Gamma_3\Rightarrow\varphi_2}\,(o)\qquad \frac{\models_{cdl}\varphi_2\to\varphi_1}{\cdot\Rightarrow\varphi_2\to\varphi_1}\,(o)$$

$$\frac{\Gamma_3\Rightarrow\varphi_2\qquad \cdot\Rightarrow\varphi_2\to[p_2]\varphi_2\qquad \cdot\Rightarrow\varphi_2\to\varphi_1}{⑧\ \Gamma_3\Rightarrow[p_2^*]\varphi_1}\,([*]i)$$

$$\frac{\frac{⑧\ \Gamma_3\Rightarrow[p_2^*]\varphi_1}{}}{\varphi_1\Rightarrow[f=1?\alpha_2][p_2^*]\varphi_1}\,(P?,\to r,\phi)\qquad \frac{\varphi_1\Rightarrow[f=1?\alpha_2][p_2^*]\varphi_1}{⑥\ \varphi_1\Rightarrow[f=1?\alpha_2;p_2^*]\varphi_1}\,([;])$$

$$\frac{\models_{cdl}\bigwedge_{\varphi\in\Gamma_1}\varphi\to\varphi_1}{\Gamma_1\Rightarrow\varphi_1}\,(o)\qquad \frac{⑥}{\cdot\Rightarrow\varphi_1\to[p_1]\varphi_1}\,(\to r)\qquad \frac{⑦\ \ldots}{\cdot\Rightarrow\varphi_1\to[p_1]c_r\prec c_o}\,(\to r)$$

$$\frac{\Gamma_1\Rightarrow\varphi_1\qquad \cdot\Rightarrow\varphi_1\to[p_1]\varphi_1\qquad \cdot\Rightarrow\varphi_1\to[p_1]c_r\prec c_o}{⑤\ \Gamma_2\Rightarrow[p_1^*][p_1]c_r\prec c_o}\,([*]i)$$

$$\frac{\frac{⑤\ \Gamma_2\Rightarrow[p_1^*][p_1]c_r\prec c_o}{}}{\Gamma_2\Rightarrow[p_1^\omega]c_r\prec c_o}\,(\pi[\omega],\pi[*]i)\qquad \frac{\Gamma_2\Rightarrow[p_1^\omega]c_r\prec c_o}{④\ \Gamma_1\Rightarrow[\alpha_1][p_1^\omega]c_r\prec c_o}\,(\phi)$$

$$\frac{\models_{cdl}\bigwedge_{\varphi\in\Gamma_2}\varphi\to\hbar(c_r\prec c_o)}{\Gamma_2\Rightarrow\hbar(c_r\prec c_o)}\,(o)\qquad \frac{\Gamma_2\Rightarrow\hbar(c_r\prec c_o)}{③\ \Gamma_1\Rightarrow[\alpha_1]c_r\prec c_o}\,(\pi)$$

$$\frac{\frac{③\ \Gamma_1\Rightarrow[\alpha_1]c_r\prec c_o\qquad ④\ \Gamma_1\Rightarrow[\alpha_1][p_1^\omega]c_r\prec c_o}{}}{②\ \Gamma_1\Rightarrow[DF]c_r\prec c_o}\,(\pi[;],\wedge r)\qquad \frac{\frac{②\ \Gamma_1\Rightarrow[DF]c_r\prec c_o}{}}{①\ \cdot\Rightarrow I\to[DF]c_r\prec c_o}\,(\to r,\wedge l)$$

$\alpha_1=(c_r|n:=4|f:=1)$, $\alpha_2=(c_r|f:=0)$, $\alpha_3=(c_o|f:=1|n:=4)$, $\alpha_4=(c_p|n:=n-1)$.
$p_1=f=1?\alpha_2;p_2^*$, $p_2=P_1?\alpha_3\cup P_2?\alpha_4$, $P_1=n=0\wedge f=0$, $P_2=n>0\wedge f=0$.
$\varphi_1=(C_1\vee C_2)\wedge c_r^n>c_o^n$, $\varphi_2=(C_1\wedge c_r^n-c_o^n>1)\vee(C_2\wedge c_r^n>c_o^n)$,
$C_1=0\le n<4\wedge f=0$, $C_2=n=4\wedge f=1$.
$\boldsymbol{v}=(c_r^n,c_r^s,c_p^n,c_p^s,c_o^n,c_o^s)$, $\boldsymbol{v}^x=((c_r^n)^x,(c_r^s)^x,(c_p^n)^x,(c_p^s)^x,(c_o^n)^x,(c_o^s)^x)$, where $x=1,2,3,4$.
$\boldsymbol{v}^x,x_1,x_2,y_1,z_1,z_2,u_1$ are new variables corresponding to their counterparts in substitutions.

$\Gamma_1: c_r^n=0,c_r^s=0,c_p^n=0,c_p^s=0,c_o^n=0,c_o^s=0$
$\Gamma_2: \Gamma_1[\boldsymbol{v}^1,x_1,x_2/\boldsymbol{v},n,1], c_r^n=(c_r^n)^1+1, c_r^s=1, c_p^n=(c_p^n)^1, c_p^s=0, c_o^n=(c_o^n)^1, c_o^s=0, n=4$
$\Gamma_3: \{\varphi_1,f=1\}[\boldsymbol{v}^2,y_1/\boldsymbol{v},f], c_r^n=(c_r^n)^2+1, c_r^s=1, c_p^n=(c_p^n)^2, c_p^s=0, c_o^n=(c_o^n)^2, c_o^s=0, f=0$
$\Gamma_4: \{\varphi_2,P_1\}[\boldsymbol{v}^3,z_1,z_2/\boldsymbol{v},n,1], c_r^n=(c_r^n)^3, c_r^s=0, c_p^n=(c_p^n)^3, c_p^s=0, c_o^n=(c_o^n)^3+1, c_o^s=1, n=4$
$\Gamma_5: \{\varphi_2,P_2\}[\boldsymbol{v}^4,u_1/\boldsymbol{v},n], c_r^n=(c_r^n)^4, c_r^s=0, c_p^n=(c_p^n)^4+1, c_p^s=1, c_o^n=(c_o^n)^4, c_o^s=0, n=u_1-1$

Fig. 6. The deduction procedure of $I\to[DF]c_r\prec c_o$

Due to the limit of space, we omit the details of the branch from node ⑦. At node ⑤, ⑧, we apply rule $([*]i)$ to eliminate the loop operator $*$. Here we need to manually decide the loop invariants φ_1,φ_2. The selecting of a suitable invariants is according to the loop body (here p_1,p_2) and the formulas we want to verify after the loop program (here $[p_1]c_1\prec c_2$, φ_1). e.g., in φ_1, we have to guarantee '$c_r^n>c_o^n$' always holds during each execution of p_1, because if not so, $[p_1]c_1\prec c_2$ would not hold for some state during the execution of p_1^*. '$C_1\vee C_2$' is to make sure that n,f can only be 'reasonable values' during the execution of p_1. At last, easy to see that each leave node is a valid QF-AFOL formula. e.g., at node ⑨, clearly from Γ_4, we have C_2 holds. In Γ_4, since $z_1=0\wedge z_2=0$(in $P_1[z_1,z_2/n,y]$), there is $(c_r^n)^3-(c_o^n)^3>1$(from $\varphi_1[\boldsymbol{v}^3,z_1,z_2/\boldsymbol{v},n,f]$). Because $c_r^n=(c_r^n)^3$, $c_o^n=(c_o^n)^3+1$, so $c_r^n>c_o^n$ holds.

For SP_2, just like in previous approaches [4,18,19], we firstly make the product of the system model DF and the clock definitions $c_{p'} \triangleq c_p\$1$, $c_{p''} \triangleq c_{p'} \propto 3$. As indicated in Fig. 1, this product can then be captured by an SEP program. A similar verification procedure as above can be carried out.

6 Related Work

Previous approaches [18,19] for the verification of CCSL specifications are mainly based on model checking, where the reachability analysis is made for the product of the system model and the CCSL specification. When the CCSL specification is unsafe, a bound needs to be set to avoid the enumeration of infinite number of states. Our approach is based on theorem proving and SMT-checking, which provides a unified framework under which both safe and unsafe CCSL specifications can be analyzed.

Another subject of analysis for CCSL is to find a schedule of a given CCSL specification [3,13,20], where no system models were involved. The earliest approach [3] combined BDD-based boolean solving and the rewriting on clock expressions, while the method in [20] was based on the rewriting logic in Maude. In [13], the schedule was found by solving an UFLIA formula that encodes the CCSL specification through an SMT-checking procedure. Comparing with [13], we propose a proof system to transform the CDL formula into QF-AFOL formulas, which are more efficient for an SMT-checking procedure to solve.

CDL is largely based on the traditional FODL [8] and its rules $(\pi[;])$, $(\pi[\cup])$, $(\pi[*]u)$, $(\pi[*]i)$ are inspired from the Differential Dynamic Temporal Logic (DDTL), a dynamic logic for verification of hybrid systems [16,21]. In DDTL, the program supports a continuous time model with differential equations embedded into it. Our SEP supports a discrete time model with synchronous mechanism which we think would be more friendly for modelling RTESs.

7 Conclusion and Future Work

In this paper, we propose a logical approach for verification of CCSL specifications. We build a variation of dynamic logic called CDL to capture the verification problem, and a proof system to provide the verification support. We give a case study to illustrate how CDL can be used for verifying CCSL specifications.

Unlike traditional synchronous programming languages, SEP only supports sequential models. We shall present a concurrent extension in a future work by adding a '$\|$' operator. We also consider mechanizing CDL with the popular theorem prover Coq in order to see more practical potentials for this method.

References

1. OMG: UML profile for MARTE: Modeling and analysis of real-time embedded systems. Technical report, OMG, June 2011. Formal 02 June 2011

2. Mallet, F.: Clock constraint specification language: specifying clock constraints with UML/MARTE. ISSE **4**(3), 309–314 (2008)
3. André, C.: Syntax and semantics of the clock constraint specification language (CCSL). Research Report RR-6925, INRIA (2009)
4. Mallet, F., de Simone, R.: Correctness issues on MARTE/CCSL constraints. Sci. Comput. Program. **106**, 78–92 (2015)
5. Mallet, F., Millo, J.V., de Simone, R.: Safe CCSL specifications and marked graphs. In: 11th ACM/IEEE International Conference on Formal Methods and Models for Codesign, pp. 157–166, IEEE (2013)
6. Zhang, M., Ying, Y.: Towards SMT-based LTL model checking of clock constraint specification language for real-time and embedded systems. In: LCTES 2017, pp. 61–70. ACM (2017)
7. Harel, D., Kozen, D., Tiuryn, J.: Dynamic logic. SIGACT News **32**(1), 66–69 (2001)
8. Harel, D. (ed.): First-Order Dynamic Logic. LNCS, vol. 68. Springer, Heidelberg (1979). https://doi.org/10.1007/3-540-09237-4
9. Halbwachs, N.: Synchronous Programming of Reactive Systems. Kluwer Academic Publisher, Dordrecht (1993)
10. Barrett, C., Fontaine, P., Tinelli, C.: The SMT-LIB standard: version 2.6. Technical report, Department of Computer Science, The University of Iowa (2017). www. SMT-LIB.org
11. Nipkow, T., Wenzel, M., Paulson, L.C. (eds.): Isabelle/HOL—A Proof Assistant for Higher-Order Logic. LNCS, vol. 2283. Springer, Heidelberg (2002). https://doi. org/10.1007/3-540-45949-9
12. Bertot, Y., Castéran, P.: Interactive Theorem Proving and Program Development - Coq'Art: The Calculus of Inductive Constructions. Texts in Theoretical Computer Science. An EATCS Series. Springer, Heidelberg (2004). https://doi.org/10.1007/978-3-662-07964-5
13. Zhang, M., Mallet, F., Zhu, H.: An SMT-based approach to the formal analysis of MARTE/CCSL. In: Ogata, K., Lawford, M., Liu, S. (eds.) ICFEM 2016. LNCS, vol. 10009, pp. 433–449. Springer, Cham (2016). https://doi.org/10.1007/978-3-319-47846-3_27
14. Berry, G., Gonthier, G.: The Esterel synchronous programming language: design, semantics, implementation. Sci. Comput. Program. **19**(2), 87–152 (1992)
15. Gentzen, G.: Untersuchungen über das logische Schließen. Ph.D. thesis, NA, Göttingen (1934)
16. Platzer, A.: Logical Analysis of Hybrid Systems - Proving Theorems for Complex Dynamics. Springer, Heidelberg (2010). https://doi.org/10.1007/978-3-642-14509-4
17. André, C., Mallet, F.: Specification and verification of time requirements with CCSL and Esterel. In: LCTES 2009, pp. 167–176. ACM (2009)
18. Suryadevara, J., Seceleanu, C., Mallet, F., Pettersson, P.: Verifying MARTE/CCSL mode behaviors using UPPAAL. In: Hierons, R.M., Merayo, M.G., Bravetti, M. (eds.) SEFM 2013. LNCS, vol. 8137, pp. 1–15. Springer, Heidelberg (2013). https:// doi.org/10.1007/978-3-642-40561-7_1
19. Zhang, Y., Mallet, F., Chen, Y.: Timed automata semantics of spatio-temporal consistency language STeC. In: TASE 2014, pp. 201–208, IEEE (2014)
20. Zhang, M., Dai, F., Mallet, F.: Periodic scheduling for MARTE/CCSL: theory and practice. Sci. Comput. Program. **154**, 42–60 (2018)
21. Platzer, A.: A temporal dynamic logic for verifying hybrid system invariants. In: Artemov, S.N., Nerode, A. (eds.) LFCS 2007. LNCS, vol. 4514, pp. 457–471. Springer, Heidelberg (2007). https://doi.org/10.1007/978-3-540-72734-7_32

Semantics and Analysis Methods

Refinement of Statecharts with Run-to-Completion Semantics

Karla Morris[1]([⊠]), Colin Snook[2], Thai Son Hoang[2], Robert Armstrong[1], and Michael Butler[2]

[1] Sandia National Laboratories, Livermore, CA, USA
{knmorri,rob}@sandia.gov
[2] University of Southampton, Southampton, UK
{cfs,t.s.hoang,mjb}@soton.ac.uk

Abstract. Statechart modelling notations, with so-called 'run to completion' semantics and simulation tools for validation, are popular with engineers for designing systems. However, they do not support formal refinement and they lack formal static verification methods and tools. For example, properties concerning the synchronisation between different parts of a system may be difficult to verify for all scenarios, and impossible to verify at an abstract level before the full details of substates have been added. Event-B, on the other hand, is based on refinement from an initial abstraction and is designed to make formal verification by automatic theorem provers feasible, restricting instantiation and testing to a validation role. In this paper, we introduce a notion of refinement, similar to that of Event-B, into a 'run to completion' Statechart modelling notation, and leverage Event-B's tool support for proof. We describe the pitfalls in translating 'run to completion' models into Event-B refinements and suggest a solution. We illustrate the approach using our prototype translation tools and show by example, how a synchronisation property between parallel Statecharts can be automatically proven at an intermediate refinement level.

Keywords: SCXML · Statecharts · Event-B · iUML-B · Refinement

1 Introduction

Formal verification of high-consequence systems requires the analysis of formal models that capture the properties and functionality of the system of interest. Although high-consequence controls and systems are designed to limit complexity, the requirements and consequent proof obligations tend to increase the complexity of the formal verification. Proof obligations for such requirements can be made more tractable using abstraction/refinement, providing a natural divide and conquer strategy for controlling complexity.

Statecharts [7] are often used for safety-critical and other high-consequence systems to provide an unambiguous, executable way of specifying functional as

© Springer Nature Switzerland AG 2019
C. Artho and P. C. Ölveczky (Eds.): FTSCS 2018, CCIS 1008, pp. 121–138, 2019.
https://doi.org/10.1007/978-3-030-12988-0_8

well as safety, security, and reliability properties. While functional properties (usually) can be tested, the need for instantiation and state space explosion can make testing of safety, security and reliability properties intractable. Therefore, such properties must be proved formally.

Here we give a binding from Statecharts to Event-B [1] so that this type of reasoning can be carried out. The binding is facilitated by translating to iUML-B [18–20], a diagrammatic modelling notation for Event-B. Hierarchical encapsulation maps well onto Statecharts in a similar way to nested state-machines in iUML-B. Binding UML Statecharts [17] to iUML-B is natural and the addition of run-to-completion semantics, expected by Statechart designers, is much of the contribution of this work. Another contribution is the augmentation of the textual and parse-able format for Statecharts, *State Chart eXtensible Markup Language* (SCXML) [22] to accommodate elements necessary to support formal analysis.

There are many formal semantics that can be bound to the Statechart graphical language [5]. While Statecharts and various semantic interpretations of Statecharts admit refinement reified as both hierarchical or parallel composition (e.g. see Argos [12]), here, as previously [18], we focus on hierarchical refinement, the form that Event-B natively admits. Here we define hierarchical composition to mean nesting new transition systems inside previously pure states, and parallel composition to be the combination in one machine of formerly separate transition systems. A hierarchical development of a system model uses refinement concepts to link the different levels of abstraction. Each subsequent level increases model complexity by adding details in the form of functionality and implementation method. As the model complexity increases in each refinement level, tractability of the detailed model can be improved by the use of a graphical representation, with rich semantics that can support an infrastructure for formal verification.

The semantics adopted here adheres closely to UML Statecharts [3] and is implemented in iUML-B. Models described in Statecharts are expressed in SCXML and translated into Event-B logic which uses the *Rodin platform* (Rodin) [2] for machine proofs. With suitable restrictions, Statecharts already provide a sound, intuitive, visual metaphor for refinement. Outfitted with a formal semantics, this work borrows from well-used Statechart practices in digital design. We previously reported [16] our early attempts to relate Statecharts to Event-B. At that stage (and similarly in [20]) we suggested the necessary extensions and basic mechanism of translation but avoided the more challenging problem of refinement with run to completion semantics. The goal of the present work is to provide usable, well-founded tools that are familiar to designers of safety-critical systems with the formal guarantees needed to ensure safety and reliability. The motivation of the work is entirely driven by the industrial partner, who feels that the current semantics for Statecharts is insufficient for formal verification.

The Event-B modelling method provides the logic and refinement theory required to formally analyse a system model. The open-source Rodin provides support for Event-B including automatic theorem provers and model checking capabilities. iUML-B augments the Event-B language with a graphical interface including state-machines.

The rest of the paper is structured as follows. Section 2 provides background information on SCXML, Event-B, and iUML-B. Section 3 presents our running example. Section 4 discusses the various challenges for introducing a refinement notion into SCXML and demonstrates our approach. In Sect. 5, we illustrate our translation of SCXML models into Event-B using the example introduced in Sect. 3. Section 6 shows how properties of the SCXML models can be specified as invariants and verified in Event-B. We summarise related work in Sect. 7, conclude in Sect. 8 and describe our plans for future work in Sect. 9.

2   Background

2.1   SCXML

SCXML is a modelling language based on Harel Statecharts with facilities for adding data elements that are manipulated by transition actions and used in conditions for their firing. SCXML follows the usual 'run to completion' semantics of such Statechart languages, where trigger events[1] may be needed to enable transitions. Trigger events are queued when they are raised, and then one is de-queued and consumed by firing all the transitions that it enables, followed by any (un-triggered) transitions that then become enabled due to the change of state caused by the initial transition firing. This is repeated until no transitions are enabled, and then the next trigger is de-queued and consumed. There are two kinds of triggers: internal triggers are raised by transitions and external triggers are raised by the environment (spontaneously as far as our model is concerned). An external trigger may only be consumed when the internal trigger queue has been emptied. Listing 1 shows a pseudocode representation of the run to completion semantics as defined within the latest W3C recommendation document [22]. Here IQ and EQ are the triggers present in the internal and external queues respectively.

```
 1  while running:
 2      while completion = false
 3          if untriggered_enabled
 4              execute(untriggered())
 5          elseif IQ /= {}
 6              execute(internal(IQ.dequeue))
 7          else
 8              completion = true
 9          endif
10      endwhile
11      if EQ /= {}
12          execute(EQ.dequeue)
13          completion = false
14      endif
15  endwhile
```

Listing 1. Pseudocode for 'run to completion'

---

[1] In SCXML the triggers are called 'events', however, we refer to them as 'triggers' to avoid confusion with Event-B.

We adopt the commonly used terminology where a single transition is called a *micro-step* and a complete run (between de-queueing external triggers) is referred to as a *macro-step*.

2.2 Event-B

Event-B [1] is a formal method for system development. Main features of Event-B include the use of *refinement* to introduce system details gradually into the formal model. An Event-B model contains two parts: *contexts* and *machines*. Contexts contain *carrier sets*, *constants*, and *axioms* constraining the carrier sets and constants. Machines contain *variables* v, *invariants* I(v) constraining the variables, and *events*. An event comprises a guard denoting its enabled-condition and an action describing how the variables are modified when the event is executed. In general, an event e has the form: **any** t **where** $G(t, v)$ **then** $S(t, v)$ **end** where t are the event parameters, $G(t, v)$ is the guard of the event, and $S(t, v)$ is the action of the event.

Machines can be refined by adding more details. Refinement can be done by extending the machine to include additional variables (*superposition refinement*) representing new features of the system, or to replace some (abstract) variables by new (concrete) variables (*data refinement*). More information about Event-B can be found in [8]. Event-B is supported by Rodin [2], an extensible toolkit which includes facilities for modelling, verifying the consistency of models using theorem proving and model checking techniques, and validating models with simulation-based approaches.

2.3 iUML-B State-Machines

iUML-B provides a diagrammatic modelling notation for Event-B in the form of state-machines and class diagrams. The diagrammatic models relate to an Event-B machine and generate or contribute to parts of it. For example a state-machine will automatically generate the Event-B data elements (sets, constants, axioms, variables, and invariants) to implement the states. Transitions contribute further guards and actions representing their state change, to the events that they elaborate. State-machines are typically refined by adding nested state-machines to states. Figure 1 shows an example of a simple state-machine with two states.

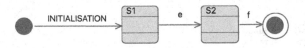

Fig. 1. An example iUML-B state-machine

Each state is encoded as a boolean variable and the current state is indicated by one of the boolean variables being set to TRUE. An invariant ensures that only one state is set to TRUE at a time. Events change the values of state variables to move the TRUE value according to the transitions in the state-machine. The Event-B translation[2] of the state-machine in Fig. 1 can be seen in Listing 2. iUML-B also provides the option of an alternative translation with a single state variable ranging over an enumerated type of states, however, the boolean representation of each state is more natural for a user to reference in SCXML guards and actions.

While the iUML-B translation deals with the basic data formalisation of state-machines it differs significantly from the aims of the work presented here. iUML-B adopts Event-B's simple guarded action semantics and does not have a concept of triggers and run-to-completion. Here we make use of iUML-B's state-machine translation but provide a completely different semantic by generating a behaviour into the underlying Event-B events that are linked to the generated iUML-B transitions.

```
1  variables S1 S2
2  invariants
3    TRUE ∈ {S1, S2} ⇒ partition({TRUE}, {S1}∩{TRUE}, {S2}∩{TRUE})
4  events
5    INITIALISATION: begin S1, S2 := TRUE, FALSE end
6    e: when S1 = TRUE then S1, S2 := FALSE, TRUE end
7    f: when S2 = TRUE then S2 := FALSE end
8  end
```

Listing 2. Translation of the state-machine in Fig. 1

3   Intrusion Detection System

An *Intrusion Detection System* (IDS) is used to illustrate the use of refinement in Statecharts and how it is supported by Event-B verification tools. The IDS is designed using an *Application-Specific Integrated Circuit* (ASIC) which connects to a buzzer and a sensor over a *Serial Peripheral Interface* (SPI) bus. The system is controlled via the ASIC on the SPI bus. At power-up, the ASIC sends commands over the SPI bus to initialise the sensor and the buzzer. After waiting for 50 ms the ASIC enters its main routine, which makes the buzzer respond to the sensor. In the early design phase the Statechart model of this system may be limited to the ASIC that captures the initialisation of the peripherals and the 50 ms wait. In the interest of simplicity, we elide all details of the main routine.

A Statechart model of this system is shown in Fig. 2a. The ASIC starts by initialising the buzzer; this involves sending a message over the SPI bus. These messages constitute an implementation detail that we elide at this abstraction level. Once the message is sent (which will be indicated by some event saying that the SPI system is done), the ASIC moves on to initialise the sensor. After that the ASIC moves into a waiting state for 50 ms, and finally moves into the state which represents normal operation. At this abstraction the **spi_done** trigger,

---

[2] Here, partition($S, T1, T2, \ldots$) means the set S is partitioned into disjoint (sub-)sets $T1, T2, \ldots$ that cover S.

which indicates that the SPI system has finished, is an internal trigger that can be fired at any time.

In a subsequent level of refinement, shown in Fig. 2b, the designer uses super-position refinement to add a parallel state representing the SPI subsystem. The SPI subsystem is usually in an **Idle** state until the **send_message** trigger is raised, at which point the SPI subsystem enters a state **Sending Message**, which represents sending the message, byte by byte. When the last byte of the message is sent, it raises the **spi_done** trigger, allowing the other parallel state to continue, while the SPI subsystem returns to idle. In the current refined model we have incorporated the implementation details for raising **spi_done** and introduced a new internal trigger **send_message**, which is non-deterministic at this point.

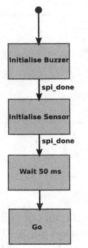

(a) ASIC component high level abstraction

(b) First refinement introducing the abstract model of the SPI subsystem

Fig. 2. Statechart diagram for IDS including the abstract representation of the ASIC and SPI components.

The model can be further refined by incorporating more details on how the initialisation states, the wait state, and the SPI subsystem operate, including how they interact with each other. The Statechart diagram for this refinement level is in Fig. 3. The **Initialise Buzzer** state constructs the SPI message to send, then raises the **send_message** trigger, and then waits. After **send_message** is raised, the SPI subsystem reacts. It spins for a while in the **Send Byte** state, looping as many times as it takes to get to the last byte in the message. When the last byte in the message is sent, it goes back to **Idle** and raises an event which allows the state machine on the left to proceed. The sensor is then initialised in a very similar manner to the buzzer. After both peripherals are initialised, the state machine goes into the **Wait 50 ms** state, where it increments a counter until it reaches some maximum, then exits.

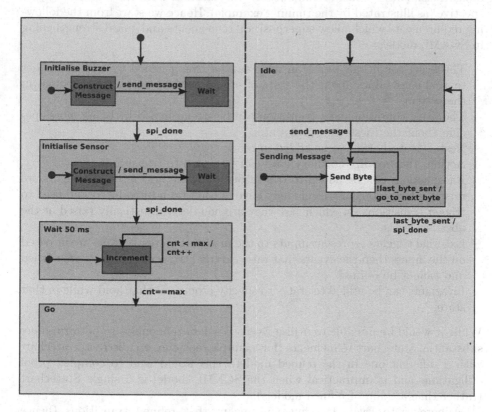

Fig. 3. Statechart diagram for IDS including implementation details for the messages sent between the system components.

The system described must send messages to complete the initialisation of the buzzer and sensor, but once the main routine is reached (**Go** state) no more messages should be sent through the SPI bus. As a result, a desirable safety property is that *when the ASIC is in the Go state the SPI subsystem must be in the Idle state*. This safety property should hold from the first refinement and be preserved in all future refinements.

4   Design Rationale

We consider the kinds of things we would like to do in SCXML refinements and what properties should be preserved. In practice, we wish to leverage existing Event-B verification tools and hence adopt a notion of refinement that can be automatically translated into an equivalent Event-B model consisting of a chain of refinements. We use particular refinement idioms at the Statechart level that correspond to Event-B's superposition refinement and thus have simple proof obligations. These refinement idioms are very natural from an engineering perspective (as illustrated by the running example). Hence we start from the following requirements which allow superposition refinements and guard strengthening in SCXML models:

- The firing conditions of a transition can be strengthened by adding further textual constraints about the state of other variables and state machines in the system.
- The firing conditions of a transition can be strengthened by being more specific about the (nested) source state,
- Nested Statecharts can be added in refinements.
- Actions that modify ancillary data can be added to transitions.
- Raise actions can be added to transitions to define how internal triggers are raised. These internal triggers may have already been introduced and used to trigger transitions, in which case they are non-deterministically raised at the abstract levels.
- External triggers represent inputs to the model. If no restrictions are imposed on the inputs then the events that raise external trigger are always unguarded and cannot be refined.
- Invariants can be added to states to specify properties that hold while in that state.

While it would be possible to utilise Event-B's data refinement to perform more substantial Statechart refinements (for example replacing an abstract Statechart with a different one in the refined model), this would lead to complex proof obligations and is impractical when the SCXML model is a single Statechart (rather than a chain of refined models).

Adherence to Event-B refinement means that refined transitions (hence micro- and macro-steps) should preserve the abstract state and new ones should not alter the abstract state. With this approach, there is an inherent difficulty in refining 'run to completion' semantics where every enabled micro-step must be completed before the next macro-step is started. The problem is that, in a refinement, we want to strengthen the conditions for a micro-step. However, by making the micro-steps more constrained we may disable them and hence make the completion of enabled ones more easily achieved. This makes the guard for taking the next macro-step weaker breaking the notion of refinement.

While it is always possible to abstract away sufficiently to reach a common semantics (see [20] for example), in this work we wish to explore verification that considers 'run to completion' behaviour as closely as possible. To simulate the 'run to completion' semantics in Event-B, we initially adopted a scheduler approach where 'engine' events decide which user transitions should be fired based on their guards. Boolean flags were then used to enable these transitions which may fire before the next step of the engine. The engine implemented the operational semantics of Listing 1 by deciding when to use internal or external triggers. To allow for transition guards to be strengthened in later refinements (hence achieving completion earlier) the scheduling engine was allowed to continue without actually firing the transitions. However, this non-deterministic completion introduced many additional behaviours making simulation difficult.

Due to these difficulties with non-deterministic completion we developed an alternative approach where a separate event is generated for each combination of transitions that could possibly be fired together in the same step. For example, if T1 and T2 are transitions that could both become enabled at the same scheduler step, four events are needed to cater for the possible combinations: neither, T1, T2 and both (where the combined event is constructed from the conjunction of guards and parallel firing of actions). To allow for strengthening of the guards in refinement we omit the negation of guards leaving the choice of lesser combinations, including the empty one, non-deterministically available in case of future refinement. For example, T1 could fire alone even if T2 is enabled since we cannot add the negation of T2's guard to T1 unless we know that it will never be strengthened. This non-determinism in the model accurately reflects the abstract run to completion where we do not yet know whether T2 will be enabled or not in future refinements. The non-determinism is useful to allow abstractions which facilitate verification proofs but must be removed in refinements to reach a design suitable for implementation. In future work we intend to add an attribute *finalised* to indicate that no further guard strengthening refinements will be made to a transition, removing non-determinism throughout the refinement chain.

Since there is only ever a single event to be fired in a particular micro-step, the scheduler can be integrated with the events that represent the transition combinations, greatly simplifying the Event-B model. Instead of explicit events to progress and implement the scheduling engine, an abstract machine is provided with events that can be refined by the translation of the user's SCXML model into events that represent combinations of transitions that can fire in the same micro-step. Each refinement produces a new set of events representing the (possibly extended) transition combinations that may occur at that level of refinement. This has benefits both for simulation (i.e. execution of the Statechart for validation) which is easier to follow having less translation artefacts and for proof where the obligations are directly associated with particular transition combinations. Another benefit is that any parallel assignments to the same variable are rejected by the Event-B static checker. The disadvantage, of course, is that there could be a combinatorial explosion in the number of events generated. In practice though, this is unlikely since, to be fired in parallel, transitions must have the same trigger and be located in parallel Statecharts. A high number of events is also not necessarily a bad thing since they are automatically generated and the main purpose of the Event-B model is for proof which could be simplified by replacing some of the unnecessary sequential steps of the model by a choice. If the number of combinations is excessive it may indicate poor modelling style which can be reduced by introducing more internal triggers. So far our examples have required few or no parallel transitions.

```
 1  context
 2   basis_c  // (generated for SCXML)
 3  sets
 4   SCXML_TRIGGER // all possible triggers
 5  constants
 6   SCXML_FutureInternalTrigger // all possible internal triggers
 7   SCXML_FutureExternalTrigger // all possible external triggers
 8  axioms
 9   partition(SCXML_TRIGGER, SCXML_FutureInternalTrigger, SCXML_FutureExternalTrigger)
10  end
```

Listing 3. Abstract basis context

The following syntax extensions are added to SCXML models to support refinement and invariant verification.

- **refinement** - an integer attribute representing the refinement level at which the parent element should be introduced,
- **invariant** - an invariant property (such as synchronisation of state with ancillary data and other state machines) that holds while in the parent state,
- **guard** - a guard condition of the parent transition (allowing transition conditions to be added at particular refinement levels).

5   SCXML Translation

The translation from SCXML to Event-B is based on an abstract 'basis' that models the 'run to completion' semantics. This basis consists of an Event-B *context* and *machine* that are the same for all input models and are refined by the specific output of the translation. The basis context, Listing 3, introduces a given set of all possible triggers that is partitioned into internal and external ones, some of which will be introduced in future refinements. Refinements partition these trigger sets further to introduce concrete triggers, leaving a new abstract set to represent the remaining triggers yet to be introduced. For example, the IDS model introduces a specific internal trigger, **spi_done**, by partitioning SCXML_FutureInternalTrigger into the singleton {**spi_done**} and a new set, SCXML_FutureInternalTrigger0, representing the remainder.

The basis machine, part of which is shown in Listing 4, declares variables that correspond to the triggers present in the queue at any given time, and a flag, SCXML_uc, that signals when a run to completion macro-step has been completed (no un-triggered transitions are enabled). After initialisation, both trigger queues are empty and SCXML_uc is set to FALSE so that un-triggered transitions are dealt with. The basis machine provides events that describe the generic behaviour of models that follow the run to completion semantics in terms of altering the trigger queues and completion flag. Since new events introduced in a refinement cannot modify existing variables, all future events generated by translation of the specific SCXML model, will refine these abstract events. The abstract event, SCXML_futureExternalTrigger represents the raising of an external trigger. The abstract event, SCXML_futureInternalTransitionSet represents a combination of transitions that are triggered by an internal trigger. The guards of this event ensure prior completion of the previous macro-step. A similar event, SCXML_futureExternalTransitionSet (not shown) represents a combination of transitions that are triggered by an external trigger and has the additional guard that the internal trigger queue is empty. These two triggered transition events reset the completion flag to ensure that any un-triggered transitions that may have become enabled have a chance to fire next. The abstract event SCXML_futureUntriggeredTransitionSet represents a combination of transitions that are un-triggered and may only be fired when the completion flag is unset (FALSE). It leaves the completion flag unset in case further combinations of un-triggered transitions are enabled. All three of these transition events also allow for raising a non-deterministic set of internal triggers. A final abstract event, SCXML_completion, sets the completion flag (TRUE) if it is not already set. At this abstract basis level, this is non-deterministically fired since we do not yet have any detail of what needs to be completed.

The translation of a specific SCXML model comprises two stages as follows. Firstly, all possible combinations of transitions that can fire together are calculated and corresponding events are generated, at appropriate refinement levels, that refine the abstract basis events. If these transitions raise internal triggers, a guard, (e.g. $\{i1, i2, ...\} \subseteq$ SCXML_raisedTrigger, where $i1, i2, ...$ have been added to the internal triggers set), is introduced that defines the raised triggers parameter. The subset constraint leaves it open for more raised triggers to be added by later refinements. For triggered transition combinations, the trigger is specified in a guard (see line 8 of Listing 5) that provides a value for the trigger parameter.

Secondly, the SCXML state-chart is translated into a corresponding iUML-B state-machine whose transitions elaborate (i.e. add state change details to) the possible transition combination events that the transition may be involved in. A transition may fire in parallel with transitions of parallel nested state-machines that have the same (possibly null) trigger. Figure 4 shows the generated iUML-B first refinement level corresponding to the IDS described in Fig. 2b. The main rules for the translation of SCXML features to iUML-B/Event-B can be summarized as follow:

Top level SCXML model: Generates a refinement chain of Event-B machines each containing an initialisation event and a iUML-B state-machine. The depth of the refinement chain is found by searching the SCXML for the maximum refinement annotation.

State: Generates a state in the iUML-B state-machine that has been produced from the container of the SCXML state. A refined state is also added in all of the refinements of the parent iUML-B state-machine. E.g. Fig. 2b, **Initialise Buzzer** → Fig. 4, InitialiseBuzzer.

State invariant: Generates an invariant in the iUML-B state corresponding to the SCXML state that contains the invariant. Added only at the refinement level defined in the invariant (defaults to first level at which containing iUML-

```
 1  machine basis_m sees basis_c // (generated for SCXML)
 2  variables
 3    SCXML_iq  // internal trigger queue
 4    SCXML_eq  // external trigger queue
 5    SCXML_uc  // run to completion flag
 6  invariants
 7    SCXML_iq ⊆ SCXML_FutureInternalTrigger // internal trigger queue
 8    SCXML_eq ⊆ SCXML_FutureExternalTrigger // external trigger queue
 9    SCXML_iq ∩ SCXML_eq= ∅     // queues are disjoint
10    SCXML_uc ∈ BOOL       // completion flag
11  events
12
13    INITIALISATION:
14    begin
15      SCXML_iq := ∅  //internal Q is initially empty
16      SCXML_eq := ∅  //external Q is initially empty
17      SCXML_uc := FALSE //completion is initially FALSE
18    end
19
20    SCXML_futureExternalTrigger:
21    any SCXML_raisedTriggers where
22      SCXML_raisedTriggers ⊆ SCXML_FutureExternalTrigger
23    then
24      SCXML_eq := SCXML_eq ∪ SCXML_raisedTriggers
25    end
26
27    SCXML_futureInternalTransitionSet:
28    any SCXML_it SCXML_raisedTriggers where
29      SCXML_it ∈ SCXML_iq
30      SCXML_uc = TRUE
31      SCXML_raisedTriggers ⊆ SCXML_FutureInternalTrigger
32    then
33      SCXML_uc := FALSE
34      SCXML_iq := (SCXML_iq ∪ SCXML_raisedTriggers) \ {SCXML_it}
35    end
36
37    SCXML_futureUntriggeredTransitionSet:
38    any SCXML_raisedTriggers where
39      SCXML_uc = FALSE
40      SCXML_raisedTriggers ⊆ SCXML_FutureInternalTrigger
41    then
42      SCXML_uc := FALSE
43      SCXML_iq := SCXML_iq ∪ SCXML_raisedTriggers
44    end
45
46  end
```

Listing 4. Abstract basis machine (part of)

B state is introduced). E.g. Fig. 4, Idle = TRUE is generated from an invariant attached (not shown) to the state **Go** of Fig. 2b.

Parallel Region: Generates an iUML-B state-machine in the state corresponding to the owner of the parallel region. The nested iUML-B state-machine is added starting from the refinement level that is annotated on the parallel region and continuing throughout subsequent refinements. E.g. Fig. 2b, right-hand region → Fig. 4, lower nested state-machine.

Initial: Generates an iUML-B initial state, and a transition from it to the iUML-B state indicated in the SCXML initial attribute. The iUML-B initial state and iUML-B transition are added at all refinement levels. The iUML-B

```
 1  spi_done_InitialiseSensor_Wait50ms:
 2  refines SCXML_futureInternalTransitionSet
 3  any SCXML_it SCXML_raisedTriggers where
 4  SCXML_it ∈ SCXML_iq
 5  SCXML_uc = TRUE
 6  SCXML_raisedTriggers ⊆ SCXML_FutureInternalTrigger
 7  InitialiseSensor = TRUE
 8  SCXML_it = spi_done    //trigger for this transition
 9  then
10  SCXML_uc := FALSE
11  SCXML_iq := (SCXML_iq ∪ SCXML_raisedTriggers) \ {SCXML_it}
12  InitialiseSensor := FALSE
13  Wait50ms := TRUE
14  end
```

Listing 5. Event-B event corresponding to internal triggered transition to **Wait 50 ms** state in refinement level 1 shown in Fig. 2a

> transitions are set to elaborate the Event-B INITIALISATION event for that refinement level. E.g. Fig. 2b, initial state and transition in right-hand region → Fig. 4, initial state and transition in lower nested state-machine.

Final: Generates an iUML-B state with a transition to a final state in the state-machine that has been generated from the containing SCXML state. The transition elaborates the same events that are linked to the transitions that exit the parent iUML-B state. The iUML-B state, final state and transition are also added as refined elements to all of the refinements of the parent iUML-B state-machine. (Not used in our example).

Transition: Generates an iUML-B transition in the state-machine that has been generated from the containing SCXML state. The iUML-B transition's source and target are those that have been generated from the SCXML transition's source and target states. The transition elaborates generated Event-B events according to the rules given in Sect. 5. The iUML-B transition and elaborated Event-B events are also added as corresponding refined elements in all of the refinements of the parent iUML-B state-machine. E.g. Fig. 2b, send_message → Fig. 4, send_message_Idle_SendingMessage.

A tool to automatically translate SCXML models into iUML-B has been produced. The tool is based on the *Eclipse Modelling Framework* (EMF) and uses an SCXML meta-model provided by Sirius [4] which has good support for extensibility. The iUML-B state-machine is subsequently translated into Event-B using the standard iUML-B translation [18] which provides variables to model the current state and guards and actions to model the state changes that transitions perform.

6   Verification of Intrusion Detection System

One of our main goals is to express properties in SCXML intermediate refinements and prove them via translation to Event-B. In this section we illustrate how this can be done in the IDS example.

Properties about the synchronisation of parallel state-machines (such as $Go = TRUE \Rightarrow Idle = TRUE$) can be difficult to verify for all scenarios via simulation in SCXML. Proof of such properties is a major benefit of translating into Event-B. Furthermore, in order to benefit from the abstraction provided by Event-B, we would like to prove such things at abstract levels before the complication of further details are introduced. Typically these further details concern the raising of internal triggers that contribute to the synchronisation we wish to verify. Therefore additional constraints, that are an abstraction of the missing details, are needed about triggers in order to perform the proof.

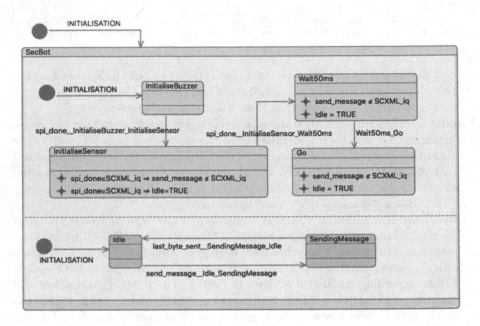

Fig. 4. State invariants to be verified at refinement level 1.

Figure 4 is the generated iUML-B showing state invariants (textual properties with a star icon inside states) to be verified. Note that the invariants are added to the SCXML model but are easier to visualise in the iUML-B with the current tooling. The main aim is to show the property $Idle = TRUE$ holds in state Go. This is true because after sending the message while in InitialiseSensor, no other messages are triggered by the ASIC, so the SPI subsystem stays in the Idle state indefinitely. To enable the provers to discharge the proof obligation we work back along the ASIC's sequence of states. That is, $Idle = TRUE$ is maintained in state Go if it holds in state Wait50ms and no send_message triggers are raised by the entry transition Wait50ms_Go nor once the ASIC subsystem is in state Go. To ensure this we add a guard $send\_message \notin SCXML\_raisedTriggers$ to Wait50ms_Go to prevent any future refinement from raising the trigger send_message. (Currently, this is added verbatim but we envision a 'doesn't raise' notation to avoid the user having to reference the translation artefact, SCXML_raisedTriggers). We also need to prevent any future transitions from raising this trigger in the state Go. To automate this for all abstract 'future' events, they could be automatically generated and added to satisfy all user invariants concerning the raising of internal triggers regardless of whether they are violated in future levels. For example, the guard Go = TRUE $\Rightarrow$ send_message $\notin$ SCXML_raisedTriggers needs to be automatically added to the three 'basis' events, SCXML_futureUntriggeredTransitionSet, SCXML_futureInternalTransitionSet and SCXML_futureExternalTransitionSet to prove they do not break the property being verified. If it is not obeyed by future transitions, guard strengthening proof obligations will fail, making it obvious where the problems lie. As indicated above, we now need to prove by similar means that Idle=TRUE holds in state Wait50ms. In this case, however, we can only say that Idle=TRUE in state InitialiseSensor after the SPI-system finishes sending the message and raises the trigger, spi_done. Hence the state invariant for InitialiseSensor becomes spi_done$\in$SCXML_iq $\Rightarrow$ Idle = TRUE. In order to prove this we again need a corresponding state invariant about send_message and need to make sure that the SPI system will never raise send_message. We also ensure it does not raise spi_done until it is finished. With these invariants and additional guards the Rodin automatic provers are able to prove all proof obligations and hence verify that the SPI system remains in Idle after servicing the 'Initialise Sensor' message.

In order to prove properties at an abstract level we constrain the behaviour to be added in later refinements. For example, we needed to add a guard to specify that a transition does not raise a particular trigger in any future refinement. The abstract constraints should not appear in later refinements when the details have been finalised. To do this we could introduce ranges into our refinement attributes.

7   Related Work

Refinement of UML Statecharts has been studied previously in [6,11,14,15,21]. In [14], the authors consider a coalgebraic description of UML Statecharts, and define an equivalence relationship and a behavioural refinement notion between Statecharts. In [21], the authors define a structured operational semantics of Statecharts based on label transition systems. Behaviour refinements are then constructed based on this semantics. The authors prove that a "safe-extension" of UML Statecharts is a correct behavioural refinement. In [11,15], formal refinement rules are developed for SysML, including Statecharts, based on the corresponding process refinement rules of the Compass Modelling Language. *The issue of run to completion with respect to refinement is not considered explicitly nor shown in any examples.* In [6], the authors propose a "purely additive" refinement process where no elements (e.g. events, guards, etc.) of the original model can be removed and the "external" behaviour of the model is therefore preserved. This refinement process is similar to Event-B "superposition" refinement which we use in our translation.

In our paper, we focus on the run-to-completion semantics of Statecharts, whereas none of the above work deals with it explicitly. Furthermore, the refinement process supported in [6,11,14,15] is based on refinement patterns (called refinement rules/laws), whereas we rely on the more general theory of refinement, given by the proof obligations of Event-B, for proving the refinement relationship between Statecharts.

8 Conclusion

We have shown how a slightly extended and annotated Statechart, with a typical 'run to completion' semantic, can be translated into the Event-B notation for verification of synchronisation properties using the Event-B theorem proving tools. Furthermore, borrowing from the refinement concepts of Event-B, we introduce a notion of refinement to Statecharts and demonstrate how the proof of a property at an abstract level, helps formulate constraints that must apply (and will be verified to do so) in further refinements.

9 Future Work

In future work we will continue to experiment with different examples to explore the alternative translation strategies in more detail. In particular, further work on refinement of the micro/macro-step and whether correspondence of macro-steps can be relaxed; whether more complex refinement techniques could be supported (for example, using ranges in refinement annotations) would be useful; supporting/comparing alternative variations of semantics (by generating a different basis/scheduler for the translation). For our interpretation of Statecharts in iUML-B, we used the 'run-to-completion' semantics of Statecharts. In particular, we have carefully designed our translated model such that the semantics is captured as a generic abstract model, which is subsequently refined by the translation of the SCXML model. An advantage of this approach is that we can easily adapt the basis model with other alternative semantics [5] without changing the translation of the SCXML model.

We will also demonstrate the scalability of the translation on more realistic industrial examples. The Haemodialysis Machine case study [13] from the ABZ 2016 conference would make a good test case since its highly sequential processes are natural for a state-chart representation and results can be compared with existing iUML-B solutions [10]. The ERTMS Hybrid Level 3 case study [9] from the ABZ 2018 conference is also an industrial example which would test the method. This case study would require lifting of the output models to a generalised set of instances using a model composition technique that we have been developing for this purpose.

All data supporting this study are openly available from the University of Southampton repository at https://doi.org/10.5258/SOTON/D0693.

Acknowledgment. The authors would like to thank Jason Michnovicz for developing the IDS example used throughout the manuscript.

References

1. Abrial, J.-R.: Modeling in Event-B: System and Software Engineering. Cambridge University Press, Cambridge (2010)
2. Abrial, J.-R., Butler, M., Hallerstede, S., Hoang, T.S., Mehta, F., Voisin, L.: Rodin: An open toolset for modelling and reasoning in Event-B. Softw. Tools Technol. Transf. **12**(6), 447–466 (2010)
3. David, A., Möller, M.O., Yi, W.: Formal verification of UML statecharts with real-time extensions. In: Kutsche, R.-D., Weber, H. (eds.) FASE 2002. LNCS, vol. 2306, pp. 218–232. Springer, Heidelberg (2002). https://doi.org/10.1007/3-540-45923-5_15
4. Eclipse Foundation: Sirius Project Website. https://eclipse.org/sirius/overview.html. Accessed Mar 2016
5. Eshuis, R.: Reconciling statechart semantics. Sci. Comput. Program. **74**(3), 65–99 (2009)
6. Hansen, C., Syriani, E., Lucio, L.: Towards controlling refinements of statecharts. CoRR, abs/1503.07266 (2015)
7. Harel, D.: Statecharts: a visual formalism for complex systems. Sci. Comput. Program. **8**(3), 231–274 (1987)
8. Hoang, T.S.: An introduction to the Event-B modelling method. In: Romanovsky, A., Thomas, M. (eds.) Industrial Deployment of System Engineering Methods, pp. 211–236. Springer, Heidelberg (2013)
9. Hoang, T.S., Butler, M., Reichl, K.: The hybrid ERTMS/ETCS level 3 case study. In: Butler, M., Raschke, A., Hoang, T.S., Reichl, K. (eds.) ABZ 2018. LNCS, vol. 10817, pp. 251–261. Springer, Cham (2018). https://doi.org/10.1007/978-3-319-91271-4_17
10. Hoang, T.S., Snook, C., Ladenberger, L., Butler, M.: Validating the requirements and design of a hemodialysis machine using iUML-B, BMotion studio, and co-simulation. In: Butler, M., Schewe, K.-D., Mashkoor, A., Biro, M. (eds.) ABZ 2016. LNCS, vol. 9675, pp. 360–375. Springer, Cham (2016). https://doi.org/10.1007/978-3-319-33600-8_31
11. Lima, L., et al.: An integrated semantics for reasoning about SysML design models using refinement. Softw. Syst. Model. **16**(3), 875–902 (2017)
12. Maraninchi, F.: The Argos language: graphical representation of automata and description of reactive systems. In: IEEE Workshop on Visual Languages (1991)
13. Mashkoor, A.: The hemodialysis machine case study. In: Butler, M., Schewe, K.-D., Mashkoor, A., Biro, M. (eds.) ABZ 2016. LNCS, vol. 9675, pp. 329–343. Springer, Cham (2016). https://doi.org/10.1007/978-3-319-33600-8_29
14. Meng, S., Naixiao, Z., Barbosa, L.S.: On semantics and refinement of UML statecharts: a coalgebraic view. In: Proceedings of the Second International Conference on Software Engineering and Formal Methods, SEFM 2004, pp. 164–173, September 2004
15. Miyazawa, A., Cavalcanti, A.: Formal refinement in SysML. In: Albert, E., Sekerinski, E. (eds.) IFM 2014. LNCS, vol. 8739, pp. 155–170. Springer, Cham (2014). https://doi.org/10.1007/978-3-319-10181-1_10
16. Morris, K., Snook, C.: Reconciling SCXML statechart representations and Event-B lower level semantics. In: HCCV - Workshop on High-Consequence Control Verification (2016)
17. Rumbaugh, J., Jacobson, I., Booch, G.: Unified Modeling Language Reference Manual, 2nd edn. Pearson Higher Education, Upper Saddle River (2004)

18. Snook, C.: iUML-B statemachines. In: Proceedings of the Rodin Workshop 2014, Toulouse, France (2014). http://eprints.soton.ac.uk/365301/
19. Snook, C., Butler, M.: UML-B: formal modeling and design aided by UML. ACM Trans. Softw. Eng. Methodol. **15**(1), 92–122 (2006)
20. Snook, C., Savicks, V., Butler, M.: Verification of UML models by translation to UML-B. In: Aichernig, B.K., de Boer, F.S., Bonsangue, M.M. (eds.) FMCO 2010. LNCS, vol. 6957, pp. 251–266. Springer, Heidelberg (2011). https://doi.org/10.1007/978-3-642-25271-6_13
21. Szasz, N., Vilanova, P.: Behavioral refinements of UML-Statecharts. Technical report RT 10–13, Universidad de la República, Montevideo, Uruguay (2010)
22. W3C: State chart XML SCXML: State machine notation for control abstraction. http://www.w3.org/TR/scxml/. Accessed Sept 2015

Abstraction Refinement with Path Constraints for 3-Valued Bounded Model Checking

Nils Timm[(⊠)] and Stefan Gruner

Department of Computer Science, University of Pretoria, Pretoria, South Africa
{ntimm,sgruner}@cs.up.ac.za

Abstract. We present an abstraction refinement-based technique for checking safety properties of software. The technique employs predicate abstraction and SAT-based 3-valued bounded model checking. In contrast to classical refinement techniques where a single state space model is iteratively explored and refined with predicates, our approach is as follows: We use a coarsely-abstracted model of the full state space where we check for abstract witness paths for the property of interest. For each detected abstract witness we construct a partial model whose state space is restricted to refinements of the witness only. On the partial models we check whether the witness is real or spurious. We eliminate spurious witnesses in the full model via constraints, which do not increase the state space complexity. Our technique terminates when a real witness in a partial model can be detected, or no more witnesses in the full model exist. The approach enables verification with a reduced state space complexity.

1 Introduction

3-valued abstraction (3VA) [12] is a technique for reducing the complexity of software verification. It proceeds by generating an abstract state space model of a software system over predicates with the possible values *true*, *false* and *unknown*, where the latter represents the loss of information due to abstraction. The evaluation of temporal logic properties on such models is known as *3-valued model checking* (3MC) [2]. Under 3VA both *true* and *false* model checking results can be transferred to the modelled software system, whereas an *unknown* result indicates that the current model is too coarse for a definite outcome. In the latter case a so-called *unconfirmed witness* is produced, which is an execution path in the abstract state space with some *unknown* transitions or predicates that characterises a potential violation of the property of interest. *Witness-guided abstraction refinement* [14] then iteratively adds further predicates to the model until a previously *unconfirmed* witness turns out to be *definite*, or no more witnesses exist. The described approach follows the classical *abstract–check–refine* paradigm where a single model that represents the entire system is iteratively refined. Since each refinement iteration involves an exponential growth of the state space to be explored, this approach can easily suffer from state explosion.

© Springer Nature Switzerland AG 2019
C. Artho and P. C. Ölveczky (Eds.): FTSCS 2018, CCIS 1008, pp. 139–157, 2019.
https://doi.org/10.1007/978-3-030-12988-0_9

Here, we present a novel abstraction refinement technique that facilitates verification with an improved state space complexity. We focus on the verification of *safety* properties of concurrent software systems. Examples are mutual exclusion and absence of deadlocks, which are vital properties in many safety-critical applications. In our approach we make use of two kinds of state space models: We use a *full model* that considers all parts of the underlying system, and we use *partial models* that are restricted to certain execution paths. Both full and partial models are subject to abstraction. But only the partial models are refined by adding predicates, whereas the full model is iteratively pruned via *path constraints* derived from partial models. For this, we define an extension of 3-valued model checking *with path constraints*. Our new technique proceeds as follows: In the same manner as in the classical approach, we start with a coarsely-abstracted full model of the system and we check whether the property of interest can be proven or refuted. If the check returns *unknown* along with an unconfirmed witness, then we derive new predicates for refinement. Now instead of refining the full model, we construct a new partial model that is narrowed down to refinements of the witness only. Checking the partial model either proves the previously unconfirmed witness to be *definite* or to be *spurious*. In the first case we are done. In the latter case we generate a constraint for ruling out the spurious witness. In the subsequent iteration we return to the full model and prune its state space via the generated *spurious witness constraint*. The procedure terminates when either no more witnesses in the full model exist or a definite witness in a partial model can be detected.

Our approach reduces the state space complexity in two ways. Refinement is only applied to *partial* models whose state space is already strongly limited by being restricted to refinements of a certain unconfirmed witness. The state space of the full model is pruned by spurious witness constraints derived from partial models. But the refinement predicates that were used in the partial model to derive these constraints do *not* have to be added to the full model. Hence, we gain precision in the full model without enlarging its state space. The price that we pay is an increased number of iterations until definite result can be obtained. The actual number depends on the *strength* of generated constraints in terms of ruling out spurious behaviour. Thus, we develop a *constraint strengthening* concept: The spuriousness of a witness typically originates from a *fragment* of the path that it represents. A constraint for excluding all paths that exhibit such a *spurious fragment* is naturally stronger than a constraint that just excludes the specific witness. Our constraint strengthening concept allows us to determine spurious fragments of witnesses and to rule them out via *spurious fragment constraints*. In general, a spurious fragment refers to a *particular position* along a path that starts in an initial state of the modelled system. Hence, a corresponding constraint would only rule out paths that exhibit the spurious fragment at *exactly this position*. We develop a second strengthening technique that is based on checking whether a spurious fragment is *initial state independent*. We show that in case of initial state independence, a constraint can be shifted such that it rules out all paths that exhibit the spurious fragment at some *arbitrary position*.

We implemented our refinement technique on top of a 3-valued bounded model checker. Our tool encodes the model checking problems to be solved in propositional logic. Hence, model checking is reduced to SAT solving. The SAT scenario allows us to efficiently conduct constraint generation and strengthening: The *spuriousness* of a witness translates to the *unsatisfiability* of a propositional logic formula. While the entire unsatisfiable formula characterises the entire spurious witness, an *unsatisfiable core* of the formula characterises a spurious fragment. Today's SAT solvers can efficiently extract small or minimal unsatisfiable cores [11], which we exploit in our approach for generating strong *spurious fragment constraints*. Likewise, checking whether a spurious fragment depends on the initial state translates into SAT-based checking whether the unsatisfiable core contains the encoding of the initial state. In experiments we show that our constraint-based verification approach allows for significant performance improvements in comparison to classical abstraction refinement.

2   Abstracted Concurrent Software Systems

We start with a brief introduction to the systems that we want to verify and the abstraction technique that we use in our work. A *concurrent system* Sys consists of a number of possibly non-uniform processes P_1 to P_n composed in parallel: $Sys = \|_{i=1}^{n} P_i$. It is defined over a set of variables $Var = Var_{Sys} \cup Var_{PC}$. Var_{Sys} is a set of arbitrary system variables, whereas Var_{PC} is a special set that holds for each process P_i a dedicated program counter variable pc_i ranging over binary control locations from a set Loc_i. Locations of a process are labelled with guarded commands with regard to system variables and with a reference to the subsequent location. The form of a guarded command is $g : v_1 := e_1, \ldots, v_m := e_m$ where $v_1, \ldots, v_m \in Var_{Sys}$ and $g, e_1, \ldots e_m$ are expressions over Var_{Sys}. The state space over Var is the set S_{Var} of all type-correct valuations of the variables. An example of a system implementing mutual exclusion is depicted below (Fig. 1).

$$y : \textsf{semaphore where } y = 1;$$

$$P_1 :: \begin{bmatrix} \textsf{loop forever do} \\ \begin{bmatrix} \textsf{0: acquire } (y,1); \\ \textsf{1: CRITICAL} \\ \quad \textsf{release } (y,1); \end{bmatrix} \end{bmatrix} \| P_2 :: \begin{bmatrix} \textsf{loop forever do} \\ \begin{bmatrix} \textsf{0: acquire } (y,1); \\ \textsf{1: CRITICAL} \\ \quad \textsf{release } (y,1); \end{bmatrix} \end{bmatrix}$$

Fig. 1. Concurrent system implementing mutual exclusion

Here we have two processes operating on a shared counting semaphore variable y. The semantics of the semaphore operations are as follows: $acquire(y,1) = (y > 0) : y := y - 1$ and $release(y,1) = (true) : y := y + 1$. We assume that for any Sys a deterministic initialisation of all its variables is given in terms of a predicate expression $Init$, e.g., $Init = (y = 1) \wedge (pc_1 = 0) \wedge (pc_2 = 0)$ for our example. A computation corresponds to a possibly infinite sequence of commands where in each step a process is non-deterministically selected and the guarded command at its current location is attempted to be executed. If the execution is not blocked by a guard, the variables are updated according to the assignment part and the process advances to the next location. A computation can be likewise considered as sequence of states $s_0 s_1 s_2 \ldots$ where the transition from s_i to s_{i+1} correctly characterises the execution of the associated guarded command.

We use *3-valued abstraction* [12] to reduce the state space complexity of our systems, which gives us abstract systems defined over predicates with the domain $3 = \{true, false, unknown\}$ which we typically abbreviate by $\{t, f, u\}$. The value u represents the loss of details due to abstraction. 3-valued abstraction generates an approximation in the sense that all definite verification results (t, f) obtained for an abstract system can be transferred to the concrete system, whereas a u result tells us that the current level of abstraction is too coarse. We now give a short overview of 3-valued abstraction which is based on the Kleene logic $\mathcal{K}_3$ [6]. Details of the technique can be found in [12]. In abstract systems guarded commands do not refer to concrete variables but to abstract predicates A_{Sys} over Var_{Sys}. Abstract commands have the form $choice(a, b)$: $p_1 := choice(a_1, b_1), \ldots, p_m := choice(a_m, b_m)$ where $p_1, \ldots, p_m \in A_{Sys}$ and $a, b, a_1, b_1, \ldots$ are expressions over A_{Sys}. $choice(a, b)$-expressions have the following semantics: $s(choice(a, b)) = t$ if $s(a) = t$, $s(choice(a, b)) = f$ if $s(b) = t$, $s(choice(a, b)) = u$ otherwise. Predicates in A_{Sys} may be set to u by an abstract command. While this abstraction reduces the complexity induced by system variables, it preserves the original control flow. For this, the set of 2-valued predicates $A_{PC} = \{(pc_i = j) \mid i \in [1, n], j \in Loc_i\}$ is used that covers all locations of the system. The overall set of predicates is thus $A = A_{Sys} \cup A_{PC}$.

3   3-Valued Bounded Model Checking

Verification tasks with regard to the abstracted systems can be formalised as model checking problems such that the model checking result correctly characterises the computational behaviour of the system [12]. In this section, we briefly review *3-valued bounded model checking* (3BMC) [15] and we introduce an extension of 3BMC, that makes use of *path constraints*. In 3BMC state spaces of abstracted systems are modelled as *3-valued Kripke structures* (KS):

Definition 1 (3-Valued Kripke Structure). *A 3-valued Kripke structure over a set of atomic predicates A is a tuple $M = (S, I, R, L)$ where*

- *S is a finite set of states,*
- *$I \subseteq S$ is a set of initial states,*
- *$R : S \times S \to 3$ is a transition function such that $\forall s \in S : \exists s' \in S$ with $R(s, s') \in \{t, u\}$,*
- *$L : S \times A \to 3$ is a labelling function that associates a truth value with each atomic predicate in each state.*

A Kripke structure representing the state space of our example system can be defined over the predicate set $A = \{(pc_1 = 0), (pc_1 = 1), (pc_2 = 0), (pc_2 = 1)\}$. Here we only have predicates over the control flow, but so far no predicates over the variable y. We assume that all states have a *unique labelling*, i.e. a pair $s, s' \in S$ with $\forall p \in A : L(s, p) = L(s', p)$ implies $s = s'$. A unique labelling is guaranteed by the abstraction technique that we use. Given an $s \in S$ and an expression pe over A, then $s(pe)$ denotes the valuation of pe in s. The set of initial states of a structure modelling our example system abstracted over A can be defined as $I = \{s \in S \mid s((pc_1 = 0) \wedge (pc_2 = 0)) = t\}$. We also introduce the function $T : S \rightarrow \mathcal{P}(A)$ where $T(s) = \{p \in A \mid L(s, p) = t\}$ and the function $F : S \rightarrow \mathcal{P}(A)$ where $F(s) = \{p \in A \mid L(s, p) = f\}$. Thus, $T(s)$ returns the set of predicates that evaluate to *true* in s, whereas $F(s)$ returns the set of predicates that evaluate to *false* in s. States are considered as parts of *paths*:

Definition 2 (Path). *Let* $M = (S, I, R, L)$ *be a 3-valued Kripke structure. A path* π *of* M *is a sequence of states* $s_0 s_1 s_2 \ldots$ *with* $s_0 \in I$ *and* $\forall i : R(s_i, s_{i+1}) \in \{t, u\}$. π_i *denotes the i-th state of* π *and* Π_M *denotes the set of all paths in* M.

While paths of a Kripke structure can be infinitely long, bounded model checking looks at finite k-prefixes $\pi_0 \ldots \pi_k$ of paths π where $k \in \mathbb{N}$ is the so-called bound. On such prefixes we can evaluate temporal logic properties. Here we use the *bounded temporal logic* BTL which corresponds to the k-bounded fragment of the linear temporal logic LTL.

Definition 3 (Syntax of BTL). *Let* A *be a predicate set and* $k \in \mathbb{N}$ *be a bound. The set of k-bounded temporal logic formulae BTL over* A *is defined as:*

- *if* $p \in A$ *and* $i \in [0, k]$ *then* $p_i \in BTL$ *and* $\neg p_i \in BTL$,
- *if* $\psi \in BTL$ *then* $\neg \psi \in BTL$,
- *if* $\psi \in BTL$ *and* $\psi' \in BTL$ *then* $\psi \vee \psi' \in BTL$ *and* $\psi \wedge \psi' \in BTL$.

Hence, a BTL formula refers to atomic predicates $p \in A$ where each p occurs indexed with values between 0 and the bound k. The 3-valued semantics of BTL in terms of prefixes of paths π is defined as follows:

Definition 4 (3-Valued Evaluation of BTL). *Let* π *be a path of a Kripke structure* $M = (S, I, R, L)$ *over* A, *let* $k \in \mathbb{N}$ *and* $i \in [0, k]$. *Then the evaluation of a k-bounded BTL formula* ψ *on* π, *written* $[\pi \models \psi]_k$, *is inductively defined as:*

$$
\begin{aligned}
[\pi \models p_i]_k &= L(\pi_i, p) \wedge \bigwedge_{j=0}^{i-1} R(\pi_j, \pi_{j+1}) \\
[\pi \models \neg p_i]_k &= \neg L(\pi_i, p) \wedge \bigwedge_{j=0}^{i-1} R(\pi_j, \pi_{j+1}) \\
[\pi \models \psi \vee \psi']_k &= [\pi \models \psi]_k \vee [\pi \models \psi']_k \\
[\pi \models \psi \wedge \psi']_k &= [\pi \models \psi]_k \wedge [\pi \models \psi']_k \\
[\pi \models \neg(\psi \vee \psi')]_k &= [\pi \models \neg\psi]_k \wedge [\pi \models \neg\psi']_k \\
[\pi \models \neg(\psi \wedge \psi')]_k &= [\pi \models \neg\psi]_k \vee [\pi \models \neg\psi']_k
\end{aligned}
$$

The evaluation of a BTL formula on a prefix of a path of a 3-valued Kripke structure can either yield t, f, or u. We primarily use BTL for specifying *properties of interest* ψ whose validity is checked for a given Kripke structure. For our example, the formula $\psi = \bigvee_{i=0}^{k} \neg Safe_i$ with $Safe_i = \neg((pc_1 = 1)_i \wedge (pc_2 = 1)_i)$ characterises the k-bounded violation of mutual exclusion. Since bounded model checking is typically performed *incrementally* with regard to k, it can be assumed that in previous bound iterations $k' < k$ no property violation could be detected. Hence, it is sufficient to check whether the formula $\psi = (\bigwedge_{i=0}^{k-1} Safe_i) \wedge \neg Safe_k$ holds in order to detect a k-bounded violation of mutual exclusion. Checking such conjunctive formulae is generally more efficient than checking disjunctive formulae.

Besides for specifying properties of interest, we also use BTL for defining *path constraints* σ. Our novel path constraint concept allows to limit the number of paths that need to be considered during model checking. In our later abstraction refinement approach, we distinguish between promising path prefixes that we want to focus on and spurious prefixes that we want to exclude. Both, *focussing on* and *excluding* certain prefixes $\pi_0 \ldots \pi_k$ can be carried out via constraints:

Definition 5 (Path Constraints Corresponding to Prefixes). *Let $\pi_0 \ldots \pi_k$ be a path prefix of a Kripke structure. Then the corresponding* focussing *constraint is*

$$\sigma(\pi_0 \ldots \pi_k) := \bigwedge_{i=0}^{k} \left(\left(\bigwedge_{p \in T(\pi_i)} p_i \right) \wedge \left(\bigwedge_{p \in F(\pi_i)} \neg p_i \right) \right)$$

and the corresponding excluding *constraint is* $\overline{\sigma}(\pi_0 \ldots \pi_k) := \neg\sigma(\pi_0 \ldots \pi_k)$.

Given a 3-valued Kripke structure M and a set of path constraints Σ, then $\Pi_M^{\Sigma} = \{\pi \in \Pi_M \mid \forall \sigma \in \Sigma : [\pi \models \sigma]_k = t\}$ is the set of paths of M that satisfy Σ. 3BMC with path constraints is now defined as follows:

Definition 6 (3-Valued Bounded Model Checking with Constraints). *Let $M = (S, I, R, L)$ be a 3-valued Kripke structure over A, $k \in \mathbb{N}$, ψ a BTL formula, and Σ a set of path constraints. The corresponding universal model checking problem is*

$$\underset{A}{\overset{\Sigma}{}}[M \models_{\forall} \psi]_k = \bigwedge_{\pi \in \Pi_M^{\Sigma}} [\pi \models \psi]_k$$

and the corresponding existential model checking problem is

$$\underset{A}{\overset{\Sigma}{}}[M \models_{\exists} \psi]_k = \bigvee_{\pi \in \Pi_M^{\Sigma}} [\pi \models \psi]_k.$$

Universal model checking can always be transformed into existential model checking based on the equation $\underset{A}{\overset{\Sigma}{}}[M \models_{\forall} \psi]_k = \neg \underset{A}{\overset{\Sigma}{}}[M \models_{\exists} \neg\psi]_k$. From now on we only consider the existential case, since it is the basis of SAT-based bounded model checking. We assume that ψ characterises the violation of a desirable property, and the form of ψ is $(\bigwedge_{i=0}^{k-1} Safe_i) \wedge \neg Safe_k$ where $Safe$ is an arbitrary expression over A and $Safe_i = Safe[p \leftarrow p_i \mid p \in A]$. We now show how 3BMC can be combined with classical abstraction refinement that iteratively extends the set A until a definite verification result for the input system abstracted over A can be obtained.

4   Abstraction Refinement

Solving $\frac{\Sigma}{A}[M \models_\exists (\bigwedge_{i=0}^{k-1} Safe_i) \wedge \neg Safe_k]_k$, where M models the state space of the input system abstracted over A, has the possible outcomes *true*, *unknown* and *false*. A *true* result indicates that there exists a path $\pi \in \Pi_M^\Sigma$ such that its k-prefix $\omega = \pi_0 \dots \pi_k$ is a *definite witness* for the formula $(\bigwedge_{i=0}^{k-1} Safe_i) \wedge \neg Safe_k$.

Definition 7 (Definite Witness). *Let* $\frac{\Sigma}{A}[M \models_\exists (\bigwedge_{i=0}^{k-1} Safe_i) \wedge \neg Safe_k]_k$ *be a 3BMC problem where Safe is over A and* $Safe_i = Safe[p \leftarrow p_i \mid p \in A]$. *A* definite witness *for the property is a prefix* $\omega = \pi_0 \dots \pi_k$ *of a path* $\pi \in \Pi_M^\Sigma$ *with*

$$\pi_k(Safe) = false \text{ and } \forall 0 \le i < k : R(\pi_i, \pi_{i+1}) = true$$

Since we assume an incremental approach with regard to k, the safety of the $(k-1)$-prefix $\pi_0 \dots \pi_{k-1}$ is guaranteed. Thus, for finding a witness we only have to check the safety of the state π_k. A definite witness implies that a safety violation has been detected, and thus, no further model checking runs are required.

An *unknown* result in 3-valued bounded model checking indicates that there exists a path $\pi \in \Pi_M^\Sigma$ such that its k-prefix $\omega = \pi_0 \dots \pi_k$ is an *unconfirmed witness* for the BTL formula $(\bigwedge_{i=0}^{k-1} Safe_i) \wedge \neg Safe_k$.

Definition 8 (Unconfirmed Witness). *Let* $\frac{\Sigma}{A}[M \models_\exists (\bigwedge_{i=0}^{k-1} Safe_i) \wedge \neg Safe_k]_k$ *be as above. An* unconfirmed witness *is a prefix* $\omega = \pi_0 \dots \pi_k$ *with either*

$$\pi_k(Safe) = unknown, \text{ or}$$
$$\pi_k(Safe) = false \text{ and } \exists 0 \le i < k \text{ with } R(\pi_i, \pi_{i+1}) = unknown$$

For our running example with $A = \{(pc_1 = 0), (pc_1 = 1), (pc_2 = 0), (pc_2 = 1)\}$, bound $k = 2$ and $Safe = \neg((pc_1 = 1) \wedge (pc_2 = 1))$ we obtain such an *unknown* result and the corresponding unconfirmed witness

$$\omega = \pi_0 \pi_1 \pi_2 = (0,0)_0 \xrightarrow{u} (1,0)_1 \xrightarrow{u} (1,1)_2.$$

In this representation $(l_1, l_2)_i$ denotes that in state π_i process P_1 is at location l_1 and P_2 is at location l_2. Moreover, $\xrightarrow{u}$ denotes an *unknown* transition between states. The witness ω is *unconfirmed* because it reaches the state π_2 where safety is definitely violated, but *unknown* transitions are taken to reach this state. An unconfirmed witness implies that the current level of abstraction, characterised by the predicate set A, is too coarse for a definite result. In this case, refinement in the sense of extending the set A is required. We then have to build the Kripke structure corresponding to the extended set A and search for a witness in its state space.

A *false* result in 3BMC indicates that there exists neither a definite nor an unconfirmed witness $\omega = \pi_0 \dots \pi_k$ for ψ. However, a property violation might still exist for a larger bound. In this case, k has to be incremented until either a definite witness can be detected or a completeness threshold is reached [9].

We now focus on the case where an *unconfirmed witness* has been detected. We present a basic abstraction refinement algorithm AR that adds predicates to the set A until a definite result can be obtained. For convenience, we assume a *fixed* bound k. In [14] we defined a procedure *analyseWitness*. It takes an unconfirmed witness as an input and, based on the guarded commands of the underlying system and the weakest precondition calculus, derives predicates for refinement. For our example with the abstracted mutual exclusion system Sys and the unconfirmed witness $\omega = \pi_0 \pi_1 \pi_2$ we get $analyseWitness(\pi_0 \pi_1 \pi_2) = \{(y > 0), \overline{(y > 0)}\}$. This is the set containing the guard $(y > 0)$, associated with the *acquire* operation in Sys, as well as its complement $\overline{(y > 0)}$[1]. The basic abstraction refinement algorithm AR that utilises *analyseWitness* is defined as follows:

Algorithm 1. $AR(Sys = \|_{i=1}^{n} P_i, Init, \psi, k)$

---

1   $A := \{(pc_i = j) \mid i \in [1, n], \; j \in Loc_i\} \cup atoms(\psi), \;\; \Sigma := \emptyset$

2   **loop forever do** /*refinement loop*/

3   **if** $_A^{\Sigma}[M \models_\exists \psi]_k = false$ **then**

4 | **return** *false*, 'no witness for safety violation of length k exists'

5   **if** $_A^{\Sigma}[M \models_\exists \psi]_k = true$ and witness ω **then**

6 | **return** *true*, 'ω is a definite witness for safety violation'

7   **if** $_A^{\Sigma}[M \models_\exists \psi]_k = unknown$ and witness ω **then**

8 | $A := A \cup analyseWitness(\omega)$

AR takes a system Sys, an initial state predicate $Init$, a BTL formula $\psi = (\bigwedge_{i=0}^{k-1} Safe_i) \wedge \neg Safe_k$ and a bound k as an input. The predicate set A is initialised with control flow predicates and with the atomic predicates that occur in ψ. The constraint set Σ remains empty throughout the run of the basic algorithm. After initialisation, the Kripke structure M representing the input system abstracted over A is built and the corresponding 3BMC problem is solved. In case of t and f results the algorithm terminates. In case of a u result, an unconfirmed witness ω is generated and new predicates are derived via *analyseWitness*. The predicate set of the next iteration is defined by the predicates of the current iteration joined with the newly derived predicates. Now the steps of model checking the Kripke structure corresponding to the extended predicates set and deriving

---

[1] In contrast to the Boolean predicates over the control flow, predicates over system variables have a *3-valued* domain as they may evaluate to u due to abstraction. In order to enable the later reduction of 3BMC to SAT, there must be a complementary predicate $\overline{p}$ with $\overline{p} \equiv \neg p$ for each predicate p over system variables [16].

new refinement predicates are repeated until a definite result can be obtained. AR can be easily extended by an outer loop that ranges over the bound k from 0 to a completeness threshold, where k gets incremented each time when the model checking result is f. Such thresholds for safety properties are linear in the number of abstract states [9]. For simplicity, we omit this extension here. The termination of AR is guaranteed for finite-state systems. In [14] we showed that the result of AR correctly characterises the computational behaviour of the input system.

For our example with $k = 2$ AR terminates with an f result after one refinement step that adds the predicates $(y > 0)$ and $\overline{(y > 0)}$. Thus, there does not exist a witness of length 2 that violates mutual exclusion. We also obtain f when we set the bound to $k = 12$, which is a completeness threshold for this model checking problem. Hence, based on an abstraction over the set $A = \{(pc_1 = 0), (pc_1 = 1), (pc_2 = 0), (pc_2 = 1), (y > 0), \overline{(y > 0)}\}$ we can conclude that mutual exclusion is not violated for the system. The major challenge in model checking is still the state explosion problem. Each additional predicate involves an exponential growth of the state space to be explored. In the next section, we introduce an enhanced abstraction refinement algorithm that allows to reduce the number of predicates that are actually considered during model checking. Our enhancement is based on our previously introduced path constraint concept.

5   Witness Refinement and Constraint Generation

The algorithm AR that we presented in the previous section is based on the classical *abstract–check–refine* loop [3]. A drawback of such an approach is that the state space grows exponentially with each loop iteration. Here we introduce an enhanced algorithm based on the loop

$$abstract—check—\big(refine\,Witness—check\,Witness\big)^* —generate\,Constraint$$

where the * denotes that the steps in brackets belong to an internal loop with potentially multiple iterations. The idea of our approach is as follows. If abstraction-based model checking on a model that covers the full state space returns an unconfirmed witness ω, then we start an internal refinement loop with a partial model that is restricted to refinements of the witness ω only. The partial model can be straightforwardly obtained by using the focussing path constraint $\sigma(\omega)$. The *witness refinement loop* either results in a definite witness, which means we are done, or it tells us that ω spurious. In the latter case, we generate a constraint $\overline{\sigma}(\omega)$ that excludes the unconfirmed witness ω from further consideration. In the next overall loop, we return to the full model and we use the constraint $\overline{\sigma}(\omega)$ in order to restrict the state space exploration. But we do not need to add the refinement predicates that we used in the partial model in order to generate the constraint. Hence, we have two forms of refinement respectively concretisation here: predicate refinement along unconfirmed witnesses in a partial model and the pruning of infeasible paths via constraints in the full model. The latter does not involve any increase of the state space. We implemented both the restriction to refinements of detected witnesses and the exclusion of spurious witnesses via our path constraint concept from Sect. 3. Our new algorithm WRC is defined as follows:

Algorithm 2. $WRC(Sys = \|_{i=1}^{n} P_i, Init, \psi, k)$

---

1   $A := \{(pc_i = j) \mid i \in [1,n],\ j \in Loc_i\} \cup atoms(\psi),\ \Sigma := \emptyset$
2   **loop forever do** /*global constraint loop*/
3   **if** $_A^{\Sigma}[M \models_\exists \psi]_k = false$ **then**
4   **return** $false$, 'no witness for safety violation of length k exists'
5   **if** $_A^{\Sigma}[M \models_\exists \psi]_k = true$ and witness ω **then**
6   **return** $true$, 'ω is a definite witness for safety violation'
7   **if** $_A^{\Sigma}[M \models_\exists \psi]_k = unknown$ and witness ω **then**
8       $A^\omega := A \cup analyseWitness(\omega)$
9       $\Sigma^\omega := \{\sigma(\omega)\}$
10   **loop forever do** /*refinement loop local to ω*/
11   **if** $_{A^\omega}^{\Sigma^\omega}[M \models_\exists \psi]_k = false$ **then**
12   /* ω is spurious */
13           $\Sigma := \Sigma \cup \{\overline{\sigma}(\omega)\}$
14   **goto 3**
15   **if** $_{A^\omega}^{\Sigma^\omega}[M \models_\exists \psi]_k = true$ and witness v **then**
16   **return** $true$, 'v is a definite witness for safety violation'
17   **if** $_{A^\omega}^{\Sigma^\omega}[M \models_\exists \psi]_k = unknown$ and witness v **then**
18           $A^\omega := A^\omega \cup analyseWitness(v)$

WRC consists of an outer constraint loop where we operate on a full state space model defined over a global predicate set A and an initially empty global constraint set Σ. While A remains constant throughout the execution of the algorithm, Σ will be gradually extended with *spurious witness constraints*. The cases where a definite result is obtained in the outer loop are identically handled as in AR. If a u result together with an unconfirmed witness ω is obtained in the outer loop, then the algorithm enters an inner refinement loop *local* to ω. In the inner loop, we use a model defined over the predicate set A^ω and the constraint set Σ^ω that are both local to the unconfirmed witness ω under current consideration. A^ω is initialised as the union of A and the refinement predicates derived from ω. Σ^ω is the set containing the constraint $\sigma(\omega)$ that restricts the feasible paths to those whose prefix is a refinement of ω. Hence, the model checking problem in the inner loop has a refined state space defined over A^ω, but the employed model is partial in the sense that the state space exploration is narrowed down to refinements of ω. In case of a f result in the inner loop, we have that ω is a spurious witness. We then extend the global constraint set Σ by the constraint $\overline{\sigma}(\omega)$, which excludes ω from further consideration, and we return to the outer loop where we operate again with the full model and the original predicate set A. In case of a t result in the inner loop, we obtain a definite witness v that is a refinement of ω. Thus, WRC can terminate. In case of a u result in the inner loop, we obtain an unconfirmed witness v that is a refinement of ω. We then derive new predicates from v and continue with a further refinement iteration local to ω. We get the following theorem with regard to the return values of AR and WRC:

Theorem 1. *Let* $input = (Sys, Init, \psi, k)$ *be a tuple consisting of a system, an initial state predicate, a safety formula and a bound. Then the following holds:*

1. $AR(input) = true$ *iff* $WRC(input) = true$
2. $AR(input) = false$ *iff* $WRC(input) = false$

Proof. See http://www.github.com/ssfm-up/TVMC/raw/master/proofs.pdf.

Hence, both algorithms return the same result for the same input. Since the correctness of AR has been shown in [14], we can conclude that also the result of WRC correctly characterises the computational behaviour of the input system.

We now illustrate how WR processes verification tasks based on our mutual exclusion example with bound $k = 2$. The initialisation of the predicate set is as follows: $A = \{(pc_1 = 0), (pc_1 = 1), (pc_2 = 0), (pc_2 = 1)\}$. The set is de facto reducible to just $\{(pc_1 = 0), (pc_2 = 0)\}$ by assuming the equivalences $(pc_1 = 1) \equiv \neg(pc_1 = 0)$ and $(pc_2 = 1) \equiv \neg(pc_2 = 0)$, but for illustrative purposes we use the expanded set A here. In the first constraint iteration, WR detects the unconfirmed witness $\omega = (0,0)_0 \xrightarrow{u} (1,0)_1 \xrightarrow{u} (1,1)_2$ with the corresponding path constraint $\sigma(\omega)$. Similar as in our illustration of the basic algorithm, WRC now derives the refinement predicates $(y > 0)$ and $\overline{(y > 0)}$. But the predicates are added to the *local* predicate set A^ω. Moreover, $\{\sigma(\omega)\}$ is used as the local constraint set Σ^ω, which gives us a partial state space model. Hence, when we are solving the refined model checking problem in the inner loop, the valuation of the control flow predicates in each state along a prefix is now fixed by $\sigma(\omega)$. This means that the complexity of the state space to be explored is solely induced by the predicates over y. Model checking yields that ω is spurious. Consequently, $\overline{\sigma}(\omega)$ is added to the global constraint set Σ, which excludes any further consideration of ω and its possible refinements. The next iteration detects another unconfirmed witness $\omega' = (0,0)_0 \xrightarrow{u} (0,1)_1 \xrightarrow{u} (1,1)_2$. WR now enters a refinement loop local to ω'. It detects that ω' is also spurious, and thus, can be excluded by the global constraint $\overline{\sigma}(\omega')$. In the final constraint iteration WRC terminates with the definite result that no witness for safety violation of length $k = 2$ exists.

With WRC we are able to reduce the number of predicates that actually contribute to the size of the state space to be explored. In our simple example, WRC had to solve model checking problems on full and partial models with a maximum number of two predicates, whereas AR had to solve a problems with maximum four predicates. The price that we pay is an increased number of model checking runs. In our experiments we will show that the savings due to the reduced number of predicates typically outweigh the extra costs due to additional model checking runs. Similar to AR, the enhanced algorithm can be straightforwardly combined with a bound iteration loop ranging over k. In general, it is not admissible to transfer generated spurious witness constraints between bound iterations: $\omega = \pi_0 \ldots \pi_k$ might be a spurious witness in iteration k, but it might be the prefix of a definite witness in some later iteration $k' > k$. Hence, we cannot simply reuse the constraint $\overline{\sigma}(\omega)$ outside the bound iteration where it was generated. In the next section, we introduce the reduction of 3-valued bounded model checking *with constraints* to SAT, which allows us to perform model checking via satisfiability solving. The reduction enables us to define path constraints as propositional logic constraints. We also introduce *constraint strengthening techniques* based on unsatisfiable cores and a concept that enables constraint reusing between bound iterations.

6   Reduction to Propositional Logic Satisfiability

In [15] we showed how a 3BMC problem *without path constraints*, denoted by $_A[M \models_\exists \psi]_k$, can be encoded as a propositional formula $_A[\![M, \psi, k]\!]$. The encoding corresponds to an implicit problem representation such that the construction of an explicit KS is avoided. The formula $_A[\![M, \psi, k]\!]$ is defined over a set of Boolean atoms *Atoms*, the constants t, f, and a special atom $\perp$ that is used to represent the *unknowns* due to abstraction. The atom $\perp$ occurs solely non-negated in $_A[\![M, \psi, k]\!]$. Based on the encoding, 3BMC can be performed via two SAT checks. The first check considers an *under-approximating completion*, marked with '$-$', where all $\perp$'s are assumed to be *false*: $_A[\![M, \psi, k]\!]^- := {}_A[\![M, \psi, k]\!][\perp \mapsto false]$ and the second check considers an *over-approximating completion*, marked with '$+$', where all $\perp$'s are assumed to be *true*: $_A[\![M, \psi, k]\!]^+ := {}_A[\![M, \psi, k]\!][\perp \mapsto true]$. Here $[\perp \mapsto z]$, $z \in \{true, false\}$ denotes the assumption that the special atom $\perp$ is assigned to z. This gives us the notion of *3-valued satisfiability* $\mathbf{sat_3}$:

Definition 9 ($\mathbf{sat_3}$). *Let* $_A[\![M, \psi, k]\!]$ *over Atoms be the propositional logic encoding of* $_A[M \models_\exists \psi]_k$. *Then* $\mathbf{sat_3}$ *is defined as:*

$$\mathbf{sat_3}\big(_A[\![M, \psi, k]\!]\big) = \begin{cases} true & \text{if} & \mathbf{sat}\big(_A[\![M, \psi, k]\!]^-\big) \\ false & \text{if} & \mathbf{unsat}\big(_A[\![M, \psi, k]\!]^+\big) \\ unknown & \text{otherwise} \end{cases}$$

In [15] the following lemma has been proven:

Lemma 1. *Let* $_A[\![M, \psi, k]\!]$ *and* $_A[M \models_\exists \psi]_k$ *be as above. Then:*

$$_A[M \models_\exists \psi]_k = \mathbf{sat_3}\big(_A[\![M, \psi, k]\!]\big)$$

Hence, by solving $\mathbf{sat_3}$ we obtain the result of the encoded 3BMC problem. If the results of the two SAT checks are $\mathbf{unsat}\big(_A[\![M, \psi, k]\!]^-\big)$ and $\mathbf{sat}\big(_A[\![M, \psi, k]\!]^+\big)$, then we can conclude that the result of the encoded problem is *unknown*. In this case, a truth assignment $\mathcal{A} : Atoms \rightarrow \{t, f\}$ that satisfies $_A[\![M, \psi, k]\!]^+$

characterises an unconfirmed witness. Thus, witness generation in the SAT-based approach is straightforward. The details on how the formula $_A[\![M, \psi, k]\!]$ is built can be found in [15]. $_A[\![M, \psi, k]\!]$ is in *conjunctive normal form* (CNF) and we assume a representation of the CNF formula as a set of sets of literals $\{\{l, \ldots, l'\}, \ldots, \{l'', \ldots, l'''\}\}$. The construction of $_A[\![M, \psi, k]\!]$ is divided into the encoding of initial states I, the encoding of k unrollings of the transition relation R and the encoding of the property ψ:

$$_A[\![M, \psi, k]\!] \; = \; [\![I]\!] \cup [\![R, k]\!] \cup [\![\psi]\!]$$

In the expanded representation, we omit the reference to the associated predicate set A, as this is clear from the context. We now show that also *3BMC problems with path constraints* $_A^\Sigma[M \models_\exists \psi]_k$ can be encoded into a formula

$$_A^\Sigma[\![M, \psi, k]\!] \; = \; [\![I]\!] \cup [\![R, k]\!] \cup [\![\psi]\!] \cup [\![\Sigma]\!]$$

such that model checking gets reduced to $\mathbf{sat_3}$. Since path constraints $\sigma \in \Sigma$ are essentially BTL formulae, the encoding $[\![\,\cdot\,]\!]$ of temporal logic properties ψ, as defined in [15], can be straightforwardly used for constraints σ. We get $[\![\Sigma]\!] := \bigcup_{\sigma \in \Sigma}[\![\sigma]\!]$, and we get the following corollary from Lemma 1 and Definition 6:

Corollary 1. *Let* $_A^\Sigma[\![M, \psi, k]\!]$ *and* $_A^\Sigma[M \models_\exists \psi]_k$ *be as above. Then:*

$$_A^\Sigma[M \models_\exists \psi]_k \; = \; \mathbf{sat_3}(_A^\Sigma[\![M, \psi, k]\!])$$

This result allows us to redefine the algorithm *WRC* as a SAT-based version *SAT-WRC*. An excerpt of the redefined algorithm, focussing on the part where a spurious witness ω is ruled out via a constraint $\overline{\sigma}(\omega)$, is depicted below.

Algorithm 3. *Excerpt of SAT-WRC($Sys = \|_{i=1}^n P_i, Init, \psi, k$)*

7 **if** $\mathbf{sat_3}(_A^\Sigma[\![M, \psi, k]\!]) = unknown$ and unconfirmed witness ω **then**
8 $\quad A^\omega := A \cup analyseWitness(\omega)$
9 $\quad [\![\Sigma^\omega]\!] := [\![\sigma(\omega)]\!]$
10 $\quad$ **loop forever do** /*refinement loop local to ω*/
11 $\quad\quad$ **if** $\mathbf{sat_3}(_{A^\omega}^{\Sigma^\omega}[\![M, \psi, k]\!]) = false$ **then**
12 $\quad\quad\quad$ /* ω *is spurious* */
13 $\quad\quad\quad$ $[\![\Sigma]\!] := [\![\Sigma]\!] \cup \overline{[\![\sigma(\omega)]\!]}$

Here we use $\overline{[\![\sigma(\omega)]\!]}$ as an abbreviation for $\mathrm{CNF}(\neg[\![\sigma(\omega)]\!])$, i.e., the transformation of $\neg[\![\sigma(\omega)]\!]$ into CNF. We now discuss the constraint generation mechanism of *SAT-WRC* and we present a concept for constraint strengthening. For convenience, we will refer to *the encoding of a constraint* by simply *a constraint*. In line 11 of the algorithm, the *false* result of $\mathbf{sat_3}(_{A^\omega}^{\Sigma^\omega}[\![M, \psi, k]\!])$ indicates that the unconfirmed witness characterised by the constraint $[\![\sigma(\omega)]\!]$ is spurious. Hence, its negation $\overline{[\![\sigma(\omega)]\!]}$ is a feasible constraint of the encoded 3BMC problem, and thus, it can be added to the encoded constraint set $[\![\Sigma]\!]$ (line 13). Since the spurious witness constraint $\overline{[\![\sigma(\omega)]\!]}$ is a disjunctive expression, it is not a very strong constraint in terms of ruling out infeasible parts of the state space. We now define a concept for *strengthening* spurious witness constraints. Our concept is based on determining *unsatisfiable cores* [11] of the encoding $\Sigma_{A^\omega}^\omega[\![M, \psi, k]\!]$.

Definition 10 (Unsatisfiable Core). *Let F be a CNF formula with $\mathsf{sat}_3(F) = f$. An unsatisfiable core is a subset $F_{uc} \subseteq F$ of clauses of F with $\mathsf{sat}_3(F_{uc}) = f$.*

Now if we obtain a *false* result in line 11 of the algorithm, we extract an unsatisfiable core $\Sigma_{A^\omega}^\omega[\![M, \psi, k]\!]_{uc} \subseteq \Sigma_{A^\omega}^\omega[\![M, \psi, k]\!]$ via a SAT solver. Regarding such an unsatisfiable core, we can define *spurious fragments* of a spurious witness ω:

Definition 11 (Spurious Fragment). *Let ω be a spurious witness and let $\Sigma_{A^\omega}^\omega[\![M, \psi, k]\!]_{uc} = [\![I]\!]_{uc} \cup [\![R, k]\!]_{uc} \cup [\![\psi]\!]_{uc} \cup [\![\sigma(\omega)]\!]_{uc}$ be an unsatisfiable core of the encoding $\Sigma_{A^\omega}^\omega[\![M, \psi, k]\!] = [\![I]\!] \cup [\![R, k]\!] \cup [\![\psi]\!] \cup [\![\sigma(\omega)]\!]$ with $[\![I]\!]_{uc} \subseteq [\![I]\!]$, $[\![R, k]\!]_{uc} \subseteq [\![R, k]\!]$, $[\![\psi]\!]_{uc} \subseteq [\![\psi]\!]$, $[\![\sigma(\omega)]\!]_{uc} \subseteq [\![\sigma(\omega)]\!]$. Then $[\![\sigma(\omega)]\!]_{uc}$ is the encoding of a spurious fragment and $[\![\sigma(\omega)]\!]_{uc}$ is the corresponding spurious fragment constraint.*

Since we have that $[\![\sigma(\omega)]\!]_{uc} \subseteq [\![\sigma(\omega)]\!]$, the spurious fragment constraint $\overline{[\![\sigma(\omega)]\!]_{uc}}$ is generally stronger than the spurious witness constraint $\overline{[\![\sigma(\omega)]\!]}$ in terms of reducing the SAT search space. We defined an improved algorithm *SAT-WRC-UC* that modifies *SAT-WRC* by replacing line 13 by $[\![\Sigma]\!] := [\![\Sigma]\!] \cup \overline{[\![\sigma(\omega)]\!]_{uc}}$.
We proved the following theorem:

Theorem 2. *Let input $= (Sys, Init, \psi, k)$ be a tuple consisting of a system, an initial state predicate, a safety formula and a bound. Then the following holds:*

1. *$AR(input) = true$ iff $SAT\text{-}WRC\text{-}UC(input) = true$*
2. *$AR(input) = false$ iff $SAT\text{-}WRC\text{-}UC(input) = false$*

Proof. See http://www.github.com/ssfm-up/TVMC/raw/master/proofs.pdf.

Hence, also our SAT-based algorithm with constraints derived from unsatisfiable cores returns correct model checking results. The computation of unsatisfiable cores also allows us to introduce a concept for reusing path constraints between bound iterations and for shifting constraints along path positions. Both are permissible if a constraint is *initial state independent*:

Definition 12 (Initial State Independence). *Let $[\![I]\!]_{uc} \cup [\![R, k]\!]_{uc} \cup [\![\psi]\!]_{uc} \cup [\![\sigma(\omega)]\!]_{uc}$ and $[\![I]\!] \cup [\![R, k]\!] \cup [\![\psi]\!] \cup [\![\sigma(\omega)]\!]$ be as above. Then the encoding of the spurious fragment $[\![\sigma(\omega)]\!]_{uc}$ is initial state independent iff $[\![I]\!]_{uc} = \emptyset$ and $[\![\psi]\!]_{uc} = \emptyset$.*

We proved the following theorem:

Theorem 3. *Let $[\![\sigma(\omega)]\!]_{uc}$ be an initial state independent encoding of the spurious fragment of ω that was generated in bound iteration k. Then it is admissible to reuse the constraint $\overline{[\![\sigma(\omega)]\!]}_{uc}$ in iterations $k' \geq k$. Moreover, position shifts of $\overline{[\![\sigma(\omega)]\!]}_{uc}$ within the bound are also admissible constraints in $k' \geq k$.*

Proof. See http://www.github.com/ssfm-up/TVMC/raw/master/proofs.pdf.

We will now illustrate the consequences of Theorems 2 and 3 based on a slightly bigger example verification task. Due to space limitations, we refrain from a formal definition of a *position shift* of a constraint, but the definition will straightforwardly follow from the example. The following system is a generalisation of our previously considered mutual exclusion system (Fig. 2).

y_1, y_2, y_3 : **binary semaphore where** $y_1 = 1$; $y_2 = 1$; $y_3 = 1$;

$$
P_1 :: \begin{bmatrix} \texttt{loop forever do} \\ \begin{bmatrix} \texttt{00: acquire } (y_1, 1); \\ \texttt{01: HOLD ONE} \\ \texttt{\quad acquire } (y_2, 1); \\ \texttt{10: CRITICAL} \\ \texttt{\quad release } (y_1, 1); \\ \texttt{11: release } (y_2, 1); \end{bmatrix} \end{bmatrix} \parallel P_2 :: \begin{bmatrix} \texttt{loop forever do} \\ \begin{bmatrix} \texttt{00: acquire } (y_2, 1); \\ \texttt{01: HOLD ONE} \\ \texttt{\quad acquire } (y_3, 1); \\ \texttt{10: CRITICAL} \\ \texttt{\quad release } (y_2, 1); \\ \texttt{11: release } (y_3, 1); \end{bmatrix} \end{bmatrix} \parallel P_3 :: \begin{bmatrix} \texttt{loop forever do} \\ \begin{bmatrix} \texttt{00: acquire } (y_3, 1); \\ \texttt{01: HOLD ONE} \\ \texttt{\quad acquire } (y_1, 1); \\ \texttt{10: CRITICAL} \\ \texttt{\quad release } (y_3, 1); \\ \texttt{11: release } (y_1, 1); \end{bmatrix} \end{bmatrix}
$$

Fig. 2. Concurrent system implementing dining philosophers

It implements a solution to the dining philosophers problem. We have three philosopher processes and each process has to acquire two semaphore forks to enter its critical section and eat. We check again for a safety violation where $Safe = \neg((pc_1 = 10) \wedge (pc_2 = 10)) \wedge \neg((pc_1 = 10) \wedge (pc_3 = 10)) \wedge \neg((pc_2 = 10) \wedge (pc_3 = 10))$. Bound iteration $k = 4$ yields the following unconfirmed witness that turns out spurious:

$$\omega = (00, 00, 00)_0 \xrightarrow{u} (01, 00, 00)_1 \xrightarrow{u} (01, 01, 00)_2 \xrightarrow{u} (10, 01, 00)_3 \xrightarrow{u} (10, 10, 00)_4$$

The corresponding propositional logic constraint $[\![\sigma(\omega)]\!]$ has an unsatisfiable core $[\![\sigma(\omega)]\!]_{uc}$ that characterises the spurious fragment ω_{uc} of ω:

$$\omega_{uc} = (01, 00, *)_1 \xrightarrow{u} (01, 01, *)_2 \xrightarrow{u} (10, 01, *)_3$$

This spurious fragment reveals that it is not possible that the processes P_2 and P_1 acquire the semaphore y_2 immediately one after another. Here the $*$ indicates that the behaviour of P_3 is not part of the spurious fragment, and thus, can be arbitrary. The corresponding spurious fragment constraint $[\![\sigma(\omega)]\!]_{uc}$ is admissible (Theorem 2) and it rules out any possible refinement of ω_{uc}, which is significantly stronger than the spurious witness constraint $\overline{[\![\sigma(\omega)]\!]}$ that just rules out refinements of ω. Moreover, we can show via a SAT solver that $[\![\sigma(\omega)]\!]_{uc}$

is *initial state independent*, which allows us to reuse $\overline{[\![\sigma(\omega)]\!]}_{uc}$ and its position shifts in all bound iterations $k \geq 4$ (Theorem 3). For our example there exist two position shifts of $\overline{[\![\sigma(\omega)]\!]}_{uc}$ within the bound $k = 4$. These shifts characterise the likewise spurious fragments $(01, 00, *)_0 \xrightarrow{u} (01, 01, *)_1 \xrightarrow{u} (10, 01, *)_2$ and $(01, 00, *)_2 \xrightarrow{u} (01, 01, *)_3 \xrightarrow{u} (10, 01, *)_4$. Hence, due to the initial state independence of the constraint we can conclude that the behaviour characterised by ω_{uc} is not only spurious for the fixed positions 1, 2, 3 along a prefix, but also spurious for all other consecutive positions $i, i + 1, i + 2$ within the bound. This allows us to introduce further constraints for limiting the search space of SAT, and thus, to reduce the number of iterations until *SAT-WRC-UC* terminates.

7 Experiments

We implemented our approach on top of the SAT-based 3-valued bounded model checker TVMC (available at http://www.github.com/ssfm-up/TVMC). In our experiments, we verified different instantiations of the dining philosopher system that we introduced in the previous section. We considered instantiations with $2 \leq n \leq 5$ philosophers and forks, and we checked two different safety properties: *mutual exclusion* in the sense that no pair of neighboured philosophers ever eats at the same time, and *absence of deadlocks* in the sense that there is no circular waiting for forks. While the first property holds, the second one fails when all philosophers are at location 01 at the same time. We compared the performance of the classical refinement algorithm (SAT-AR) and our constraint-based algorithm with constraint strengthening (SAT-WRC-UC). Both algorithms were integrated into a bound incrementation loop ranging from zero up to a completeness threshold (Table 1).

Table 1. Experimental results

Case study	n	SAT-AR			SAT-WRC-UC		
		Refinement iterations	Maximum predicates	Time	Constraint iterations	Maximum predicates	Time
MUTUAL EXCLUSION	2	2	8	6.22 s	6	4	5.82 s
	3	3	12	25.7 s	18	6	16.2 s
	4	4	16	42 m	24	8	8.5 m
	5	5	20	137 m	30	10	29 m
ABSENCE OF DEAD-LOCKS	2	1	8	3.73 s	1	4	3.55 s
	3	1	12	5.02 s	1	6	4.89 s
	4	1	16	14.5 s	1	8	8.41 s
	5	1	20	42.4 s	1	10	18.7 s

In terms of the mutual exclusion case study, we see that SAT-WRC-UC needs a substantially higher number of iterations than SAT-AR to prove the property. On the other hand, the model checking problems to be solved by SAT-AR require up to twice as much predicates as the problems to be solved by SAT-WRC-UC. This implies a significant complexity reduction due to SAT-WRC-UC, as a linear increase of the number of predicates involves an exponential increase of the size of the state space. The reduced amount of predicates results from the fact that SAT-WRC-UC makes use of a full model that is solely defined over a set of initial predicates, and of partial models where the initial predicates are fixed by an unconfirmed witness and only the refinement predicates contribute to the state space complexity. When it comes to the trade-off between computational costs induced by the number of iterations and by costs induced by the state space, we see that our new approach clearly outperforms the classical approach with regard to the overall verification time. This applies particularly to the larger verification tasks. In terms of the deadlock case study, we see that both approaches are capable of detecting the property violation within one iteration. But again, SAT-WRC-UC needs less predicates and achieves a better time performance.

8 Related Work

Our verification technique is related to existing approaches for improving the classical *abstract–check–refine* paradigm [3,13]. *Lazy abstraction* [4,7,8,10] is a concept that builds and refines a single abstract model where different parts of the model exhibit different degrees of precision. This is achieved by adding refinement predicates only at parts where they are required for proving the spuriousness of witnesses. The major difference to our approach is that we work with one full and multiple partial models. Only the partial models are refined in order to *prove* whether a particular witness is spurious or not. In the full model we take proven spuriousness as a *fact* in order to prune the state space. The separation of proving and eliminating spuriousness enables us to conduct verification on smaller models in comparison to lazy abstraction where only a single model is used. Another related approach is *local abstraction refinement* [5] which extends the lazy abstraction idea. The technique also adds predicates only to relevant parts of the model. While a new predicate typically splits an abstract state in two refined states, local abstraction refinement uses heuristics for determining whether a single refined state is sufficient for the underlying verification task. This enables smaller state spaces. The approach is still based on a single model, and thus, does not have the same state space reduction capabilities as our multi-model approach. Our work also is related to *conditional model checking* (CMC) [1], which reformulates model checking as follows: If model checking fails (due to state explosion) to fully prove or disprove the property of interest, then it at least returns a condition under which the property holds. This allows for a sequential combination of model checking runs where a first run generates a condition and a second run checks whether the condition holds. Our approach can be regarded as an application and generalisation of the CMC idea in the context of abstraction refinement. We take unconfirmed witnesses as conditions for our partial models and we use conditions for excluding spurious witnesses in the full model.

9   Conclusion and Outlook

We introduced an iterative abstraction refinement technique for the verification of safety properties of concurrent systems. The novelty of our approach is that we use separate models for producing abstract witness paths and for checking whether witnesses are definite or spurious. Our partial models are restricted to refinements of particular witnesses only. The abstract state space of our full model is pruned via constraints derived from partial models. We hereby gain precision in the full model without increasing its state space. Our multi-model approach allows for a significant reduction of the state space complexity in comparison to single-model approaches. It comes at the cost of an increased number of iterations. Our new constraint strengthening concept enables us to diminish this number, which gives us a space- *and* time-efficient verification technique.

As future work we intend to do a performance comparison of our approach with related abstraction refinement techniques.

References

1. Beyer, D., Henzinger, T.A., Keremoglu, M.E., Wendler, P.: Conditional model checking: a technique to pass information between verifiers. In: Proceedings of the ACM SIGSOFT 20th International Symposium on the Foundations of Software Engineering, FSE 2012, pp. 57:1–57:11. ACM, New York (2012)
2. Bruns, G., Godefroid, P.: Model checking partial state spaces with 3-valued temporal logics. In: Halbwachs, N., Peled, D. (eds.) CAV 1999. LNCS, vol. 1633, pp. 274–287. Springer, Heidelberg (1999). https://doi.org/10.1007/3-540-48683-6_25
3. Clarke, E., Grumberg, O., Jha, S., Lu, Y., Veith, H.: Counterexample-guided abstraction refinement. In: Emerson, E.A., Sistla, A.P. (eds.) CAV 2000. LNCS, vol. 1855, pp. 154–169. Springer, Heidelberg (2000). https://doi.org/10.1007/10722167_15
4. Degiovanni, R., Ponzio, P., Aguirre, N., Frias, M.: Improving lazy abstraction for SCR specifications through constraint relaxation. Softw. Test. Verif. Reliab. **28**(2), e1657 (2018)
5. Fecher, H., Shoham, S.: Local abstraction-refinement for the μ-calculus. In: Bošnački, D., Edelkamp, S. (eds.) SPIN 2007. LNCS, vol. 4595, pp. 4–23. Springer, Heidelberg (2007). https://doi.org/10.1007/978-3-540-73370-6_3
6. Fitting, M.: Kleene's three valued logics and their children. Fundamenta Informaticae **20**(1–3), 113–131 (1994)
7. Henzinger, T.A., Jhala, R., Majumdar, R., Sutre, G.: Lazy abstraction. In: Proceedings of the 29th ACM SIGPLAN-SIGACT Symposium on Principles of Programming Languages, POPL 2002, pp. 58–70. ACM, New York (2002)
8. Hsu, K., Majumdar, R., Mallik, K., Schmuck, A.: Lazy abstraction-based control for reachability. CoRR abs/1804.02722 (2018)

9. Kroening, D., Ouaknine, J., Strichman, O., Wahl, T., Worrell, J.: Linear completeness thresholds for bounded model checking. In: Gopalakrishnan, G., Qadeer, S. (eds.) CAV 2011. LNCS, vol. 6806, pp. 557–572. Springer, Heidelberg (2011). https://doi.org/10.1007/978-3-642-22110-1_44

10. Madhukar, K., Srivas, M., Wachter, B., Kroening, D., Metta, R.: Verifying synchronous reactive systems using lazy abstraction. In: 2015 Design, Automation Test in Europe Conference Exhibition (DATE), pp. 1571–1574, March 2015

11. Nadel, A.: Boosting minimal unsatisfiable core extraction. In: Proceedings of the 2010 Conference on Formal Methods in Computer-Aided Design, FMCAD 2010, pp. 221–229. FMCAD Inc., Austin (2010)

12. Schrieb, J., Wehrheim, H., Wonisch, D.: Three-valued spotlight abstractions. In: Cavalcanti, A., Dams, D.R. (eds.) FM 2009. LNCS, vol. 5850, pp. 106–122. Springer, Heidelberg (2009). https://doi.org/10.1007/978-3-642-05089-3_8

13. Shoham, S., Grumberg, O.: 3-valued abstraction: more precision at less cost. Inf. Comput. **206**(11), 1313–1333 (2008)

14. Timm, N., Gruner, S.: Three-valued bounded model checking with cause-guided abstraction refinement (manuscript submitted for publication). http://www.github.com/ssfm-up/TVMC/raw/unbounded/SCICO2018.pdf

15. Timm, N., Gruner, S., Harvey, M.: A bounded model checker for three-valued abstractions of concurrent software systems. In: Ribeiro, L., Lecomte, T. (eds.) SBMF 2016. LNCS, vol. 10090, pp. 199–216. Springer, Cham (2016). https://doi.org/10.1007/978-3-319-49815-7_12

16. Wehrheim, H.: Bounded model checking for partial Kripke structures. In: Fitzgerald, J.S., Haxthausen, A.E., Yenigun, H. (eds.) ICTAC 2008. LNCS, vol. 5160, pp. 380–394. Springer, Heidelberg (2008). https://doi.org/10.1007/978-3-540-85762-4_26

Model Transformation

Model Transformation with Triple Graph Grammars and Non-terminal Symbols

William da Silva[1,2(✉)], Max Bureck[1], Ina Schieferdecker[1,2],
and Christian Hein[1]

[1] Fraunhofer Fokus, Berlin, Germany
{william.bombardelli.da.silva,max.bureck,ina.schieferdecker,
christian.hein}@fokus.fraunhofer.de
[2] Technische Universität Berlin, Berlin, Germany

Abstract. This work proposes a new graph grammar formalism, that introduces non-terminal symbols to triple graph grammars (TGG) and shows how to apply it to solving the model transformation problem. Our proposed formalism seems to suit code generation from models well, outperforms the standard TGG in the grammar size in one evaluated case and is able to express one transformation that we could not express with TGG. We claim, that such advantages make a formal specification written in our formalism easier to validate and less error-prone, what befits safety-critical systems specially well.

Keywords: NCE graph grammars · Triple graph grammars ·
Model transformation · Model-based development

1 Introduction

Quality of service is a very common requirement for software projects, especially for safety-critical systems. A technique that aims to assure and enhance quality of software is the model-based development approach, which consists of the use of abstract models to specify aspects of the system under construction. The use of such models often allows for cheaper tests and verification as well as facilitates discussions about the system, for more abstract models tend to reduce the complexity of the actual object of interest.

The construction of a system with model-based development commonly requires the creation of various models at different levels of abstraction, in which case we are interested in generating models automatically from other models. One example of such a situation is the transformation of a UML diagram into source-code or the compilation of source-code into machine-code. This problem is known as model transformation. For safety-critical systems, automatic model transformation is attractive, because transformers can be verified for correction carefully once and used many times, whereas manually or ad-hoc transformations have to be checked each time.

© Springer Nature Switzerland AG 2019
C. Artho and P. C. Ölveczky (Eds.): FTSCS 2018, CCIS 1008, pp. 161–177, 2019.
https://doi.org/10.1007/978-3-030-12988-0_10

Several approaches to solving the model transformation problem have been proposed so far. Some of them consist of using the theory of graph grammars to formalize models and describe relations between them. One of which is the triple graph grammar (TGG) approach [20], which consists of building context-sensitive grammars of, so-called, triple graphs.

Triple graphs are composed of three graphs, the source and the target graphs, representing two models, and the correspondence graph that connects the source and the target through morphisms. A triple graph can be used to express the relationship between two graphs through the morphisms between their vertices. In this sense, a TGG describes a language of pairs of graphs whose vertices have a certain relationship. For the context of model transformation, in which one is interested in defining a translator from a source model to a target model, a TGG can be used to describe the set of all correctly translated source models and its correspondent target models, in form of a language of triple graphs.

Despite the various positive aspects of TGG, like a well-founded theory and a reasonable tool support [1], they may sometimes get too big or too difficult to be constructed correctly. We judge, this downside stems from the absence of the concept of non-terminal symbols in the TGG formalism. This concept allows, in the theory of formal languages, for a very effective representation of abstract entities in string grammars.

So, motivated by this benefit, we present in this paper a novel formalism that redefines the standard triple graph grammars and introduces the notion of non-terminal symbols to create a context-free triple graph grammar formalism, that has in some cases a smaller size and with which we could describe one transformation that we could not with standard TGG.

Our approach consists of (1) mixing an already existent context-free graph grammar formalism, called NCE graph grammar [15], with the standard TGG formalism [20], to create the NCE TGG and (2) constructing a model transformer that interprets a NCE TGG to solve the model transformation problem.

The remainder of this paper is as follows, in Sect. 2, we present the research publications related to this topic, in Sect. 3, we give the main definitions necessary to build our approach, in Sect. 4, we propose our modified version of TGG, the NCE TGG, in Sect. 5 we argue that our approach can be used for model transformation, in Sect. 6 we evaluate our results and, finally, in Sect. 7 we summarize and close our discussion.

2   Related Works

In this section, we offer a short literary review on the graph grammar and triple graph grammar approaches that are more relevant to our work. We focus, therefore, on the context-free node label replacement and the hyperedge replacement approaches for graph grammars, although, there is a myriad of different alternatives to it, for example, the algebraic approach [8]. We refer to context-free grammars, inspired by the use of such classification for string grammars, in a relaxed way without any compromise to any definition.

In the node label replacement context-free formalisms stand out the *node label controlled graph grammar* (NLC) and its successor *graph grammar with neighborhood-controlled embedding* (NCE). NLC is based on the replacement of one vertex by a graph, governed by embedding rules written in terms of the vertex's label [19]. For various classes of these grammars, there exist polynomial-time top-down and bottom-up parsing algorithms [11,12,19,22]. The recognition complexity and generation power of such grammars have also been analyzed [10,17]. NCE occurs in several formulations, including a context-sensitive one, but here we focus on the context-free formulation, where one vertex is replaced by a graph, and the embedding rules are written in terms of the vertex's neighbors [15,21]. For some classes of these grammars, polynomial-time bottom-up parsing algorithms and automaton formalisms were proposed and analyzed [4,16]. In special, one of these classes is the *boundary graph grammar with neighborhood-controlled embedding* (BNCE), that is used in our approach for model transformation.

Hyperedge replacement graph grammars (HRG) are context-free grammars with semantics based on the replacement of hyperedges by hypergraphs governed by morphisms [7]. Prominent polynomial-time top-down and shift-reduce parsing techniques for classes of such grammars can be found in [5,6]. In particular, Engelfriet and Rozenberg [9] shows that BNCE and HRG have the same generative power.

Regarding TGG [20], a 20 years review of the realm is put forward by Anjorin et al. [1]. In special, advances are made in the direction of expressiveness with the introduction of application conditions [18] and of modularization [2]. Furthermore, in the algebraic approach for graph grammars, we have found proposals that introduce inheritance [3,13] and variables [14] to the formalisms. Nevertheless, we do not know any approach that introduces non-terminal symbols to TGG with the purpose of gaining expressiveness or usability. In this sense, our proposal brings something new to the current state-of-the-art.

3   Graph Grammars and Triple Graph Grammars

In this section, we introduce important definitions that are used throughout this paper. First, we present definitions regarding graphs [19], second, we introduce the NCE graph grammar [15,16] and then, we express our understanding of TGG [20].

Definition 1. *A directed labeled graph G over the finite set of symbols Σ, $G = (V, E, \phi)$ consists of a finite set of vertices V, a set of labeled directed edges $E \subseteq V \times \Sigma \times V$ and a total vertex labeling function $\phi : V \to \Sigma$.*

We refer to directed labeled graphs often simply as graphs. For a fixed graph G we refer to its components as V_G, E_G and ϕ_G. For two graphs G and H, we write $G \subseteq H$ if, and only if, $V_G \subseteq V_H, E_G \subseteq E_H$ and $\phi_G \subseteq \phi_H$. Furthermore, G and H are disjoint if, and only if, $V_G \cap V_H = \emptyset$. If $\phi_G(v) = a$ we say v is labeled by a. Two vertices v and w are neighbors if, and only if, $(v, l, w) \in E_G$

or $(w, l, v) \in E_G$. In this case, we say (v, l, w) and (w, l, v) are adjacent edges to v and to w. In special, we do not allow loops (vertices of the form (v, l, v)), but multi-edges with different labels are allowed and we denote the set of all graphs over Σ by $\mathcal{G}_\Sigma$.

Definition 2. *A morphism of graphs G and H is a total mapping $m : V_G \to V_H$.*

Definition 3. *An isomorphism of directed labeled graphs G and H is a bijective mapping $m : V_G \to V_H$ that maintains the connections between vertices and their labels, that is, $(v, l, w) \in E_G$ if, and only if, $(m(v), l, m(w)) \in E_H$ and $\phi_G(v) = \phi_H(m(v))$.*

If there exists an isomorphism of G and H, then G and H are said to be isomorphic and we denote the equivalence class of all graphs isomorphic to G by $[G]$. Notice that, contrary to isomorphisms, morphisms do not require bijectivity nor label or edge-preserving properties.

Definition 4. *A graph grammar with neighborhood-controlled embedding (NCE graph grammar) $GG = (\Sigma, \Delta \subseteq \Sigma, S \in \Sigma, P)$ consists of a finite set of symbols Σ that is called alphabet, a subset of the alphabet $\Delta \subseteq \Sigma$ that holds the terminal symbols (we define the complementary set of non-terminal symbols as $\Gamma := \Sigma \setminus \Delta$), a special symbol of the alphabet $S \in \Sigma$, that is called start symbol, and a finite set of production rules P of the form $(A \to R, \omega)$ where $A \in \Gamma$ is called left-hand side, $R \in \mathcal{G}_\Sigma$ is called right-hand side and $\omega : V_R \nrightarrow 2^{\Sigma \times \Sigma}$ is the partial embedding function from R's vertices to pairs of edge and vertex labels.*

A production rule $(A \to R, \omega)$ can be applied on a graph G to generate another graph H. In this case, we say G *concretely derives* in one step into H. A concrete derivation can be informally understood as the replacement of a non-terminal vertex v and all its adjacent edges in G by the graph R plus edges e between former neighbors w of v and some vertices t of R, provided e's label and w's label are in the embedding specification $\omega(t)$. That is, the embedding function ω of a rule specifies which neighbors of v are to be connected with which vertices of R, according to their labels and the adjacent edges' labels. The process that governs the creation of these edges is called embedding and can occur in various forms in different graph grammar formalisms. We opted for a rather simple approach, in which the edges' directions and labels are maintained.

Formally, a concrete derivation is defined as follows.

Definition 5. *Let $GG = (\Sigma, \Delta, S, P)$ be a NCE graph grammar and G and H be two graphs over Σ that are disjoint to all right-hand sides from P, G concretely derives in one step into H with rule r and vertex v, we write $G \overset{r,v}{\Rightarrow}_{GG} H$ and call it a concrete derivation step, if, and only if, the following holds:*

$$r = (A \to R, \omega) \in P \text{ and } A = \phi_G(v) \text{ and}$$
$$V_H = (V_G \setminus \{v\}) \cup V_R \text{ and}$$
$$E_H = (E_G \setminus (\{(v, l, w) \mid (v, l, w) \in E_G\} \cup \{(w, l, v) \mid (w, l, v) \in E_G\}))$$

$$\cup E_R$$
$$\cup \{(w, l, t) \mid (w, l, v) \in E_G \wedge (l, \phi_G(w)) \in \omega(t)\}$$
$$\cup \{(t, l, w) \mid (v, l, w) \in E_G \wedge (l, \phi_G(w)) \in \omega(t)\} \ and$$
$$\phi_H = (\phi_G \setminus \{(v, x) \mid x \in \Sigma\}) \cup \phi_R$$

Without loss of generality, we set $\omega(t) = \emptyset$ for all vertices t without an image defined in ω. Furthermore, let H' be isomorphic to H, if G *concretely derives* in one step into H, we say G *derives* in one step into H' and write $G \stackrel{r,v}{\Rightarrow}_{GG} H'$.

When GG, r or v are clear in the context or irrelevant we might omit them and simply write $G \Rightarrow H$ or $G \Rightarrow H$. Moreover, we denote the reflexive transitive closure of $\Rightarrow$ by $\Rightarrow^*$ and, for $G \Rightarrow^* H'$, we say G *derives into* H'.

Definition 6. *A derivation D in the grammar GG is a non-empty sequence of derivation steps and is written as*

$$D = (G_0 \stackrel{r_0, v_0}{\Rightarrow} G_1 \stackrel{r_1, v_1}{\Rightarrow} G_2 \stackrel{r_2, v_2}{\Rightarrow} \ldots \stackrel{r_{n-1}, v_{n-1}}{\Rightarrow} G_n)$$

Finally, we define, for convenience, the start graph of GG as $Z_{GG} := (\{v_s\}, \emptyset, \{v_s \mapsto S\})$. Then, we can discourse about the language of a graph grammar.

Definition 7. *The language $L(GG)$ generated by the grammar GG is the set of all graphs containing only terminal vertices derived from the start graph Z_{GG}, that is*

$$L(GG) = \{H \ is \ a \ graph \ over \ \Delta \ and \ Z_{GG} \Rightarrow^* H\}$$

Notice that, in the original definition of NCE graph grammars [15], the left-hand sides of the productions were allowed to contain any connected graph. Moreover, only undirected graphs without edge labels were allowed. So, strictly speaking, our definitions characterize actually a 1-edNCE graph grammar, that contains only one element in the left-hand side and a directed edge-labeled graph in the right-hand side. Nevertheless, for simplicity, we use the denomination NCE graph grammar, or simply graph grammar, to refer to a 1-edNCE graph grammar along this paper. Moreover, vertices from the right-hand sides of rules labeled by non-terminal (terminal) symbols are said to be non-terminal (terminal) vertices.

In the following, we present our concrete syntax inspired by the well-known Backus-Naur form to denote NCE graph grammar rules. Let $GG = (\{A, B, a, b, c, l, m\}, \{a, b, c, l, m\}, A, \{p, q\})$ be a graph grammar with production rules $p = (A \rightarrow G, \omega)$ and $q = (A \rightarrow H, \zeta)$ where $G = (\{v_1, v_2, v_3\}, \{(v_1, l, v_2), (v_2, m, v_3)\}, \{v_1 \mapsto B, v_2 \mapsto b, v_3 \mapsto c\})$, and $H = (\{u_1\}, \emptyset, \{u_1 \mapsto a\})$, we denote p and q together as

Observe that, we use squares for non-terminal vertices, circles for terminal vertices, position the respective label inside the shape and the (possibly omitted) identifier over it. Near each edge is positioned its respective label. The embedding function is not included in the notation, so it is expressed separately, if necessary.

Below, we give one example of a grammar whose language consists of all chains of one or more vertices with interleaved vertices labeled with a and b.

Example 1. $GG = (\{S, A, B, a, b, c\}, \{a, b, c\}, S, P)$, where $P = \{r_0, r_1, r_2, r_3, r_4, r_5\}$ is denoted by

with $\omega_0 = \omega_1 = \emptyset$, $\omega_2(u_{21}) = \omega_3(u_{31}) = \{(c, b)\}$ and $\omega_4(u_{41}) = \omega_5(u_{51}) = \{(c, a)\}$ being the complete definition of the embedding functions of the rules, $r_0, r_1, r_2, r_3, r_4, r_5$ respectively.

The graph $G = $ ⓐ $\xrightarrow{c}$ ⓑ $\xrightarrow{c}$ ⓐ belongs to $L(GG)$ because it contains only terminal vertices and Z_{GG} *derives* into it using the following derivation:

Building upon the concepts of graphs and graph grammars, we present, in the following, our understanding over triple graphs and triple graph grammars, supported by the TGG specification from Schürr [20].

Definition 8. *A directed labeled triple graph* $TG = G_s \xleftarrow{m_s} G_c \xrightarrow{m_t} G_t$ *over* Σ *consists of three disjoint directed labeled graphs over* Σ *(see Definition 1), respectively, the source graph* G_s*, the correspondence graph* G_c *and the target graph* G_t*, together with two injective morphisms (see Definition 2)* $m_s : V_{G_c} \to V_{G_s}$ *and* $m_t : V_{G_c} \to G_{G_t}$.

We refer to directed labeled triple graphs are often simply as triple graphs in this paper and we might omit the morphisms' names in the notation. Moreover, we define the special empty triple graph as $\varepsilon := E \xleftarrow{m_s} E \xrightarrow{m_t} E$ with $E = (\emptyset, \emptyset, \emptyset)$ and $m_s = m_t = \emptyset$ and we denote the set of all triple graphs over Σ by $\mathcal{TG}_\Sigma$. We also point out that in the literature, triple graphs are often modeled as typed graphs, but we judge that, for our circumstance, labeled graphs fit better.

Below, we introduce the standard definition of TGG.

Definition 9. *A triple graph grammar* $TGG = (\Sigma, \Delta \subseteq \Sigma, S \in \Sigma, P)$ *consists of, analogously to graph grammars (see Definition 4), an alphabet* Σ*, a set of terminal symbols* Δ*, a start symbol* S *and a set of production rules* P *of the form* $L \to R$ *with* $L = L_s \xleftarrow{\sigma_l} L_c \xrightarrow{\tau_l} L_t$ *and* $R = R_s \xleftarrow{\sigma_r} R_c \xrightarrow{\tau_r} R_t$ *and* $L_s \subseteq R_s, L_c \subseteq R_c, L_t \subseteq R_t, \sigma_l \subseteq \sigma_r$ *and* $\tau_l \subseteq \tau_r$.

As the reader should notice, this definition of TGG does not fit our needs optimally, because it defines a context-sensitive graph grammar, whereas we wish a context-free graph grammar to use together with the NCE graph grammar formalism. Hence, we refine it, in the next section, to create a NCE TGG, that fits our context better.

4   NCE TGG: A TGG with Non-terminal Symbols

In this section, we put forward our first contribution, that is the result of mixing the NCE and the TGG grammars.

Definition 10. *A triple graph grammar with neighborhood-controlled embedding (NCE TGG) $TGG = (\Sigma, \Delta \subseteq \Sigma, S \in \Sigma, P)$ consists of an alphabet Σ, a set of terminal symbols Δ (also define $\Gamma := \Sigma \setminus \Delta$), a start symbol S and a set of production rules P of the form $(A \to (R_s \leftarrow R_c \to R_t), \omega_s, \omega_t)$ with $A \in \Gamma$ being the left-hand side, $(R_s \leftarrow R_c \to R_t) \in \mathcal{TG}_\Sigma$ the right-hand side and $\omega_s : V_{R_s} \nrightarrow 2^{\Sigma \times \Sigma}$ and $\omega_t : V_{R_t} \nrightarrow 2^{\Sigma \times \Sigma}$ the partial embedding functions from the right-hand side's vertices to pairs of edge and vertex labels.*

For convenience, define also the start triple graph of TGG as $Z_{TGG} := Z_s \overset{ms}{\leftarrow} Z_c \overset{mt}{\to} Z_t$ where $Z_s = (\{s_0\}, \emptyset, \{s_0 \mapsto S\})$, $Z_c = (\{c_0\}, \emptyset, \{c_0 \mapsto S\})$, $Z_t = (\{t_0\}, \emptyset, \{t_0 \mapsto S\})$, $ms = \{c_0 \mapsto s_0\}$ and $mt = \{c_0 \mapsto t_0\}$.

The most important difference between the traditional TGG and the NCE TGG is that the former allows any triple graph to occur in the left-hand sides, whereas the latter only one symbol. In addition to that, traditional TGG requires that the whole left-hand side occur also in the right-hand side, that is to say, the rules are monotonic. Therewith, embedding is not an issue, because an occurrence of the left-hand side is not effectively replaced by the right-hand side, instead, only new vertices are added. On the other hand, NCE TGG has to deal with embedding through the embedding function.

In the following, the semantics for NCE TGG is presented analogously to the semantics for NCE graph grammars.

Definition 11. *Let $TGG = (\Sigma, \Delta, S, P)$ be a NCE TGG and $G = G_s \overset{g_s}{\leftarrow} G_c \overset{g_t}{\to} G_t$ and $H = H_s \overset{h_s}{\leftarrow} H_c \overset{h_t}{\to} H_t$ be two triple graphs over Σ that are disjoint to all right-hand sides from P, G concretely derives in one step into H with rule r and distinct vertices v_s, v_c, v_t, we write $G \overset{r, v_s, v_c, v_t}{\Rightarrow}_{TGG} H$ if, and only if, the following holds:*

$$r = (A \to (R_s \overset{r_s}{\leftarrow} R_c \overset{r_t}{\to} R_t), \omega_s, \omega_t) \in P \text{ and}$$
$$A = \phi_{G_s}(v_s) = \phi_{G_c}(v_c) = \phi_{G_t}(v_t) \text{ and}$$
$$V_{H_s} = (V_{G_s} \setminus \{v_s\}) \cup V_{R_s} \text{ and}$$
$$V_{H_c} = (V_{G_c} \setminus \{v_c\}) \cup V_{R_c} \text{ and}$$
$$V_{H_t} = (V_{G_t} \setminus \{v_t\}) \cup V_{R_t} \text{ and}$$

$$E_{H_s} = (E_{G_s} \setminus (\{(v_s, l, w) \mid (v_s, l, w) \in E_{G_s}\} \cup \{(w, l, v_s) \mid (w, l, v_s) \in E_{G_s}\}))$$
$$\cup E_{R_s}$$
$$\cup \{(w, l, t) \mid (w, l, v_s) \in E_{G_s} \wedge (l, \phi_{G_s}(w)) \in \omega_s(t)\}$$
$$\cup \{(t, l, w) \mid (v_s, l, w) \in E_{G_s} \wedge (l, \phi_{G_s}(w)) \in \omega_s(t)\} \text{ and}$$
$$E_{H_c} = (E_{G_c} \setminus (\{(v_c, l, w) \mid (v_c, l, w) \in E_{G_c}\} \cup \{(w, l, v_c) \mid (w, l, v_c) \in E_{G_c}\}))$$
$$\cup E_{R_c} \text{ and}$$
$$E_{H_t} = (E_{G_t} \setminus (\{(v_t, l, w) \mid (v_t, l, w) \in E_{G_t}\} \cup \{(w, l, v_t) \mid (w, l, v_t) \in E_{G_t}\}))$$
$$\cup E_{R_t}$$
$$\cup \{(w, l, t) \mid (w, l, v_t) \in E_{G_t} \wedge (l, \phi_{G_t}(w)) \in \omega_t(t)\}$$
$$\cup \{(t, l, w) \mid (v_t, l, w) \in E_{G_t} \wedge (l, \phi_{G_t}(w)) \in \omega_t(t)\} \text{ and}$$
$$h_s = (g_s \setminus \{(v_c, x) \mid x \in V_{G_s}\}) \cup r_s$$
$$h_t = (g_t \setminus \{(v_c, x) \mid x \in V_{G_t}\}) \cup r_t$$
$$\phi_{H_s} = (\phi_{G_s} \setminus \{(v_s, x) \mid x \in \Sigma\}) \cup \phi_{R_s} \text{ and}$$
$$\phi_{H_c} = (\phi_{G_c} \setminus \{(v_c, x) \mid x \in \Sigma\}) \cup \phi_{R_c} \text{ and}$$
$$\phi_{H_t} = (\phi_{G_t} \setminus \{(v_t, x) \mid x \in \Sigma\}) \cup \phi_{R_t}$$

Without loss of generality, we set $\omega(t) = \emptyset$ for all vertices t without an image defined in ω. And, analogously to graph grammars, if $G \overset{r, v_s, v_c, v_t}{\Rightarrow}{}_{TGG} H$ and $H' \in [H]$, then $G \overset{r, v_s, v_c, v_t}{\Rightarrow}{}_{TGG} H'$, moreover the reflexive transitive closure of $\Rightarrow$ is denoted by $\Rightarrow^*$ and we call these relations by the same names as before, namely, derivation in one step and derivation. We might also omit identifiers.

A concrete derivation of a triple graph $G = G_s \overset{g_s}{\leftarrow} G_c \overset{g_t}{\rightarrow} G_t$ can be informally understood as concrete derivations (see Definition 5) of G_s, G_c and G_t according to the right-hand sides R_s, R_c and R_t. The only remark is the absence of an embedding mechanism for the correspondence graph, whose edges are not important for our approach. Nevertheless, the addition of such a mechanism for the correspondence graph should not be a problem if it is desired.

Definition 12. *A derivation D in the triple graph grammar TGG is a non-empty sequence of derivation steps*

$$D = (G_0 \overset{r_0, s_0, c_0, t_0}{\Rightarrow} G_1 \overset{r_1, s_1, c_1, t_1}{\Rightarrow} G_2 \overset{r_2, s_2, c_2, t_2}{\Rightarrow} \dots \overset{r_{n-1}, s_{n-1}, c_{n-1}, t_{n-1}}{\Rightarrow} G_n)$$

Definition 13. *The language $L(TGG)$ generated by the triple grammar TGG is the set of all triple graphs containing only terminal vertices derived from the start triple graph Z_{TGG}, that is*

$$L(TGG) = \{H \text{ is a triple graph over } \Delta \text{ and } Z_{TGG} \Rightarrow^* H\}$$

Our concrete syntax for NCE TGG is similar to the one for NCE graph grammars and is presented below by means of the Example 2. The only difference is at the right-hand sides, that include the morphisms between the correspondence graphs and source and target graphs depicted with dashed lines.

Example 2. This example illustrates the definition of a NCE TGG that characterizes the language of all *Pseudocode* graphs together with their respective *Controlflow* graphs. A *Pseudocode* graph is an abstract representation of a program written in a pseudo-code where vertices refer to *actions*, *ifs* or *whiles* and edges connect these items together according to how they appear in the program. A *Controlflow* graph is a more abstract representation of a program, where vertices can only be either a *command* or a *branch*.

Consider, for instance, the program *main*, written in a pseudo-code, and the triple graph *TG* in Fig. 1. The triple graph *TG* consists of the *Pseudocode* graph of *main* connected to the *Controlflow* graph of the same program through the correspondence graph in the middle of them. In such graph, the vertex labels of the *Pseudocode* graph p, i, a, w correspond to the concepts of *program, if, action* and *while*, respectively. The edge label f is given to the edge from the vertex p to the program's first statement, x stands for *next* and indicates that a statement is followed by another statement, p and n stand for *positive* and *negative* and indicate which assignments correspond to the positive of negative case of the *if*'s evaluation, finally l stands for *last* and indicates the last action of a loop.

In the *Controlflow* graph, the vertex labels g, b, c stand for the concepts of *graph, branch* and *command*, respectively. The edge label r is given to the edge from the vertex g to the first program's statement, x, p and n mean, analogous to the former graph, *next, positive* and *negative*.

In the correspondence graph, the labels pg, ib, ac, wb serve to indicate which labels in the source and target graphs are being connected through the triple graph's morphism.

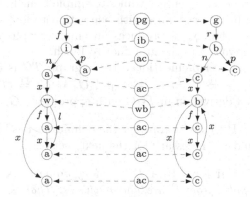

program *main(n)*
if $n < 0$ then
    return Nothing
else
    $f \leftarrow 1$
    while $n > 0$ do
        $f \leftarrow f * n$
        $n \leftarrow n - 1$
    end while
    return Just f
end if

Fig. 1. A program written in pseudo-code on the left and its correspondent triple graph with the *PseudoCode* and the *ControlFlow* graphs on the right

The TGG that specifies the relation between these two types of graphs is $TGG = (\{S, A, p, a, i, w, g, b, c, f, x, n, l, r, pg, ac, ib, wb\}, \{p, a, i, w, g, b, c, f, x, n, l, r, pg, ac, ib, wb\}, S, P)$, where $P = \{r_i \mid 0 \le i \le 5\}$ is denoted by

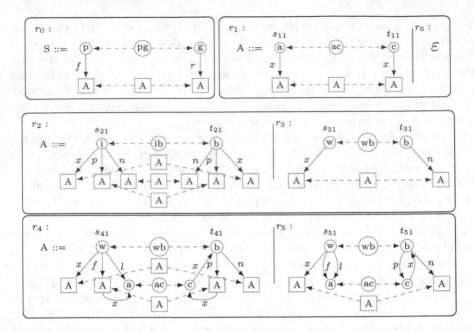

with $\sigma_0 = \emptyset$, $\sigma_1(s_{11}) = \sigma_2(s_{21}) = \sigma_3(s_{31}) = \sigma_4(s_{41}) = \sigma_5(s_{51}) = \{(f,p),(x,a),$ $(x,i),(x,w),(p,i),(n,i),(l,w),(f,w)\}$ and $\tau_1(t_{11}) = \tau_2(t_{21}) = \tau_3(t_{31}) = \tau_4(t_{41})$ $= \tau_5(t_{51}) = \{(r,g),(x,c),(x,b),(p,b),(n,b)\}$ being the complete definition of the source and target embedding functions of the rules r_0 to r_5, respectively.

The rule r_0 relates programs to graphs, r_1 actions to commands, r_2 ifs to branches, r_3 empty whiles to simple branches, r_4 filled whiles to filled loops with branches, r_5 whiles with one action to loops with branches with one command and, finally, r_6 produces an empty graph from a symbol A, what allows any derivation in the grammar to finish.

The aforementioned triple graph TG is in $L(TGG)$, because the derivation $Z_{TGG} \overset{r_0}{\Rightarrow} G_1 \overset{r_2}{\Rightarrow} G_2 \overset{r_6}{\Rightarrow} G_3 \overset{r_1}{\Rightarrow} G_4 \overset{r_6}{\Rightarrow} G_5 \overset{r_1}{\Rightarrow} G_6 \overset{r_4}{\Rightarrow} G_7 \overset{r_1}{\Rightarrow} G_8 \overset{r_6}{\Rightarrow} G_9 \overset{r_1}{\Rightarrow} G_{10} \overset{r_6}{\Rightarrow} TG$ is a derivation in TGG with appropriate G_i for $1 \leq i \leq 10$.

Ultimately, consider the definitions of Γ-boundary graphs and BNCE TGG, that are necessary for the next section.

Definition 14. *A Γ-boundary graph G is such that vertices labeled with any symbol from Γ are not neighbors. That is, the graph G is Γ-boundary if, and only if, there is no $(v,l,w) \in E_G$ with $\phi_G(v) \in \Gamma$ and $\phi_G(w) \in \Gamma$.*

Definition 15. *A boundary triple graph grammar with neighborhood-controlled embedding (BNCE TGG) is such that non-terminal vertices of the right-hand sides of rules are not neighbors. That is, the NCE triple graph grammar TGG is boundary if, and only if, for all its rules' right-hand sides $R_s \leftarrow R_c \rightarrow R_t$, R_s, R_c, and R_t are Γ-boundary graphs.*

5 Model Transformation with NCE TGG

As already introduced, TGG can be used to characterize languages of triple graphs holding correctly transformed models. That is, one can interpret a TGG as the description of the correctly-transformed relation between two sets of models S and T, where two models $G \in S$ and $T \in T$ are in the relation if, and only if, G and T are respectively, source and target graphs of any triple graph of the language $L(TGG)$. That being said, we are interested in this section on defining a model transformation algorithm that interprets a NCE TGG TGG to transform a source model G into one of its correspondent target models T according to the correctly-transformed relation defined by TGG.

For that end, let $TGG = (\Sigma = \Sigma_s \cup \Sigma_t, \Delta, S, P)$ be a triple graph grammar defining the correctly-transformed relation between two arbitrary sets of graphs S over Σ_s and T over Σ_t. And let $G \in S$ be a source graph. We want to find a target graph $T \in T$ such that $G \leftarrow C \rightarrow T \in L(TGG)$. To put in words, we wish to find a triple graph holding G and T that is in the language of all correctly transformed models. Hence, the model transformation problem is reduced—according to the definition of triple graph language (see Definition 13)—to the problem of finding a derivation $Z_{TGG} \Rightarrow^*_{TGG} G \leftarrow C \rightarrow T$.

Our strategy to solve this problem is, first, to get a derivation for G with the source part of TGG and, then, construct the derivation $Z_{TGG} \Rightarrow^*_{TGG} G \leftarrow C \rightarrow T$. For this purpose, consider the definition of the s function, that extracts the source part of a production rule.

Definition 16. *Let $r = (A \rightarrow (G_s \leftarrow G_c \rightarrow G_t), \omega_s, \omega_t)$ be a production rule of a triple graph grammar, $s(r) = (A \rightarrow G_s, \omega_s)$ gives the source part of r. Moreover, $s^{-1}((A \rightarrow G_s, \omega_s)) = r$ gives the original rule of a source rule.*

In order for s^{-1} to be well defined, we require that all source parts $(A \rightarrow G_s, \omega_s)$ be unique. This does not affect the generality of the formalism, for right-hand side graphs G_s are still allowed to be isomorphic.

Definition 17. *Let $TGG = (\Sigma, \Delta, S, P)$ be a triple graph grammar, $S(TGG) = (\Sigma, \Delta, S, s(P))$ gives the source grammar of TGG.*

Furthermore, consider the definition of the non-terminal consistent (NTC) property for TGG, which assures, that non-terminal vertices of the correspondent graphs are connected to vertices with the same label in the source and target graphs.

Definition 18. *A triple graph grammar $TGG = (\Sigma, \Delta, S, P)$ is non-terminal consistent (NTC) if and only if, for all rules $(A \rightarrow (G_s \xleftarrow{ms} G_c \xrightarrow{mt} G_t), \omega_s, \omega_t) \in P$, the following holds:*

1. *$\forall c \in V_{G_c}$. if $\phi_{G_c}(c) \in \Gamma$ then $\phi_{G_c}(c) = \phi_{G_s}(ms(c)) = \phi_{G_t}(mt(c))$ and*
2. *For the sets $N_s = \{v \mid \phi_{G_s}(v) \in \Gamma\}$ and $N_t = \{v \mid \phi_{G_t}(v) \in \Gamma\}$, the range-restricted functions $(ms \triangleright N_s)$ and $(mt \triangleright N_t)$ are bijective.*

Finally, the following result gives us an equivalence between a derivation in TGG and a derivation in its source grammar $S(TGG)$, which allows us to construct our goal derivation of $G \leftarrow C \rightarrow T$ in TGG using the derivation of G in $S(TGG)$.

Theorem 1. *Let* $TGG = (\Sigma, \Delta, S, P)$ *be a NTC TGG and* $k \geq 1$,
$D = Z_{TGG} \overset{r_0, s_0, c_0, t_0}{\Rightarrow} G^1 \overset{r_1, s_1, c_1, t_1}{\Rightarrow} \ldots \overset{r_{k-1}, s_{k-1}, c_{k-1}, t_{k-1}}{\Rightarrow} G^k$ *is a derivation in*
TGG if, and only if, $\overline{D} = Z_{S(TGG)} \overset{s(r_0), s_0}{\Rightarrow} G_s^1 \overset{s(r_1), s_1}{\Rightarrow} \ldots \overset{s(r_{k-1}), s_{k-1}}{\Rightarrow} G_s^k$ *is a*
derivation in $S(TGG)$.

Proof. We want to show that if D is a derivation in $TGG = (\Sigma, \Delta, S, P)$, then $\overline{D}$ is a derivation in $SG := S(TGG) = (\Sigma, \Delta, S, SP)$, and vice-versa. We prove it by induction in the following.

First, for the induction base, since, $Z_{TGG} \overset{r_0, s_0, c_0, t_0}{\Rightarrow}_{TGG} G^1$, then expanding Z_{TGG} and G^1, we have

$$Z_s \leftarrow Z_c \rightarrow Z_t \overset{r_0, s_0, c_0, t_0}{\Rightarrow}_{TGG} G_s^1 \leftarrow G_c^1 \rightarrow G_t^1, \text{ then, by Definition 11,}$$
$$r_0 = (S \rightarrow (R_s \leftarrow R_c \rightarrow R_t), \omega_s, \omega_t) \in P \text{ and, by Definition 16,}$$
$$s(r_0) = (S \rightarrow R_s, \omega_s) \in SP$$

Hence, using it plus the configuration of $\phi_{Z_s}(s_0)$, $V_{G_s^1}$, $E_{G_s^1}$ and $\phi_{G_s^1}$ and the equality $Z_s = Z_{SG}$, we have, by Definition 5, $Z_{SG} \overset{s(r_0), s_0}{\Rightarrow}_{SG} G_s^1$.

In the other direction, we choose c_0, t_0 from the definition of Z_{TGG}, with $\phi_{Z_c}(c_0) = S$ and $\phi_{Z_t}(t_0) = S$. In this case, since,

$$Z_{SG} \overset{s(r_0), s_0}{\Rightarrow}_{SG} G_s^1, \text{ then by Definition 5,}$$
$$s(r_0) = (S \rightarrow R_s, \omega_s) \in SP \text{ and, using the bijectivity of } s, \text{ we get}$$
$$r_0 = s^{-1}(s(r_0)) = (S \rightarrow (R_s \leftarrow R_c \rightarrow R_t), \omega_s, \omega_t) \in P$$

Hence, using it plus the configuration of $\phi_{Z_{SG}}(s_0)$, $V_{G_s^1}$, $E_{G_s^1}$ and $\phi_{G_s^1}$, the equality $Z_s = Z_{SG}$ and constructing $V_{G_c^1}$, $V_{G_t^1}$, $E_{G_c^1}$, $E_{G_t^1}$, $\phi_{G_c^1}$, $\phi_{G_t^1}$ from Z_c and Z_t according to the Definition 11 $Z_{TGG} \overset{r_0, s_0, c_0, t_0}{\Rightarrow}_{TGG} G_s^1 \leftarrow G_c^1 \rightarrow G_t^1$.

Now, for the induction step, we want to show that if $Z_{TGG} \Rightarrow_{TGG}^* G^i$ $\overset{r_i, s_i, c_i, t_i}{\Rightarrow}_{TGG} G^{i+1}$ is a derivation in TGG, then $Z_{SG} \Rightarrow_{SG}^* G_s^i \overset{s(r_i), s_i}{\Rightarrow}_{SG} G_s^{i+1}$ is a derivation in SG and vice-versa, provided that the equivalence holds for the first i steps, so we just have to show it for the step $i + 1$.

So, since, $G^i \overset{r_i, s_i, c_i, t_i}{\Rightarrow}_{TGG} G^{i+1}$, that is

$$G_s^i \overset{ms_i}{\leftarrow} G_c^i \overset{mt_i}{\rightarrow} G_t^i \overset{r_i, s_i, c_i, t_i}{\Rightarrow}_{TGG} G_s^{i+1} \leftarrow G_c^{i+1} \rightarrow G_t^{i+1}, \text{ then, by Definition 11}$$
$$r_i = (S \rightarrow (R_s \leftarrow R_c \rightarrow R_t), \omega_s, \omega_t) \in P, \text{ and by Definition 16,}$$
$$s(r_i) = (S \rightarrow R_s, \omega_s) \in SP$$

Hence, using it plus the configuration of $\phi_{G^i}(s_i)$, $V_{G_s^{i+1}}$, $E_{G_s^{i+1}}$ and $\phi_{G_s^{i+1}}$, we have, by Definition 5, $G_s^i \overset{s(r_i), s_i}{\Rightarrow}_{SG} G_s^{i+1}$.

In the other direction, we choose, using the bijectivity from the range restricted function s, stemming from the NTC property, $c_i = ms_i^{-1}(s_i), t_i = mt_i(c_i)$. Moreover, since TGG is NTC, and because, by induction hypothesis, $Z_{TGG} \Rightarrow^*_{TGG} G^i$ is a derivation in TGG and $\phi_{G^i}(s_i) \in \Gamma$, it is clear that $\phi_{G^i_s}(s_i) = \phi_{G^i_c}(c_i) = \phi_{G^i_t}(t_i)$.

In this case, since

$$G^i_s \overset{s(r_i),s_i}{\Rightarrow} {}_{SG} G^{i+1}_s, \text{ then, by Definition 5,}$$

$$s(r_i) = (A \to R_s, \omega_s) \in SP \text{ and, using the bijectivity of } s, \text{ we get}$$

$$r_i = s^{-1}(s(r_i)) = (A \to (R_s \leftarrow R_c \to R_t), \omega_s, \omega_t) \in P$$

Hence, using, additionally, the configuration of $\phi_{G^i_s}(s_i)$, $\phi_{G^i_c}(c_i)$, $\phi_{G^i_t}(t_i)$, $V_{G^{i+1}}$, $E_{G^{i+1}}$ and $\phi_{G^{i+1}}$ and constructing $V_{G^{i+1}_s}$, $V_{G^{i+1}_t}$, $E_{G^{i+1}_s}$, $E_{G^{i+1}_t}$, $\phi_{G^{i+1}_s}$, $\phi_{G^{i+1}_t}$ from G^i_c and G^i_t according to the Definition 11, we have

$$G^i_s \leftarrow G^i_c \to G^i_t \overset{r_i,s_i,c_i,t_i}{\Rightarrow} {}_{TGG} G^{i+1}_s \leftarrow G^{i+1}_c \to G^{i+1}_t$$

This finishes the proof.   □

Therefore, the problem of finding a derivation $D = Z_{TGG} \Rightarrow^* G \leftarrow C \to T$ in TGG is reduced to finding a derivation $\overline{D} = Z_{S(TGG)} \Rightarrow^* G$ in $S(TGG)$, what can be done with the procedure from Rozenberg and Welzl [19]. The final construction of the triple graph $G \leftarrow C \to T$ becomes then just a matter of creating D out of $\overline{D}$.

The complete transformation procedure is presented in the Algorithm 1. Thereby, it is required that the TGG be a BNCE TGG (see Definition 15) and be neighborhood preserving (NP) [19,21], what poses no problem to our procedure, since any BNCE graph grammar can be transformed into the neighborhood preserving normal form.

Algorithm 1. Transformation Algorithm for NP NTC BNCE TGG

Require: TGG is a valid NP NTC BNCE triple graph grammar
Require: G is a valid graph over Σ
    function $transform(TGG = (\Sigma, \Delta, S, P), G = (V_G, E_G, \phi_G))$: $Graph$
      $SG \leftarrow S(TGG)$ ▷ see Definition 16
      $\overline{D} \leftarrow parse(SG, G)$ ▷ use procedure in [19]
      if $\overline{D} = Z_{SG} \Rightarrow^*_{SG} G$ **then**   ▷ if parsed successfully
          From $\overline{D}$, construct $D = Z_{TGG} \Rightarrow^*_{TGG} G \leftarrow C \to T$ ▷ see Theorem 1
          return Just T
      else
          return Nothing   ▷ no T satisfies $(G \leftarrow C \to T) \in L(TGG)$
      end if
    end function
Ensure: $return$ is either Nothing or Just T, such that $(G \leftarrow C \to T) \in L(TGG)$

Table 1. Results of the usability evaluation of the BNCE TGG formalism in comparison with the standard TGG for the model transformation problem

Transformation	Standard TGG		BNCE TGG	
	Rules	Elements	Rules	Elements
Pseudocode2Controlflow	45	1061	**7**	**185**
BTree2XBTree	**4**	**50**	5	80
Star2Wheel	—	—	**6**	**89**
Class2Database	**6**	**98**	—	—

6   Evaluation

In order to evaluate the usability of the proposed BNCE TGG formalism, we compare the number of rules and elements (vertices, edges, and mappings) we needed to describe some model transformations in BNCE TGG and in standard TGG without application conditions. Table 1 presents these results. We cannot claim that our evaluation has a strong statistical validity, for the studied transformations are not very representative in general, but it should demonstrate the potential of our approach.

In the case of *Pseudocode2Controlflow*, our proposed approach shows a clear advantage against the standard TGG formalism. We judge that similarly to what happens to programming languages, this advantage stems from the very nested structure of *Pseudocode* and *Controlflow* graphs. That is, for instance, in rule the r_2 of this TGG (see Example 2), a node in a positive branch of an *if*-labeled vertex is never connected with a node in the negative branch. This disjunctive aspect allows every branch to be defined in the rule (as well as effectively parsed) independently of the other branch. This characteristic makes it possible for BNCE TGG rules to be defined in a very straightforward manner and reduces the total number of elements necessary.

In addition to that, the use of non-terminal symbols gives BNCE TGG the power to represent abstract concepts very easily. For example, whereas the rule r_1 encodes, using only few elements, that after each *action* comes any statement A, which can be another *action*, an *if*, a *while* or nothing (an empty graph), in the standard TGG without application condition or any special inheritance treatment, we need to write a different rule for each of these cases. For the whole grammar, we need to consider all combinations of *actions*, *ifs* and *whiles* in all rules, what causes the great number of rules and elements.

The *BTree2XBTree* transformation consists of lifting binary trees to graphs by adding edges between siblings. In this scenario, our approach performed slightly worse than TGG. The *Star2Wheel* transformation consists of transforming star graphs, which are complete bipartite graphs $K_{1,k}$—where the partitions are named center and border—to wheel graphs, that can be constructed from star graphs by adding edges between border vertices to form a minimal cycle. We could not describe this transformation in standard TGG, especially because of the rules' monotonicity (see Definition 9). That is, we missed the possibility to erase edges in a rule, feature that we do have in the semantics of BNCE TGG through the embedding mechanism.

The *Class2Database* transformation consists of transforming class diagrams, similar to UML class diagrams, to database diagrams, similar to physical entity-relationship diagrams. We could not describe this transformation in BNCE TGG by the fact that the information about the production of a terminal vertex is owned exclusively by one derivation step. That is, this information cannot be used by other derivation steps (the BNCE grammar is context-free). Thus, in the case of *Class2Database*, in which an *association* is connected to two *classes*, each been produced by two different derivation steps, we could not connect one association with two classes.

7   Conclusion

We present in this paper a new triple graph grammar formalism, called NCE TGG, that is the result of mixing NCE graph grammars [15] with TGG [20] and that introduces for the first time, as far as we know, non-terminal symbols to TGG. Furthermore, we demonstrate how BNCE TGG can be used in the practice to solve the model transformation problem.

An experimental evaluation in Sect. 6 assesses the usability of BNCE TGG in comparison with standard TGG and reveals that our proposed approach has potential. In special, we could express one transformation with BNCE TGG that we could not with TGG. And, from the other three evaluated transformations, BNCE TGG outperformed TGG in one use case with a much smaller grammar. In our view, smaller and less complex rules tend to be easier to comprehend and validate, what in turn makes formal specifications in BNCE TGG more suitable for safety-critical systems.

We are aware that this disadvantage for TGG comes from the absence of (negative and positive) application conditions, but we also argue that such mechanisms are often unhandy for tools and researchers that want to reason about it. In this sense, the use of non-terminal symbols seems to be a neater alternative to it.

As a future work, we intend to carry out a broader usability and performance evaluation of our approach and extend NCE graph grammars with an application condition mechanism that should allow it to express more languages than it can now. Finally, although the extension of our approach for the bidirectional transformation problem is straightforward, the same does not seem to be true for the model synchronization problem. Whereas the former consists of simply performing transformation from source to target and from target to source, the latter consists of transforming already generated models in both directions without creating them from scratch and using only the information of the modifications. Therefore, we are also interested in studying how our approach can be used to solve it.

References

1. Anjorin, A., Leblebici, E., Schürr, A.: 20 years of triple graph grammars: a roadmap for future research. Electron. Commun. EASST **73** (2016). https://doi.org/10.14279/tuj.eceasst.73.1031

2. Anjorin, A., Saller, K., Lochau, M., Schürr, A.: Modularizing triple graph grammars using rule refinement. In: Gnesi, S., Rensink, A. (eds.) FASE 2014. LNCS, vol. 8411, pp. 340–354. Springer, Heidelberg (2014). https://doi.org/10.1007/978-3-642-54804-8_24

3. Bardohl, R., Ehrig, H., de Lara, J., Taentzer, G.: Integrating meta-modelling aspects with graph transformation for efficient visual language definition and model manipulation. In: Wermelinger, M., Margaria-Steffen, T. (eds.) FASE 2004. LNCS, vol. 2984, pp. 214–228. Springer, Heidelberg (2004). https://doi.org/10.1007/978-3-540-24721-0_16

4. Brandenburg, F.J., Skodinis, K.: Finite graph automata for linear and boundary graph languages. Theor. Comput. Sci. **332**(1–3), 199–232 (2005). https://doi.org/10.1016/j.tcs.2004.09.040

5. Drewes, F., Hoffmann, B., Minas, M.: Predictive top-down parsing for hyperedge replacement grammars. In: Parisi-Presicce, F., Westfechtel, B. (eds.) ICGT 2015. LNCS, vol. 9151, pp. 19–34. Springer, Cham (2015). https://doi.org/10.1007/978-3-319-21145-9_2

6. Drewes, F., Hoffmann, B., Minas, M.: Predictive shift-reduce parsing for hyperedge replacement grammars. In: de Lara, J., Plump, D. (eds.) ICGT 2017. LNCS, vol. 10373, pp. 106–122. Springer, Cham (2017). https://doi.org/10.1007/978-3-319-61470-0_7

7. Drewes, F., Kreowski, H.J., Habel, A.: Hyperedge replacement graph grammars. In: Handbook Of Graph Grammars and Computing by Graph Transformation: Volume 1: Foundations, pp. 95–162. World Scientific (1997). https://doi.org/10.1142/9789812384720_0002

8. Ehrig, H., Rozenberg, G., Kreowski, H.J., Montanari, U.: Handbook of Graph Grammars and Computing by Graph Transformation, vol. 3. World Scientific, Singapore (1999). https://doi.org/10.1142/3303

9. Engelfriet, J., Rozenberg, G.: A comparison of boundary graph grammars and context-free hypergraph grammars. Inf. Comput. **84**(2), 163–206 (1990). https://doi.org/10.1016/0890-5401(90)90038-J

10. Flasiński, M.: Power properties of NLC graph grammars with a polynomial membership problem. Theor. Comput. Sci. **201**(1–2), 189–231 (1998). https://doi.org/10.1016/S0304-3975(97)00212-0

11. Flasiński, M.: On the parsing of deterministic graph languages for syntactic pattern recognition. Pattern Recognit. **26**(1), 1–16 (1993). https://doi.org/10.1016/0031-3203(93)90083-9

12. Flasiński, M., Flasińska, Z.: Characteristics of bottom-up parsable edNLC graph languages for syntactic pattern recognition. In: Chmielewski, L.J., Kozera, R., Shin, B.-S., Wojciechowski, K. (eds.) ICCVG 2014. LNCS, vol. 8671, pp. 195–202. Springer, Cham (2014). https://doi.org/10.1007/978-3-319-11331-9_24

13. Hermann, F., Ehrig, H., Taentzer, G.: A typed attributed graph grammar with inheritance for the abstract syntax of UML class and sequence diagrams. Electron. Notes Theor. Comput. Sci. **211**, 261–269 (2008). https://doi.org/10.1016/j.entcs.2008.04.048

14. Hoffmann, B.: Graph transformation with variables. In: Kreowski, H.-J., Montanari, U., Orejas, F., Rozenberg, G., Taentzer, G. (eds.) Formal Methods in Software and Systems Modeling. LNCS, vol. 3393, pp. 101–115. Springer, Heidelberg (2005). https://doi.org/10.1007/978-3-540-31847-7_6

15. Janssens, D., Rozenberg, G.: Graph grammars with neighbourhood-controlled embedding. Theor. Comput. Sci. **21**(1), 55–74 (1982). https://doi.org/10.1016/0304-3975(82)90088-3

16. Kim, C.: Efficient recognition algorithms for boundary and linear eNCE graph languages. Acta Inform. **37**(9), 619–632 (2001). https://doi.org/10.1007/PL00013320

17. Kim, C.: On the structure of linear apex NLC graph grammars. Theor. Comput. Sci. **438**, 28–33 (2012). https://doi.org/10.1016/j.tcs.2012.02.038

18. Klar, F., Lauder, M., Königs, A., Schürr, A.: Extended triple graph grammars with efficient and compatible graph translators. In: Engels, G., Lewerentz, C., Schäfer, W., Schürr, A., Westfechtel, B. (eds.) Graph Transformations and Model-Driven Engineering. LNCS, vol. 5765, pp. 141–174. Springer, Heidelberg (2010). https://doi.org/10.1007/978-3-642-17322-6_8

19. Rozenberg, G., Welzl, E.: Boundary NLC graph grammars-basic definitions, normal forms, and complexity. Inf. Control. **69**(1–3), 136–167 (1986). https://doi.org/10.1016/S0019-9958(86)80045-6

20. Schürr, A.: Specification of graph translators with triple graph grammars. In: Mayr, E.W., Schmidt, G., Tinhofer, G. (eds.) WG 1994. LNCS, vol. 903, pp. 151–163. Springer, Heidelberg (1995). https://doi.org/10.1007/3-540-59071-4_45

21. Skodinis, K., Wanke, E.: Neighborhood-preserving node replacements. In: Ehrig, H., Engels, G., Kreowski, H.-J., Rozenberg, G. (eds.) TAGT 1998. LNCS, vol. 1764, pp. 45–58. Springer, Heidelberg (2000). https://doi.org/10.1007/978-3-540-46464-8_4

22. Wanke, E.: Algorithms for graph problems on BNLC structured graphs. Inf. Comput. **94**(1), 93–122 (1991). https://doi.org/10.1016/0890-5401(91)90035-Z

Author Index

Printed in the United States
By Bookmasters